This study examines the views of politics presented by young people in contemporary Britain. Kum-Kum Bhavnani argues that previous studies of youth and youth culture have been limited by too great a reliance on simple survey techniques, and by lack of attention to conceptions of politics amongst young people, and to politics as a series of lived relationships rather than a set of external objects. Instead, she uses ethnographic approaches and open-response interviewing within the broad theoretical framework of social representations. The political is taken to refer to the ways in which people regulate, and attempt to regulate with a view to challenging, unequal social relationships. Within this the specific issues examined are employment, unemployment, youth training schemes, democracy and voting, racism, and marriage. Bhavnani's analysis, organised by themes such as disposable income and social and personal control, tackles questions of power in the research process; and a notion of discursive configurations as distinct from social representations.

European Monographs in Social Psychology
Talking politics

European Monographs in Social Psychology

Executive Editors:
I. RICHARD EISER and KLAUS R. SCHERER
Sponsored by the European Association of Experimental Social Psychology

This series, first published by Academic Press (who will continue to distribute the numbered volumes), appeared under the joint imprint of Cambridge University Press and the Maison des Sciences de l'Homme in 1985 as an amalgamation of the Academic Press series and the European Studies in Social Psychology, published by Cambridge and the Maison in collaboration with the Laboratoire Européen de Psychologie Sociale of the Maison.

The original aims of the two series are still valid: to provide a forum for the best European research in different fields of social psychology and to foster the interchange of ideas between different developments and different traditions. The Executive Editors also expect that it will have an important role to play as a European forum for international work.

Other titles in this series:

Unemployment by Peter Kelvin and Joanna E. Jarrett
National characteristics by Dean Peabody
Experiencing emotion by Klaus R. Scherer, Harald G. Wallbott and Angela B. Summerfield
Levels of explanation in social psychology by Willem Doise
Understanding attitudes to the European Community: a social-psychological study in four member states by Miles Hewstone
Arguing and thinking: a rhetorical approach to social psychology by Michael Billig
Non-verbal communication in depression by Heiner Ellgring
Social representations of intelligence by Gabriel Mugny and Felice Carugati
Speech and reasoning in everyday life by Uli Windisch
Account episodes. The management or escalation of conflict by Peter Schönbach
The ecology of the self: relocation and self-concept change by Stefan Hormuth
Situation cognition and coherence in personality: an individual centred approach by Barbara Krahé

Talking politics

A psychological framing
for views from youth
in Britain

Kum-Kum Bhavnani

*Department of Applied Social Studies,
University of Bradford*

The right of the
University of Cambridge
to print and sell
all manner of books
was granted by
Henry VIII in 1534.
The University has printed
and published continuously
since 1584.

Cambridge University Press

Cambridge

New York   Port Chester   Melbourne   Sydney

Editions de la Maison des Sciences de l'Homme

Paris

Published by the Press Syndicate of the University of Cambridge
The Pitt Building, Trumpington Street, Cambridge CB2 1RP
40 West 20th Street, New York, NY 10011-4211, USA
10 Stamford Road, Oakleigh, Melbourne 3166, Australia
and Editions de la Maison des Sciences de l'Homme
54 Boulevard Raspail, 75270 Paris Cedex 06

First published 1991

Printed in Great Britain at the University Press, Cambridge

British Library cataloguing in publication data
Bhavnani, Kum-Kum
Talking politics: a psychological framing for views from working-class
youth in Britain.
(European monographs in social psychology).
1. Great Britain. Working class adolescents. Attitudes.
Psychological aspects
I. Title   II. Series
305.235

Library of Congress cataloguing in publication data
Bhavnani, Kum-Kum
Talking politics: a psychological framing for views from working-class
youth in Britain. / Kum-Kum Bhavnani.
        p.   cm. – (European monographs in social psychology)
Includes bibliographical references and index.
ISBN 0 521 38044 8 hardback
1. Youth – Great Britain – Attitudes.   2. Youth – Employment – Great
Britain.   I. Title.   II. Series.
HQ799.8.G7B47   1990
305.23'5'0941 – dc20   90-2040

ISBN 0 521 38044 8 hardback
ISBN 2 7351 0310 2 hardback (France only)

UP

*For my mother and late father
who both taught me that politics
is the stuff of life*

The epigraphs have been wrongly placed and should read as follows:

Chapter 1
In activity there is good fortune   Arab Proverb

Chapter 2
A minority, that is to say a group that finds itself in opposition, can submit itself
and obey when it feels that the majority represents and is building a national
community. Otherwise one big gang has power over a small gang, that is all.
This, I must warn you, is the philosophical approach. But without this you cannot
understand politics. And what is philosophy today becomes reality tomorrow.

C. L. R. James
At the Rendezvous of Victory

Chapter 3
You see, I have survived so long,
my habit of observation grown so strong
that sometimes I think I almost belong.
I know exactly how a tiger drinks
how a tiger walks, smiles and thinks,
but find somehow that I cannot ape
that unthinking pride or its manifest shape.
I fully understand the Tigrish Cause
and keep my distance from those massive jaws.

Suniti Namjoshi
'Among Tigers'

Chapter 4
Nevertheless and notwithstanding differences of power, money, race, gender, age
and class, there remains one currency common to all of us. There remains one
thing that makes possible exchange, shared memory, self-affirmation and collective
identity – our language.   June Jordan
On Call. Political Essays

Chapter 5
What is life?
A friend tells me, 'Life means finding happiness in hardships.'
'No!' I say. 'Life is an endless battle with fate.'   Zhang Jie
Leaden Wings

Chapter 6
We, the older generation, did not yet understand, as most men do, and as young
women are learning today, that work and the longing for love can be
harmoniously combined, so that work remains as the main goal of existence.

Alexandra Kollontai
Autobiography of a Sexually Emancipated Woman

Chapter 7
For my family, my strength
For my comrades, my light
For the sisters and brothers whose fighting spirit was my liberator
For those whose humanity is too rare to be destroyed by walls, bars, and death
houses
And especially for those who are going to struggle until racism and class
Injustice are forever banished from our history.   Angela Y.Davis
Angela Davis: an Autobiography

Contents

Preface

The book is a report of a study I conducted in the mid 1980s. The project was an empirical exploration of the ways in which young working-class people discussed issues in the domain of the political. Sitting as I am, writing this introduction at a time when I am teaching courses in feminist epistemologies and social psychology – my two major academic passions – I'm reminded of the question which I am asked with a certain regularity: 'What does this project have to do with your interests in "race" and gender?' This is, surprisingly perhaps, more difficult to answer than it appears. To say that over the past twenty years I've been involved politically and academically with a range of educational institutions and other organisations on issues of racism, black struggle, and feminist challenges to prevailing inequalities seems to avoid the question. To reply that such a history means that the research project could not help but be informed by such issues suggests that there was no conscious attempt on my part to think through some of the implications of my personal biography for my academic work. But I now realise that it is the question itself which needs unpacking. The question contains an implicit notion that feminism within an academic context must be expressed through research projects which focus only on women. And one means of keeping feminist ideas alive in the academic arena is certainly through such projects as well as through Women's Studies courses (but see Coulson and Bhavnani 1989 for some cautionary comments). Gendered inequalities also express themselves, however, in the *relationships* between women and men, and the process of conducting research can also demonstrate this. Often, this can be done by the project simultaneously inverting *and* subverting the most commonly encountered of such relationships; in this way, such a project is able to contribute to the development of feminist ideas.

I hope the work discussed in this book is one such project. Further, the way in which certain feminist analyses and practices are able to infuse academic work is also by using these insights within the more longer established disciplines.

Social psychology is one area of thought which could certainly benefit from such insights. Despite some recent and very exciting work in psychology which I have read both for this book and more recently (e.g. Billig 1987, 1989; Gallagher 1987; Griffin 1986c; Parker 1989; Parker and Shotter 1990; Phoenix 1988; Reicher 1988; Squire 1989), it is the case that (much of the above work being exceptions) the questions raised by many academic feminists (e.g. Hartsock 1983; Harding 1987; Smith 1987) – who are often viewed as being outside of psychology – are defined as marginal, more like the 'icing' on the basic cake of experimental methods and operational definitions. The 'basic cake' approach reflects a limited notion of what constitutes social psychology, and suggests that the parochialism apparent within much of feminism and Women's Studies (see the arguments of e.g. Moraga and Anzaldua 1981; Davis 1981; Grewal et al. 1988; hooks 1989; Hull et al. 1982; Sandoval 1982 for differing, yet often complementary analyses of such parochialism) is also a key aspect of that universe of discourse which is labelled social psychology.

The project of this book was to show that it is necessary to break out of such intellectual parochialism, and the study is an attempt to demonstrate one means of doing exactly that. This study is an interdisciplinary one, drawing as it does on a range of arguments within the human sciences. However the goal of the project, to undermine psychological parochialism, requires that I specifically address social psychological analyses. Hence the focus on psychological understandings – in both the empirical and theoretical literature.

The arguments and interviews presented in this book were developed between early 1984 and early 1988. The motivation to conduct the project stemmed from my anxiety about the dramatic rise in youth unemployment in Britain as well as a desire to explore how those young peole most immediately affected by this rise would discuss it. However, in looking at the academic and more popular literature, it was clear that there was conceptual and methodological confusion about young people and the ways in which young people understood issues in the domain of the political. In other words, the frequent use of standardised questionnaires in much of the work I have read has a tendency to turn the gaze away from the ways in which politics, for example, is about lived relationships (Hall 1984). Such research strategies whilst having considerable strengths, can not show how people seek to understand, accommodate to and change the institutional and social relationships, often rooted in inequality, which shape their everyday lives. This seems to be a task with which social psychology can grapple.

The developments within European social psychology, specifically the discussions and debates around Social Representations appeared to be the theoretically most promising starting point for such questions. As I argue both in chapter 3 and in the final chapter, social representations theory need not be understood solely in the context of a Durkheimian functionalism, but rather may be a means for seeing that human agency is integral to the relationship between 'ideas' and 'practices'. That is, social representations theory is a starting point for understanding how knowledges about the world are both constituted within the world, as well as being used to reconstitute the world. In this book, I suggest that 'social representations' be recast as 'discursive configurations' in order to account both for human agency in the context of powerful institutional forces, as well as to understand such agency as existing within unequal power relationships.

Substantively, chapters 5 and 6 show that the young people interviewed were prepared to discuss in dynamic and exciting ways issues in the domain of the politial, often very wittily. They were engaged with the topics – un/employment, democracy, racism, marriage, their futures – and frequently talked at length and with considerable liveliness about their own views and analyses of these issues. The main proviso seemed to be that the discussions not be restricted to a notion of political which was only concerned with parliamentary parties. In other words, their words, it can be seen that non-involvement with political parties, for example, must not be understood solely as an indication of indifference but may be an active and at times politically self-conscious means for dealing with the social world.

But such insights are not developed by analysing the interviews, *in vacuo*. The existence of the researcher, and the very act of conducting interviews, demands a reflexivity in the analysis. The interviews themselves can then be situated, and the comments of the interviewees understood as complex themes which are produced within the specific context of a particular research relationship. It was this commitment to a reflexivity in analysis of 'data' which led me to think through some of the possible implications of a black woman interviewer, in her mid thirties (defined as 'middle class' in Registrar General's terms by virtue of being associated with a university) talking with 16-year-olds. From the pilot work in Sheffield and the time spent 'hanging around' in the shopping centre it was clear that some thought needed to be given to the reasons why particular themes might arise and be used in the interviews. That is, the *process of intellectual production* in this research context needed to be peeled open in order to reveal greater analytic insights into the 'data'. But in doing that (see Bhavnani 1990) it became clear that *all* research studies need to analyse the context in which the 'data' is obtained. In other words, the apparent unusual-ness of a black woman interviewing white men, as in this study, seems to demand analysis and comment. But as the 'phenomenon' is analysed and examined, it becomes clear that it is the more commonly occurring research relationships which mask the shifting relationships of power inequalities in the conduct of social research. At the risk of labouring the point, all research requires such commentary in order to better understand it. Such a suggestion is not new (e.g. Clifford and Marcus 1986), but it is a discussion which has not even begun to happen within social psychology, despite the urgings of some anti-racist psychologists when they were working to counter the ideas of Jensen and Eysenck in the early 1970s (e.g. Richardson, Spears and Richards 1972).

And this then leads to the point about 'race'. Sensititivity to a culturally inherited sexual division of labour can be expressed, as I have argued above, by demonstrating that the work is informed by feminist agendas. This is true of this study – the ways in which the research questions were developed (section 2.6), the self-conscious inclusion of both women and men, black and white as interviewees, as well as in the topics, the interviews and their analysis. Further, the discussion of reflexivity in the research process is a direct consequence of many arguments from within 'feminist research'. It is clearly much harder to specify some of the agendas for 'anti-racist' research strategies without making global, general statements with which very few readers of this book would disagree. Further, Meg Coulson and I have argued (Bhavnani and Coulson 1986) for an understanding of racism based on the notion of racially structured capitalist patriarchies. To be sensitive to 'race' stereotypes within a research project such as this still, however, demands careful thought in order to challenge the processes by which women become invisible within the category 'youth', callenging a 'victimology' understanding of young black people in relation to unemployment, as well as to challenge descriptions of black youth which feed in to racist discourses via the process of pathologisation. In other words, there is a need to avoid static concepts of 'race' and ethnicity, which are defined as static and unchanging. I hope I have succeeded in this task, while at the same time recognising and analysing the specific ways in which the 'multiple axes of oppression' (Frankenberg 1988), which include racism, are constitutive, constituted, immanent, and resisted.

Thus, this project, in working on the boundaries of feminism, social psychology and 'anti-racism' is one which has been both productive and stimulating. The frequent exclusions of women from consideration of youth culture are dealt with, the oft-assumed inevitability of the views of young black women and men about unemployment are re-examined, and the necessity to complicate and thus clarify social psychological understandings of human agency, specifically in relation to social representation have been some of the key goals in writing this book. The ways in which different constituencies may receive the work (see Mani 1990 for an invigorating analysis of this issue in relation to her own work) is something I shall have to wait for to find out. In the meantime, I hope you enjoy the book.

Acknowledgements

The young women and men interviewed for this study provided me with endless hours of stimulation, interest and challenge. I am extremely grateful to them for sharing their ideas and their time with me, and I should also like to thank the head teachers and the teachers of the Middington[1] schools for their co-operation.

Sally Roberts gave unstintingly of her time and energy, especially in the final stages of the write-up of this whole project, and did this with a calmness and efficiency which was very good for me. The same is also true of Stephanie Macek and Sarah Pyett who always found time when proofreading had to be done, or bibliographies checked.

This book was originally submitted as a Ph.D. dissertation in February 1988 at the University of Cambridge, England. That work would not have been started, or completed, without the committed support of my supervisor, Colin Fraser. The examiners – Michael Billig and Ray Jobling – provided many enthusiastic comments and urged me to publish the dissertation as a book. This is the result of their urging.

The research work was financially supported by the Barrow and Geraldine S. Cadbury Trust, the Economic and Social Research Council, King's College and the Joseph Rowntree Trust. I would like to thank, in particular the secretaries of those Trusts – Anthony Wilson and Wallace Johnson – as well as the Senior, Financial and Graduate Tutors at King's College.

My mother, and my sisters, Manju and Reena, along with Nilratan, Arun and Ashoke Ghosh, as well as Ian Douglas have been endlessly generous, loving and patient in the past few years. Thank you.

There are numerous other people who have been supportive, critical, encouraging and impatient – who have always been prepared to discuss my ideas with me – and who all seem to share a desire to see a finished dissertation. Thanks, in particular, to Tess Adkins, Molly Andrews, Chetan Bhatt, Joan Brown, June Cattell, Margaret Coulson, Willem Doise, Ruth Frankenberg, Tony Giddens, Chris Griffin, Di Gowland, Bill Gulam, Colleen Heenan, Gus John, Chris Jones, Jim Kincaid, Liliane Landor, Gail Lewis, Joa Luke, Stephanie Macek, Lata Mani, Bill McGuire, Ros Morpeth, Maria Noble, Tony Novak, Shirley Prendergast, Sarah Pyett, Steve Reicher, Esther

---

[1] Middington is the fictional name of the town where much of the work was conducted. All the names – of towns and schools – have been altered to fictional names in order to preserve confidentiality.

Saraga, Elinor Scarborough, Andy Shallice, Jane Shallice, Richard Vogler, Shaun Waterman and Jocelyn Watson.

1   Unemployment in Britain and its psychological and political consequences for the unemployed

A minority, that is to say a group that finds itself in opposition can submit itself and obey when it feels that the majority represents and is building a national community. Otherwise one big gang has power over a small gang, that is all. This, I must warn you is the philosophical approach. But without this you cannot understand politics. And what is philosophy today becomes reality tomorrow.

C.L.R. James   *At the Rendezvous of Victory*

1.1   The context: unemployment

In the last ten years, unemployment has grown significantly in many sections of the world, reaching a high point of approximately 3,237,154 in Britain in November 1987. However, other calculations suggest that an estimate of 5 million out of a potentially economically active population of 25 million would be a more accurate figure (*Labour Research*, December 1982).

Unemployment in Britain rose from 4.9% to 10.6% of the economically active population between 1977 and 1982, an increase of 104% (*Economic Trends Annual Supplement*, 1987). It was in November 1982 that the method of counting the unemployed was changed to include only those who were claiming benefit and not those registered at Job Centres. This excluded approximately 250,000 people at the time: that is, those who register, but do not claim. In addition, the base from which the percentage totals are calculated has changed from a base of Employed Labour Force to a base which consists of the 'Working Population', this latter including an estimate for the self-employed. Between August 1977 and August 1987, the numbers of the officially unemployed, seasonally adjusted, rose from 1,413,800 (*Economic Trends*, October 1977) to 2,832,900 (*Department of Employment Gazette*, October 1987). The Unemployment Unit, has, however, estimated that the true figure for August 1987 would be 3,302,100 – a difference of 469,200 (Unemployment Unit Briefing – Statistical Supplement, August/September 1987).[1] Thus, the number of those defined as unemployed has increased by approximately 235% in the past decade.

Clearly, there are regional variations. Official unemployment levels in the South East of England, in August 1987, seasonally adjusted, were 7.2%, (8.2% in Greater London, 7.5% in East Anglia) while they were 12.8% in the North West, 12.6% in Wales, 11.5% in Yorkshire and Humberside, with a level of 18.2% in the North of Ireland. The *Department of Employment*

---

[1]   The Unit has pointed out that the methods for counting the unemployed have included at least nineteen changes since 1979, and argues that the Unemployment Unit Index measures a 'truer' level of unemployment.

Gazette (October 1987) statistics show that the national rate of unemployment in August 1987, seasonally adjusted, was 10.2%; amongst women, however, it was 7.6% and 12.0% amongst men. This apparently lower rate of unemployment amongst women has been considered by Hirsch (1983) in a framework which includes issues of eligibility for registration, 'discouraged' workers, as well as women's lower participation in the workforce. For example, between June 1979 and September 1982, the number of women in employment fell by 650,000, whereas the numbers of women signing on as unemployed increased by only 410,000.

For women with children, there have always been social pressures against being employed outside the home. In addition, women's responsibility for the domestic sphere, including child care, has meant that these social pressures are intensified when unemployment levels are rising so rapidly. Also, there is a high propensity for women not to register as unemployed because of their ineligibility for benefit, often due to their lack of National Insurance contributions. A married woman in this position has no separate entitlement to benefit, and has to rely on her husband's income. The General Household Survey in 1981 found that for 100 registered unemployed individuals, another 16 did not register because they were not entitled to benefit; 86% of these were married women. Another difficulty which women who live with children may experience is to prove their availablilty for work when claiming benefit. They have to demonstrate that they have adequate child-care arrangements, and are not otherwise entitled to benefit. Thus, this group of women would not be included in the count of the unemployed.

As a result of these points and a number of others besides, *Labour Research* (December 1982) suggested that there is a total of 540,000 people who do not register, and estimates another 700,000 of 'discouraged' workers.[2] This number, if added into the official figures would increase unemployment by 1.24 million, approximately a third as much again of the registered total.

Brittan (cited in Deacon 1981) has suggested that between 1945 and 1970, whenever unemployment rose above 500,000, remedial measures were instigated to keep the number below this level. This 'acceptable' unemployment figure had risen to one million by 1974, something that can be deduced from Blackaby's comment in 1974 when he told a conference that:

There is a risk that politicians will discover that they can

---

[2]   The issues surrounding job discouragement are further discussed in the *Employment Gazette* of October 1985 and August 1986.

run the country with one million unemployed *without*
committing political suicide.

Cited in Deacon 1981: 67

Up until 1970, this 'suicidal level' was an unemployment level of
500,000; by 1974, the level had been raised to an unemployment level of
one million, and, more recently, Gudgin (1983) has suggested that when the
number of the unemployed is 6 million, then, the figure would be 'too large'
to be contained or ignored. The point seems to be that there is no *absolute*
figure which indicates when unemployment is unacceptable and considered
to be a source of political anxiety. As can be seen from the above examples,
this figure has been revised upwards by a significant amount in the last
decade.

Historians and others have made comparisons between the 1930s and the
1980s (e.g. Seabrook 1982) whilst Garratty (1978) has documented the
development of unemployment as a public issue over the last two thousand
years. Blackwell and Seabrook (1985) have, more recently, discussed the
ways in which the working class has undergone a profound reconstruction,
the reasons for which they locate within a global restructuring of the
division of labour. Gorz (1982) argues that as a result of mass
unemployment, work is already being abolished, and that restoring skill and
creativity to work is no longer an option. In his book, he explores the
potential disappearance of the working class in the context of his objectives,
which are 'the liberation of time and the abolition of work'. He discusses his
nine theses on these themes, and argues that the working class only
possesses an organic unity when viewed from above. This challenging
argument has not been without its critics, including Cooley (1980) who
suggests that Gorz has not considered carefully enough the possibilities of
future reorganisation of employment and the desire of many workers to
develop a creativity in their work, this possibly resulting in satisfaction for
the worker. Sociologists have discussed the impact of recent unemployment
levels in a number of different ways such as its presupposed effect on the
'informal economy' (Gershuny and Pahl 1979/80), on women's presence in
the labour market (e.g. Beechey 1984), on the entry of school leavers into
the labour market as employed or as unemployed (e.g. Hirsch 1983), on the
transition from school to work (Willis 1984a; Brown 1986) on the
relationship between unemployment and racism (e.g. Brah 1984), on the
consequences of unemployment for marital and family relations (McKee and
Bell 1983), on the possible restructuring of gender roles (Wallace 1986), and
for young black people, with the concomitant implications for social policy

(Solomos 1986). In addition, Griffin (1985b), a psychologist, has explored the ways in which young women are experiencing school to labour market transition in the context of unemployment.

1.2   Consequences of unemployment: the contribution of psychology

Psychologists, have, on the whole, concentrated on mental well-being and its relationship to unemployment. Warr and his colleagues in Sheffield have developed ways of demonstrating that, in general, mental well-being decreases with unemployment. One of the standard tools of measurement used by the workers at the Medical Research Council unit in Sheffield is the General Health Questionnaire, and they have investigated the effects of unemployment on individuals' scores on this measure. They have also noted that the degree of negative feelings associated with unemployment was greatest for those middle-aged men who had a strong commitment to work (Warr and Jackson 1984). Banks and Jackson (1982) have also demonstrated that unemployment is causally responsible for psychological change, rather than simply associated with it.

Jahoda's (1979) discussion of the latent functions of employment is an interesting theory which has generated empirical work on the relation between psychological change and unemployment (e.g. Miles 1983). Her theory, which Fryer (1986a and b) suggests is a Deprivation Theory, argues that there are five latent functions of employment:

(a)   It imposes a time structure on the working day;
(b)   It compels contact and shared experiences with others outside the nuclear family;
(c)   It links an individual to goals and purposes which transcend their own;
(d)   It imposes status and social identity;
(e)   It enforces activity.

This outline of the latent functions of employment has an intuitive appeal. However, the theory has been criticised by, for example, Coffield (1983) and Fryer (1986a and b). Coffield argues that these latent functions are only crucial for the psychological well-being of individuals if the employment is satisfying, and the conditions of employment are not too stressful. Thus, the implication of his argument is that an individual who is employed, say, on a factory production line, or in a service industry, may feel that their time structure is too rigid, may have little social contact with other workers, may feel no desire to share in the goals of their employer and may wish to conceal the identity that that particular occupation may confer. That individual may, indeed, only be in that employment for the purposes of individual may, indeed, only be in that employment for the purposes of earning a living.

Fryer's (1986a and b) systematic critique of Jahoda's theory suggests that it confuses cause and effect; he argues that to extrapolate from the evidence which links inactivity or social isolation with unemployment is not justified for it implies that it is employment alone which enforces such social contact or activity. Fryer considers Miles's (1983) study which argued that it was the individual's access to these five latent functions of employment which determine the adaptation to unemployment. This study, of 300 men in Brighton, used interviews, time-budget diaries and self-completion measures to establish these results. This empirical evidence, which appears to support Jahoda's theory, is commented upon by Fryer:

> it seems best to interpret (Miles') study as showing further evidence that unemployed people suffer psychological problems, rather than [being] convincing evidence that it is deprivation of employment imposed structure which is responsible.
>
> Fryer 1986a: 12

Fryer continues by outlining his 'agency theory' of the psychological impact of unemployment stating that his assumptions are that people interpret their social environment so as to take into account a range of possible outcomes. Jahoda's (1986) concise reply to Fryer's analysis, Fryer's response to that, and Jackson's comment on both Jahoda and Fryer's approaches, alongside his own reservations about the work by Kelvin and Jarrett (1985), are presented in one issue of a journal. Jahoda states:

> Fryer's critique... can be summarised in one sentence: he stands for a cognitive social psychology that refrains from systematic analysis of social institutions.
>
> Jahoda 1986: 27

Thus, latent functions of employment, and 'agency theory', are the main themes which inform the limited theoretical debates about the psychology of unemployment.

Whilst the question may be discussed in a number of ways, it seems important to bear in mind that there is one central point at issue. The majority of psychological research on unemployment has documented the despair, gloom and fatalism which often accompanies unemployment. It is important that this should be documented. However, it can also lead to a stigmatisation of the unemployed: not only are they without a job, they are also, by implication, probably unable to cope with their lives (Bhavnani 1985). Fryer makes this point in a different way:

> The employed become less and less likely to risk unemployment by industrial action and, hence, their working conditions and living standards deteriorate... The deprivation theory can act, irrespective of the wishes of its supporters, as the tool of a reactionary world view.
>
> Fryer 1986a: 20

Fryer, in classifying Jahoda's approach as a 'deprivation theory', has, however, created a problem. Deprivation theories, over a decade ago, were criticised by those who asked '*who* is deprived of what?' (Keddie 1973). It was argued that deprivation theories, in particular the concept of cultural deprivation, tended to end up 'blaming the victim' (Ryan 1971). It is this implication to which Fryer objects – an implication of immobilisation and inadequacy amongst those who are defined as deprived. However, following Jahoda's comments, there is a parallel danger within agency theory: the theory could be interpreted as arguing that all individuals should be able to rise beyond their situation, despite the social, economic, political and ideological contexts. If this does not appear to be happening, individualistic explanations are sought out, and a 'victim-blaming' explanation arrived at. In other words, 'agency theory' tries to avoid being deterministic, but ends up by being voluntaristic. Thus, both latent functions and personal agency may end up as 'tools of a reactionary world view'. The task would seem to be, rather, to examine the ways in which individuals, and groups of individuals are *interpreting* their material reality: defining the task in this way necessitates an analysis of both the material reality as well as an analysis of its interpretation, and hence contributes towards an understanding of human agency in a context of social institution analysis.

Platt (1983) is a psychologist who seems to be aware of such dangers. He has analysed the demographic, clinical and other characteristics of parasuicide patients admitted to Edinburgh's Regional Poisoning Treatment Centre from 1968-82. In a preliminary report he suggests:

> These findings undoubtedly point to a significant relationship between parasuicide and unemployment, and suggest that long term unemployment, rather than recent job loss, is the key factor.
>
> Platt 1983: 3

He acknowledges that the existence of an association does not constitute proof of a causal link, and continues his article with an examination of other possible explanations. However, he concludes:

> Whatever the nature of the association between unemployment and parasuicide, it has been shown that these long-term jobless currently run more than 18 times the risk of parasuicide than the employed...But while (more resources) might make unemployment more bearable, these measures do not address the fundamental underlying problem namely the depressed state of the economy. *Urgent government action is required to reduce the level of unemployment...*
>
> Platt 1983: 5 (my emphasis)

The studies of the impact of unemployment on those who are unemployed have been, in general, a demonstration of the poverty, despair and resignation which can often develop as a consequence of unemployment. Given my comments on Fryer and Jahoda, it is clear that to understand how unemployment may be contested, the political responses of the unemployed need to occupy a more central position in these studies.

1.3 Consequences of unemployment: political responses of the unemployed

1.3.1 Early empirical evidence

A search of the literature on the impact of unemployment (Showler and Sinfield 1981; Hayes and Nutman 1981) reveals that there is, in general, very little reference to empirical evidence on political reactions to unemployment; it appears that very little work has been carried out to date on this issue (see Fraser 1980 for his comments on this).

The work that has been done has, on the whole, been conducted in North America, and in periods when levels of unemployment were not at the levels they are in the mid 1980s. As Marsh, Fraser and Jobling (1985) point out, it is not possible to translate the full meanings of survey results from North America to Britain. However, a closer consideration of North American work may permit the development of some insights into their meaning for the British context.

The general findings of much survey work in North America since the 1960s implied that unemployment produced political cynicism and apathy. When the research reports are read carefully, however, it is found that there is *not* a unified set of results. This work will be initially discussed by examining some of the more general studies, and will then move on to look at black people's responses to unemployment. The reason for looking at black people's responses is that the evidence from these studies suggests that political cynicism need not be synonymous with political apathy.

Rosenstone (1982) has considered the data from the November 1974 Current Population Survey in the U.S. He examined the literature on economic adversity and voter turnout from the perspective of whether the former:

(a)   increases voter turnout (mobilisation);
(b)   decreases voter participation (withdrawal);
(c)   has no relationship to voter turnout (no effect).

He argued that the 'conflicting and weak empirical findings make it difficult to choose one over the others' (p. 29). The rest of his paper is a well-documented analysis of economic adversity, which he defined through an examination of:

(a)   those worse off financially;
(b)   unemployment levels;
(c)   poverty.

He pointed to the notion that economic adversity is correlated with age, sex, marital status, 'race', ethnicity, education and occupation – all characteristics which will affect whether an individual will vote or not. From the results of his statistical analysis he argued that voter turnout decreases at times of economic adversity and that this is manifested by the lower voting levels among the unemployed. He accepts that in part, this decrease may be due to those who become unemployed consequently moving to, for example, cheaper housing. Thus part of the impact of unemployment on voting behaviour is through the effects of mobility. He concludes that economic adversity is most likely to lead to a withdrawal from politics.

> Theories of democracy generally view political participation as a way for citizens to constrain elected officials and influence public policy. In most instances, intensity of concern increases the likelihood that people will become politically active; but when people suffer economic adversity, the very process that is foremost in their minds impedes their participation in the political process.
>
> Rosenstone 1982: 44

Whilst this position is convincingly argued, the assertion that political participation is synonymous with voting is not plausible. The experience of those who have voted who find that their personal situation has not changed as a result of their voting, could lead to a decision not to vote. This does not automatically imply a low commitment to political analysis and action, and could, indeed be indicative of protest.

The issue of voting behaviour, and whether personal concerns affect an individual's voting behaviour has been explored by Brody and Sniderman (1977). However, in amongst a number of inhibition and activation hypotheses, it could be suggested that the argument they present is circular, such that their predictions can *only* be upheld. They state, for example,

> We suggest that personal problems are likely to affect political choices *to the extent that citizens hold government responsible* for helping them cope with the problems they face.
>
> Brody and Sniderman 1977: 539

This circularity can be highlighted by arguing that *if* citizens hold a government responsible for their individual (personal) problems, then, these problems, by definition, are no longer personal; they have been defined by the citizen as being located in the public sphere. Thus, once the individual defines their own problems as originating from governmental action, or, that the solution lies in government action, it should not be surprising then that personal problems affect political choices. For example; if I define the cause of my fears of walking out at night due to poor street lighting, then my personal fear may lead me to vote for a party which claims that it will improve street lighting in the vicinity. However, if I have the same fear, but see it as a consequence of an early childhood experience, I am unlikely to attribute the cause of my fear to the lack of street lighting. If so, it is not unexpected that, having defined the issue as a personal problem, I do not consider the government as able to help me, and so do not recognise the view of a particular political party towards street lighting as a basis for preferring that party. What their paper does point up, however, is the importance of considering voters' personal perceptions of issues; thus, if a political party takes on board the centrality of potential voters' perceptions of issues, it could deal with apparently personal anxieties by demonstrating the political roots of such anxieties. In this way, issues could come to be redefined by demonstrating to individuals that their concerns are not 'isolated', and that there are political solutions for such concerns.

One interpretation of this study is that the authors do not demonstrate 'the relevance of personal concerns for voting behaviour',[3] but rather, they demonstrate how strongly personal concerns are consistently seen as having

---

[3] The subtitle of their paper.

individual solutions. An interesting question which follows from such a demonstration is to ask why this should be so. Buss, Hofstetter and Redburn (1980) have presented some data obtained from redundant steel workers in Ohio. They argue that workers who are permanently laid off will experience:

(a)   a sense of powerlessness in respect of the political system;
(b)   a sense of cynicism which involves distrust and disaffection with the political system;
(c)   a sense of anomie such that the basic principles of the social and political system no longer work effectively.

In the study, they try to explore *why* this passivity should occur. Rather than implicitly accept such passivity as part of the 'natural order', they outline some possible reasons which could underly it: aspects such as fear of 'black'-listing, age, ('too young to retire, but too old to work'), the belief that it was not 'really happening', and so on. In addition, much public emphasis was being given to potential community economic developments, with the consequence that many of the workers thought that more jobs were about to be created in the region. Buss *et al.* acknowledge that much of their argument is specific to Youngstown, Ohio, and are aware that they have not looked at how strong the above aspects are for workers who have 'sat in' when they have lost their jobs. However, their discussion of the greater anomie of the younger workers due to their differential occupational socialisation merits some consideration. This issue is discussed in chapter 2.

Further, the instruments used to investigate 'anomie' and 'cynicism' in the study have been developed without enough consideration being given to the theoretical underpinnings of these concepts. That is, the operationalisation of such concepts requires, initially, a careful definition before measurement scales are developed. The weakness of the paper appears to lie in the reliance on a range of scales to measure and quantify anomie and cynicism. If scales are operationalised from an inadequate theoretical discussion, there is a danger that the quantitative analyses which follow will mask the paucity of the theoretical basis for the scales. In other words, measurement, and its refinement comes to be seen as a goal in itself, rather than as a means to understand aspects of human behaviour and thought.

This is not a problem in Heffernan's early 1970s paper. In this, he discusses the political behaviour of the poor, and argues that the concepts of political participation used in earlier work are 'fuzzy'. Indeed, he goes further and says that such conceptions are 'middle class in orientation and structure'.

Political participation is many things – the old men talking politics in the shade of the crossroads county store, the housewives discussing the need for more classrooms in the local school, the farm family attending a campaign BarBQ, the Negro student joining the 'sit-in' demonstration at a drugstore counter... all are taking part in the daily process of a democratic government.

> Matthews and Prothro 1964, cited in
> Heffernan, n.d: 3

Thus he develops a scale for measuring political participation, which is based on a cumulative principle, that is, that an individual

(a) talks politics *and*
(b) votes *and*
(c) takes part in campaigns *and*
(d) Belongs to a political group.

He then attempts to relate where groups and individuals are on this scale to 'per person income'. In so doing, he shows that there is not much difference between those who are on incomes of less than $500 ('deprivation'), and those who are on incomes of over $1500 ('comfort') in terms of their political interest and involvement (on five categories, ranging from 'strong liberal' to 'strong conservative'). He shows that the poor are more evenly distributed along the political spectrum, whereas the 'comfort' group is clearly skewed to the conservative end of the scale. In discussing the 'political ignorance of the poor', Heffernan refers to the work of Matthews and Prothro to argue that in response to hypothesized scenarios, the poorest groups in the study responded in personal terms; the 'rich' spoke in terms of access to political decision makers, and the well-off spoke in terms of access to organisations with power. He comments:

> (The poor) do not face a conventional political situation - their life situation is more than normally dependent on the decisions of governmental actors, and their resources for influencing governmental situations are considerably less than normal, thus producing a tragic imbalance... We know that people tend either to retreat from or to attack forces controlling their lives which they cannot affect and which are not inescapable. For this reason we typically find the poor either standing aloof from the political scene or engaged in what has been called 'protest politics'.
> Heffernan, n.d.: 9/10

Despite a certain lack of clarity in Heffernan's argument, namely his argument that the poor are more likely to perceive problems in personal rather than political terms, simultaneously suggesting that the poor will involve themselves in 'protest' rather than 'conventional' politics, Heffernan raises important issues to challenge the view that the reason the poor (or, it may be suggested, the unemployed) do not involve themselves in political activity is due to a lack of knowledge on their part.

The general lack of clarity about alienation, cynicism and political activity may also be seen in Aiken and Ferman's (1966) study on 'the reaction of older negroes to unemployment'. Based on data they collected in Detroit in 1958, they conclude:

> The objective realities of the more adverse labour market experiences of Negroes was expressed in greater political alienation, greater economic liberalism, greater political extremism and a high incidence of choosing whites as targets for frustration.
>
> Aiken and Ferman 1966: 345

Here, one is not clear whether the authors are viewing 'alienation' in the same way as much of the previous literature, that is, as being virtually synonymous with cynicism, and therefore with political apathy. 'Cynicism' implies some form of political analysis and therefore some level of interest, even if the consequences of such cynicism are that the individual decides not to vote. Apathy, however, implies a lack of interest in the political system which could also result in the individual not voting. Thus, even though the two behaviours may be identical, the motivation underlying such behaviours is based on differing approaches to the political system. There are other studies from the USA which do, however, throw light on the issue of the inappropriate equation between cynicism and political apathy. For example, Orum and Cohen (1973) found that regardless of socio-economic status or age, black people aged between 7 and 17 years scored higher on political cynicism than did white people of a similar age: however, from this it cannot be concluded that they were, therefore, more likely to be politically apathetic.

Jackson (1973) in a paper entitled 'Alienation and Black Political Participation' also points out that political scientists have tended to treat alienation (or cynicism) as one aspect of political inefficacy. But whilst this may hold true for white people, he cites studies such as those of Agger (cited in Jackson 1973) in which the most politically cynical of law students were black students, who were also the ones who were especially active and interested in entering politics. He concludes:

The Southern black youths are alienated in one highly specific sense of the term political cynicism, and a moderately large number are highly anomic. They show an interesting and perhaps realistic appraisal of the situation when they score fairly high on personal morale and very high on political efficacy while being cynical of the government. There is every reason to believe that these cynicism rates represent a growth in this form of alienation over the last few years.

Jackson 1973: 881

Later, he continues,

The black young people tapped in this study may be expected to flex some political muscle while remaining skeptical of those currently in power.

Jackson 1973: 884

The above point is a major aspect of much of the research discussed earlier: that is, the display of 'cynical' attitudes is not necessarily an indication of political apathy, or even political inactivity. Thus, cynicism may be seen as justified ('realistic' in Jackson's paper), and may even act as an *impetus* for political activity. The more usual equation of cynicism with political apathy, or seeing it as a reflection of populist ideas should be viewed as only *one* interpretation. For example, taking on board some of Piven and Cloward's (1977) arguments about political movements, one could argue that the Civil Rights movement in the United States in the late fifties and early sixties provided an overt and clear focus for those black people whose 'cynical' approach to politics represented a 'realistic' one; that is the existence of a political movement aided the expression of a cynicism which was based on accuracy of perception. Whether the anti-Vietnam movement provided a similar focus needs further discussion and thought, because the difference may lie in the fact that that movement was a 'single issue' one. However, it could be argued that although very different, the feminist movement in the United States has, through a form of 'cynicism', had an impact on white women akin to the impact of the Civil Rights Movement for black people.

The above discussion of political cynicism suggests that if individuals are to identify with and be active in protest movements, a certain level of cynicism or, perhaps, critical awareness, needs to be developed before they get involved in such movements. It could then be argued that the way in which protest movements have an impact is by trying to develop 'political cynicism' amongst target groups. Thus, any simple equation of political cynicism with political apathy is analytically confusing and misleading.

Leggett's (1964) study on the development of working-class consciousness is also one which attempts to go beyond the mere equation of political cynicism with inactivity. He defined working-class consciousness as a series of states running from class verbalisation through to scepticism, ('the present distribution of wealth is such as to primarily benefit the middle class'), to militancy (a disposition on the part of the individual to act such that they advance class interests), to egalitarianism ('wanting the redistribution of wealth such that everyone has the same amount, and in such a way that there is a material basis for the full development of human creativity'). In trying to relate economic insecurity to such levels of consciousness, Leggett found that 41% of the unemployed in contrast to 31% of the employed were 'militant egalitarians'. Thus, he argued that economic insecurity leads to the development of class consciousness. Criticisms can be made of his data analysis (Fraser, personal communication); a further point is that Leggett's argument is based on the fifty-one subjects who were in his 'unemployed' group. Such a controversial argument requires more empirical evidence perhaps before it can be demonstrated that it is economic insecurity *per se* which leads to a development of class consciousness. There are a number of instances when this has not been demonstrated to be the case; the economic insecurity of the white workers at the Peugeot plant in France in 1984 resulted in their trades union demanding that the black workers employed at the plant be sent to North Africa so that there would be enough jobs for white workers. Clearly, economic insecurity, as indicated by fear of job-loss, did not appear to develop class consciousness or class solidarity in that instance.[4]

1.3.2 More recent empirical evidence
Klandermans's (1980) study of the unemployed and of an unemployed movement in the Netherlands, whilst not looking directly at 'political cynicism' is one which attempts to examine the attributions made when individuals consider reasons for unemployment. He discusses internal and external attributions as reactions to unemployment, and then goes on to state that the existence of a social movement can lead to the development of external attributions, and therefore, by implication, to political activity. It

---

[4] It should be noted that much of the reported American literature on the political responses of the unemployed has equated an individual's non-involvement in electoral politics with political apathy. A notable exception to this has been Piven and Cloward's (1977) analysis of social movements, including the unemployed workers' movement in the 1930s.

should be noted, however, that the study was carried out in a region where the Communist Party had been strong and active. Thus, Klanderman's ideas on the development of external attributions may only be generalisable to a politically militant population, or to a sample located in an area of considerable political militancy. The notion that whether attributions are made to external or internal sources is a point which is raised by Moscovici (1984) and is discussed in chapter 3, and the relationship between the political attitudes of individuals and the political 'culture' of the community has been developed further by Marsh, Fraser and Jobling (1985).

One comparatively large and fairly recent study examining the political attitudes of the unemployed is by Schlozman and Verba (1979) in the United States. The study has been widely reviewed (e.g. Blackburn 1982; Bowler 1981; Brody 1980; Burstein 1982; Leggett 1981), an indication of its significance for research in this area. The book explores the relationships between political responses and unemployment, with 'class' presented as a mediator. The data were gathered in the Spring of 1976 in a telephone survey of the urban workforce in the United States. There were 1,370 completed interviews: 571 with the unemployed, and 799 with the employed. The main question posed by the authors is that, given the comparatively high rates of unemployment, why have the political responses of the unemployed been so minimal, weak, disorganised and ineffective. They outline a model which involves a series of steps through which 'those who have interests in common become an effective political force'. Their model may be viewed as one which outlines how an individual takes political action; that is, how the individual is 'recruited' into such action. For people to mobilise in this way, they must, argue Schlozman and Verba,

    (i) share an objective condition
    (ii) experience the condition as stressful
    (iii) perceive it as shared by others, and as an appropriate object of government action
    (iv) decide on a programme for action based on shared policy preferences
    (v) mobilise

                    Schlozman and Verba 1979: 13

They also state that:

We have specified that consciousness begets mobilisation, but it is undoubtedly the case that mobilisation begets consciousness.

                    p. 20

The writers are clear that unemployment produces considerable hardship and indicate clearly via argument and evidence how the unemployed problem-solve: slimming back on personal spending, working with others to generate resources, obtaining cash from family or friends, and receiving food stamps or 'welfare'. However, a critique of their work can be presented from a number of viewpoints. The first is that the authors do not examine 'consciousness' in the manner in which they imply they will from the quotation cited above (Schlozman and Verba 1979:20). They also do not adequately examine steps (iv) and (v), and so are unable to draw well-founded conclusions on the link between 'mobilisation' and 'class/group consciousness'.

There can be major objections to their use of a telephone survey, with its 28% refusal rate, a level similar to that in many face-to-face surveys. Firstly an analysis of the demographic characteristics of this 'refusal' group would have allowed the writers to see whether they had any systematic biassing of their sample. Secondly, aside from the important comments made by Leggett (1981) on the weakness of such methods there are other issues; for example, how many unemployed people will have a telephone – particularly among the long-term unemployed – and how willing would non-native English speakers be to speak to strangers on the telephone.[5] Thirdly, a 30–40-minute interview, involving 101 questions effectively prevents an interviewee from enlarging on areas where there may be misunderstanding of what is being asked, and prevents the interviewer from realising there may be a misunderstanding. Non-verbal means of indicating ambiguity and ambivalence are lost. But it is not 'lost' data which is the only criticism of telephone interviews. There is also a fourth issue, which is of relevance to most of the other studies cited earlier, which is that of respondents being objectified within the research. Oakley (1981) has discussed this issue, and some of the arguments she raises will be considered in detail in chapter 4.

A fifth weakness of many of the earlier surveys is in their definition of 'political'. If one sees involvement in trade unions, or, voting for the Democrats (regardless of the specific policies and manifestos of the organisations) as the essence of being political, then it is acceptable to ask of individuals who they vote for, how involved they are/were in their trade union and leave it at that. But if it is agreed that 'political' includes community organising, or, that the issues of power and conflict are included

---

5   Over 95% of US households have a telephone. However, there may be likely to be a higher proportion amongst the long-term unemployed who do not have a telephone, and, thus, the sample of the unemployed could be skewed in a way that the sample of the employed will not be.

in the term 'political' and that these issues then go hand-in-hand with a range of organisational possibilities, then a 30-minute question-and-answer session, via a telephone, may tell us very little. For example, if someone is active in their local community centre, they may not view this as political activity, for it may be defined by the individual as simply 'doing my bit', and so they may not tell their telephone interviewer about such activity. However, in arguing that involvement in such community activities is a part of political activity, there is an implication that the term embraces not only specific targets such as the government, but also, social relations. It is when there is face-to-face contact that there is some chance that the interviewer will ask the same question in a number of different ways, using different vocabularies, and thus be more likely to elicit a wide range of responses relevant to the issue which is being considered.

A sixth reservation relates to the actual questions in the questionnaire used by these two authors. For example, question 87:

> Many people who have been out of work have found that when they were around the house more there was more family tension. Since you have been unemployed, has there been more family tension, less tension or hasn't it made any difference?

The preamble to this question is one which can only suggest to the respondent that there is a 'correct' answer: namely, more tension in the family. Thus if it is then reported that 48% of the unemployed sample reported an increase in family tension, the reader is not clear how much of this apparent reported increase is explicable as an artefact of the question.

Or, question 18:

> Thinking about your earnings on that job, would you say you were paid less than you deserved, about what you deserved, or more than you deserved?

This was the question which seems to have been used to assess 'satisfaction with income'. However, to derive an assessment of income satisfaction from a question about 'deserved income' involves a conceptual leap. For example, I *may* feel I deserve a part-time income for part-time employment, but I may not be satisfied with it. Similarly, I may feel that I do not deserve the income I receive for my employment (because I consider that some of it should be given to those who are poorer than me). Am I satisfied or dissatisfied with my income?

This sixth reservation can be also used to examine the questions which are claimed to deal directly with 'political issues'. One point is the issue of political sensitivity – questions 76 and 77, for example.

> Have you ever picketed or taken part in a demonstration on some political issue?
> Are you a member of a labor union?

followed by:

> Are you an active group member...that is, do you attend meetings or participate in other activities?

Someone who is politically aware may well feel that they do not wish to answer such questions over the telephone, or indeed, reveal that information to anyone who is asking for it. This concern is no doubt sharpened by the context of Watergate, 'dirty-tricks' telephone-tapping, and other fairly well known instances of political surveillance and control in the United States. That this is similar for Britain in the 1980s seems plausible. Thus to ask such questions especially over the telephone seems to be an indication of political insensitivity.[6] The 28% refusal rate is one which needs to be re-considered. Whilst there are bound to be a range of reasons why refusals occurred, suspicion of the survey and its motives should not be ruled out. In addition, those who feel they are very busy and not have the time to answer survey questions - for example, women with small children – might have been disproportionately represented amongst those who refused to participate.

The above issues are not new for many researchers. A seventh reservation regarding the study arises from the coding of answers to questions about political parties and individuals' allegiances to specific parties or groups. Individuals were asked if they considered themselves to be 'Republican', 'Democrat', or 'Other'. If the last, then they were defined as being politically 'independent'. This 'independent' category contained the largest number of respondents, almost half the sample, from both the employed and the unemployed groups: 335 out of 799, and 221 out of 571 respectively. Schlozman and Verba's question 91 then follows:

> Do you think of yourself as closer to the Republican or to the Democratic party?

---

[6]   Many of these points are applicable to survey research in general, and are not specific to telephone interviews.

The coding of the replies to this question are:
(a)   Closer to the Republican
(b)   Closer to the Democratic
(c)   Neither/Can't decide
(d)   No answer.
It is coding (c) which is of interest. If someone defines themselves as being, for example, on the 'far left' of the political spectrum, and thus perceives both political parties as representing the same sets of interests, then they may feel that they are not close to either one of the two parties, and thus answer 'neither'. However, this response would be coded in the same way as an individual who cannot decide/is uncertain as to their 'distance' from the two main parties. Thus, a question which might have revealed something of interest in respect of non-party political allegiance was organised in a way that it misrepresented those respondents who might have defined themselves as being outside the framework of the two main parties. The coding of answers thus builds into the analysis a researcher's assumptions about the issue under consideration.

An eighth reservation relates to their data presentation and analysis. In an earlier section, I discussed the complex of issues which need to be considered when discussing levels of unemployment and have suggested that the 'invisibility' of women's unemployment has often been ignored. This study illustrates the point. Schlozman and Verba do not state clearly how many women were in their samples. Whilst they specify two categories for women on p. 77 (that is, women with dependent children who = main wage earners, and married women who = non-main wage earners) they do not state how many of their 'urban youth', 'unskilled workers with a history of joblessness' and how many of the 'college graduates' were women. Further, they have no index entry for part-time workers, the majority of whom are likely to be women, in spite of the authors including a specific question:

Would you prefer to have a full-time job?

They also do not inform us how many of the sample were in part-time employment, or in search of part-time employment, due to domestic responsibilities. This is not merely due to an oversight in their reporting. It is also that women are defined in their sample as wives and mothers. The contribution of feminist theory and writing in the past ten to fifteen years within the social sciences, the critiques of the stereotypes associated with women, and the 'invisibility' of women in such research seems to have been ignored by these two researchers. For example, Table 2-5 (p. 40) indicates that 35% of the unemployed sample were non-main wage earners. Yet there is no information on how they were divided between women and men. From some simple calculations it is possible to calculate that 127 of the main wage earners who live with children are men. But the fact that Schlozman and Verba do not allow us to explore this issue with any ease is, at best, a disappointment. The authors provide a breakdown according to age, occupational level, 'race', length of unemployment and party identification, but no breakdown for sex. They are not unaware of the disproportionate representation of women amongst the unemployment figures:

> The unemployed are not perfectly representative of the work force: as a group they are less male, less old, less white and less occupationally skilled than the work force from which they are drawn.
> Schlozman and Verba 1979: 45

This statement could be rephrased so that its meaning becomes clearer: as a group, the unemployed are more likely to be women, young, black and of lower skill than the workforce from which they are drawn.

If unemployment is affecting women disproportionately, then the implications this may have for their political attitudes is an important issue in this area of enquiry. One impact of the post-1960s feminist movements has been a redefinition and expansion of the idea of 'political activity' (Wainwright, Segal and Rowbotham 1979). By using too narrow a definition of 'political' and by not providing a clear breakdown of the samples by sex, Schlozman and Verba's study cannot be used to explore this idea reflecting Leggett's and Burstein's point that the study lacks 'social movement periodicity'. If the writers had rooted their analysis within a framework which acknowledged the existence of social and political movements, their definition of 'political' would have necessitated an examination of protest outside the more conventional forms, thus producing a richer and more challenging study.

In Britain more recently, the Economist Intelligence Unit questioned 1,043 of Britain's registered unemployed about their political views in 106 areas of the country in September 1982, reported in *The Economist* (December 1982). Whilst the setting up of a sample which only includes the registered unemployed is fraught with weaknesses, notably the under-representation of women and those of non-British origin who are prevented from claiming benefits, the survey can be seen as still working on the assumption that non-voting is synonymous with political apathy. That this may not necessarily be the case has been discussed earlier. The survey points out that most of the unemployed are traditional Labour voters,

> but, *astonishingly,* they do not seem to have become more
> anti-Thatcher through their experience.
>   *The Economist,* December 1982: 23 (my emphasis)

Of the sample, 16% said they would not vote at all if there was a General Election the next day, and another 16% said they did not know if they would vote. The *Economist* editorial suggests that the 'jobless are too placid', and are not getting angry about their situation. However, this conclusion does not appear to have been empirically demonstrated – the 30% who say they will not vote may have a number of reasons for this behaviour, of which political placidity may be only one. The fact that 45% of the sample did not think a Labour government would have made much difference to current levels of unemployment could mean that some of those who said they would not vote are also those who did not feel that a Labour Government would make much difference to their situation. If this is the case, then it seems appropriate to suggest that this non-voting is not due to political apathy but, rather, to a lack of confidence in particular political parties in Britain. This is not the same as placidity or apathy. Thus it is necessary to probe deeper into the perceptions of non-voters, and their definitions of 'political activity' and 'politics'; it is also necessary to explore the reasons and arguments for such perceptions and definitions.

1.4 Conclusions

The first conclusion which may be drawn from the work discussed in this chapter is that the ways in which 'politics', and 'political activity' are defined need to be made explicit in this area of enquiry. Further, in order to avoid an over-restricted view of 'politics', respondents could be encouraged to discuss social issues; from this, researchers can use analyses with the aim of uncovering the respondents' notions of the political domain, and then include such notions in the report of the research.

Moreover much of the work reviewed suggests a need to explore what are defined as personal and political concerns, and the possible differences between the employed and the unemployed as to the boundaries between these. Similarly, there may be some differences amongst the unemployed on the location of this boundary. A major impact of the Civil Rights Movement in the United States was that personal behaviour often indicated political activity. The issue of legislating to ensure that individuals would sell their houses on a non-discriminatory basis is an oft-cited example demonstrating that personal decisions have considerable political implications. Whilst the more conventional indicators may provide some insights into aspects of politicisation, it is being argued that these, by themselves, provide too narrow an assessment. Thus, an examination of apparently personal issues could help to develop insights into the ways in which 'politics' is intimately involved in the lives of the unemployed. This could be carried out in conjunction with an examination of involvement in political parties, trades unions and community organisations.

The final substantive, as distinct from methodological, point to be drawn from the studies discussed above is the confusion and confounding of terms such as 'alienation', 'apathy' and 'cynicism'. The assumption underlying the use of these terms is that they are quasi-synonymous. Well over a decade ago, Olsen (1969) conceptualised 'alienation' as 'attitudes of estrangement from the political system' and considered these attitudes to fall into two broad categories: political incapability and discontent. What lies behind discontent with political systems needs further exploration. Whilst discontent may be defined as 'political' if it occurs along with membership of a 'far-left' grouping, the ways in which individuals deal with their discontent is also indicative of their definitions of 'political'.

1.5   Summary

Following an examination of the present context of unemployment in Britain, this chapter has argued that most psychological writings on the consequences of unemployment have constructed a picture of despair, fatalism and withdrawal as the main consequences of unemployment. The approach and assumptions inherent in such work have been questioned. In a period of high unemployment, it has been argued that an examination of issues within the domain of the 'political' could provide a more accurate set of insights into how individuals are interpreting their material and social environments.

However, from the examples in section 1.3, I have suggested that there are a number of difficulties with some of the existing research on the political attitudes of the unemployed. Broadly speaking, the issues raised are:

(a)   The equation of political activity, political involvement, and political choice with voting behaviour, e.g. Rosenstone (1982)

(b)   A failure to examine systematically the process by which personal concerns do or do not come to be seen as political issues, e.g. Brody and Sniderman (1977)

(c)   The assumed synonymity between political cynicism and political apathy, e.g. Jackson (1973)

(d) The value of large scale survey techniques in tracing the contours of political involvement, e.g. Schlozman and Verba (1979)

(e) The lack of acknowledgement that the unemployed is a heterogeneous group, especially in respect of age, gender and 'race'.

2 Youth, unemployment, and political views

Nevertheless and notwithstanding differences of power, money, race, gender, age and class, there remains one currency common to all of us. There remains one thing that makes possible exchange, shared memory, self-affirmation and collective identity – our language.

June Jordan   *On Call. Political Essays*

2.1 Youth unemployment

Discussions about unemployment often focus on the unemployment of young people. Youth unemployment is defined as a major problem throughout Britain, and indeed, throughout the world. Regardless of the political persuasion of those who write about it, discuss it, or are in the business of developing social policies in relation to it, this is an agreed starting point. Clearly, however, it is part of the issue of unemployment as a whole, which has increased dramatically in the past decade. Youth unemployment levels are directly tied to levels of unemployment in general. Makeham (1980) has pointed to figures produced by the Department of Employment which have indicated that when unemployment rises by one percentage point for women, it rises by 3 percentage points for women under 20. Similarly, for men under 20, it rises by 1.7 percentage points. Whilst it used to be argued that this relationship also held true when unemployment was falling, that is, that levels of youth unemployment rise and fall in a clear relationship to overall levels of unemployment, Finn (1983) has suggested that youth·unemployment has become 'structural' in that levels of youth unemployment are now less directly related to overall levels of unemployment. How region and 'race' intercut with age and sex is not clear: considerable analysis is still necessary.

In July 1987, 29% of 16–18-year-olds in Britain were not in full-time paid employment: 15.4% being on Youth Training Schemes and 13.6% registered as unemployed.[1] It can also be seen that of 16-year-olds, 27.1% were on training schemes, and 10.7% were registered as unemployed;[2] a total of at least 37.9% of all 16-year-olds in Britain were therefore not in 'proper' jobs. This contrasts sharply with an overall figure of 10.2% unemployment amongst the whole of the labour force. This level of 37.9% drops to 23.9% for 17-year-olds (10.3% on the Youth Training Scheme and 13.6% registered

---

[1]   All the figures in this paragraph are taken from the September 1987 *Department of Employment Gazette*.

[2]   The first section of chapter 1 has considered the arguments surrounding the definitions and the methods of counting the unemployed.

unemployed) and drops still further to 16.5% for 18-yearolds (0.2% on the Youth Training Scheme and 16.3% registered unemployed). However, it can be seen that the overall decrease incorporates an overall increase in the percentage of registered unemployed between the ages of 16 and 18 years.

The *Labour Market Quarterly* of June 1987 produced by the Manpower Services Commission has a breakdown of unemployment rates by age and sex in the spring of 1986. Using the 1986 Labour Force Survey, it is shown that women's unemployment amongst 16–19-year-olds was 19% at that time, with a level of 20% for men of the same age. This almost negligible difference between women and men becomes greater, however, amongst 20–24-year-olds, when unemployment was at 14% for women and 18% for men. The Labour Force Survey of 1986 also provides figures for rates of unemployment by ethnic origin: when unemployment was at 11% for the white men, and 10% for white women, and 11% for 'all origins', it was 19% for black women and 20% for black men. That is, it was, overall, at 22% for those of West Indian or Guyanese origin, 20% for those of Indian, Pakistani or Bangladeshi origin, and 18% for other non-white ethnic origins.[3] These figures are greater than, but still reflect the differences found by the Commission for Racial Equality in 1980. This study found that amongst 16–20-year-olds, those of Afro-Caribbean origin were one and a half times more likely to be employed as white 16–20-year-olds. Hirsch (1983) cites the work of Campbell and Jones in Bradford, who found that 17-year-olds of Indian sub-continental origin were less than half as likely to have a job as their white peers. Thus, as levels of unemployment amongst under-20-year-olds have risen in the present decade, they have risen more amongst young black people.

A number of temporary employment schemes have been set up for youth, the level of state spending on them having increased dramatically since the uprisings in the summer of 1981. Ryan (1983) points out that:

> [in recent years] we find that the gross expenditure by the state upon the former group [16–17-year-olds] has amounted...to more than four times that upon the latter [18–64-year-olds].
>
> Ryan 1983: 10

What is of especial interest here is that there has been a relatively large expenditure on youth, at a period when the present government in Britain

---

[3]   The difference between black women and black men in their rates of unemployment is small, with the level of registered unemployment amongst black women being lower than that of black men by between 1 and 3 percentage points according to ethnic group.

has been adopting a clearly deflationary and monetary policy, fully aware of the implications of such a policy for unemployment.

These temporary employment schemes – the Youth Opportunities Programmes, and the Youth Training Schemes – have been criticised in a number of ways, most particularly that there is no job guaranteed on completion of the scheme, and that the present allowance is only £28.50 per week for the first thirteen weeks changing to £35.00 per week on a one-year scheme. On a two-year scheme the rate is £28.50 per week for the first six months and £35.00 per week for the remaining time. These special and lower rates of remuneration for young people are rationalised by an unjustified assumption that the young employees will have a lower rate of productivity than older workers, and that employers need to be encouraged to hire and train young people (Marsden and Ryan 1986). Commentators who have analysed the YTS, such as Farish (1984), and Rees and Atkinson (1982) have argued that despite the training element of the Youth Training Scheme, the schemes are important for both inculcating work discipline and for perpetuating racial and gender stratifications in the labour force. Farish argues that there is an explicit agenda of the Youth Training Schemes which reinforces the work ethic, and Ryan (1983) argues that the desire to instil the work ethic into young workers is achieved by 'the workings of an overstocked labour market' (Ryan 1983: 14).

It is working-class youth that the dramatic rise in youth unemployment in the last decade has affected the most. Between 1979 and 1982, unemployment amongst the under 25s rose from approximately 11.7% to 21.2%, with 312,000 of them having been unemployed for more than a year up to October 1982. School leaver unemployment increased from 78,000 to 197,300 a rise of 153%. If one examines unemployment rates amongst young women at that time, one can see that 24% of those under 20 were unemployed as compared to 27% of men under 20; in contrast, 16% of the 19–24-year-old women were unemployed as compared to 22% of men in the same age group.[4]

Ashton and Maguire (1983a and b) and Finn (1983) argue that current levels of unemployment are due to a shrinking number of jobs available to young people. The most visible response of governments to youth unemployment has been to develop a number of schemes mostly through the auspices of the Manpower Services Commission (MSC). Finn's analysis (1983) of the spending levels of the MSC demonstrates that the Conservative

---

[4] The lower rates of unemployment documented in the 1986 figures cited earlier are, it is argued, a reflection of the changes in the ways in which unemployment is counted rather than an indication that youth unemployment has fallen between 1982 and 1986.

government of 1979 cut the budget of the MSC on entry to office in 1979/80, but that following on from the urban uprisings of 1981, the government altered its policies and expanded provision for the young.

Finn's argument is that the Youth Training Scheme (YTS), which has developed from the Youth Opportunities Programme, is:

> more likely to be seen as a 'gangplank to the dole' than a bridge to work.
>
> Finn 1984: 23

In addition, Finn argues that these YTS schemes are extending the period when youth are unable to find jobs, and that developing perceptions of youth unemployment are moulding the ways in which working class young people are having the status of adult denied to them, thus furthering the hidden agendas of the Special Measures for young people.

> The MSC has not, therefore, been a simple palliative. It represents a bureaucratic response to the political problems posed by unemployment.
>
> Finn 1986: seminar paper

The issue here is to what extent this forced reduction of school leavers' expectations can lead to this group not viewing unemployment as a political issue.

This point emerges from Finn's analysis, which is that not only was the MSC structuring the perceptions of older people about youth unemployment but that, in addition,

> the M.S.C. was attempting to structure and define their [youth's] response to the experience of cheap labour and unemployment.
>
> Finn 1986: seminar paper

Such an argument requires *systematic* investigation which takes into account the restructuring of youth employment, and the ways in which the notions of cultural reproduction and resistances may permit a greater understanding of these points. Finn's assertion, however, has an intuitive appeal and seems more plausible when one notes that the MSC is now funding many centres for the unemployed and laying down strict criteria ensuring that any political campaigning work on the part of these centres will lead to a withdrawal of funds. Ridley (1979/80) also analyses the life skills approach being encouraged by the MSC, and states:

> the whole campaign to make young people more 'employable' is irrelevant to the underlying, structural causes of juvenile unemployment, and runs the risk of misleading those concerned with youth programmes.
>
> Ridley 1979/80: 24

This can be coupled with Hartley's (1980) reference to temporary employment schemes for the young:

> It may not be sufficient to provide school leavers with 'meaningful activity' (work) since the lack of a 'real' employment relationship (based on market value) means that they may feel subsidised and that they are not being taken seriously as working adults.
>
> Hartley 1980: 413

If school leavers are not being allocated to 'meaningful activity' now, it is necessary to examine what, if any, effects this lack of both work and employment has on their views of the world. Clearly, therefore, youth unemployment provides a particular context to questions about the political responses of the young. However, before one can analyse recent work which investigates the attitudes of the young in the context of their unemployment it is necessary to examine the emergence of 'youth' as a category.

2.2   Analyses of 'youth' and studies of youth cultures

There is an implication in many writings that the 'youth question' is something entirely unprecedented. Analyses of the ways in which youth were viewed in the late nineteenth century up to the mid-twentieth century in Britain (e.g. Pearson (1983), Humphries (1981), Dyhouse (1981) and White (1980)) suggest however that this is not an accurate perception. Humphries points to:

> a powerful undercurrent of resistance [which] cannot be dismissed simply as an expression of the ignorance, immorality, and immaturity that middle class commentators have commonly attributed to working class youth...[this resistance can be seen as] a discriminating response to the contradictions and inequality that were experienced in all spheres of life
>
> Humphries 1981: 293

That youth, even working-class youth, is not a unitary category is not a new issue. Nava (1981) suggests that the term 'youth' has always had connotations of masculinity and delinquency. By an historical analysis of 'youth', she demonstrates how white girls are presented as less of a 'street problem' than boys, and indicates some of the means by which young women are controlled both within a household and within youth clubs. Thus, while both young women and young men are located in the same category, that of youth, it is clear that their experiences and how they are perceived is different. There is a certain amount of literature which suggests the same point can be seen in relation to black youth and white youth, and this is discussed later.

Within psychology, the most common approach has been to look at adolescence, with an attempt to relate the biological changes at puberty with social, intellectual (cognitive), and political development through the teenage years (e.g. Conger 1973). In addition, many people have viewed this period of the life-span as one fraught with 'storm and stress' for the young person, which is most frequently expressed through the concept of the 'identity crisis'. Erikson's (1971) argument that this period of development may be viewed as a moratorium during which the individual can 'try out' different life styles before having to 'settle down' and deal with financial and employment responsibilities is appealing. However, work by Coleman and Coleman (1984) and Weinreich-Haste (1982) has indicated that storm and stress coupled with a rebellious approach to authority is not necessarily the norm for many young people in Western industrialised societies. The work of Palmonari et al. (1984) with young people in Italy has also adopted a more wide-ranging approach than is often found in psychology. Such analyses and approaches are gaining more credence within psychology, although conventional wisdom, as reflected in journalistic approaches to youth, has not, as yet, altered significantly.[5]

An early attempt to examine the notion of 'adolescent culture' was the study reported by Elkin and Westley (1955). In their work, they challenge the idea that there is *one* adolescent culture epitomised by 'storm and stress' and that this is a widespread and dominant pattern among American

---

[5] One example of such an approach is the feature in the *Sunday Times* of 1 November 1981, where the colour magazine contained a substantial 'photo-essay' entitled Youth – Scenes From the Life of a Beleaguered Generation. Whilst the article has an introductory paragraph on the historical reasons for the setting up of the Boys Brigades and the Scouts, it manages to concentrate on behaviours usually termed 'anti-social' and manifested by youth. It could be argued that there are journalistic imperatives for Jack and McCullin (the authors of this article) to interview punks, borstal attenders, and so on; however, it seems appropriate to delve a little further and explore how such an approach seems to be the 'obvious' one to adopt. The argument here is that anxieties about youth spanning 100 years have become consolidated, via social scientific enquiry, into possessing a reality not always supported by systematic empirical work.

adolescents' life. They say:

> The assumption of a link between the needs of the
> adolescent and the youth culture leads to a biased selection
> of illustrations...[other] writers tend to ignore deferred
> gratification patterns, the internalisations of adults' modes
> of thought and behaviour, positive relationships with
> authority figures, instances of family solidarity, or 'inner
> directed' interests which may set an adolescent apart from
> his [sic] agemates.
>
> > Elkin and Westley 1955: 681

Having reported their findings of adolescent socialisation in a middle-class suburban community of Montreal, Canada, they argue that the '*current model* of adolescent culture represents an erroneous conception'. (My emphasis, note singular of model.)

Whilst the above section has discussed 'youth' and 'young people', not only is this not a homogeneous group, but the implicit biological and psychological assumptions underlying these notions disguise the ways in which the transitions between childhood and adulthood are social rather than natural. Bates et al. (1984) argue that youth is the result of social arrangements aimed at regulating the transition of child to worker and citizen in industrialised nation states, and not a transition of child to adult in any universal sense. Such an analysis can appear too stark. However, in stressing this aspect of youth, Bates et al. may be seen as redressing the balance of an otherwise ahistorical set of conceptions about youth and adolescence. They argue that it is a social transition and, in this context, youth is a social product which accompanied the rise of mass schooling. The potential labour power of the child is transformed into the actual labour power of the adult. Thus, this transition is a social process, but is not a single social process, and is differentiated by class, 'race' and gender in Britain. These shape the process of the transition, such as its length, the institutions in which it is experienced (school, college, university) and the different destinations, including the directions encountered within it. So, Bates et al. point to the fact that there are a number and variety of transitions from school to beyond school.

Much of the research concerning young people and the transition from school to work has centred on education and the labour market, such as that of Watts (1978), while some has included an analysis of leisure activities (Corrigan 1979; Jenkins 1983a). Looking at unemployment and young people, one can see that most writers have either ignored young women entirely (see McRobbie 1978) or young men have been taken as the norm against which women's experiences must be judged (Willis, 1984a and 1984b). The consequence of this is that theories which are presented as being universal are, in fact, gender specific; and Griffin (1985c) has argued that young women's experiences do not fit easily into these models. At the same time, she points out (and the analysis is expanded in Griffin, 1986b) that, whilst being gender specific, these theories have little to say about gender relations (see Connell 1983 and Willis 1977 for exceptions).

This criticism of adolescent culture as a monolithic concept has been accepted in some sociological analyses of British youth. Brake (1980, 1985) examines a variety of youth cultures in Britain and North America as well as the differing analyses of these cultures. Brake's argument is that youth cultures contain many subcultures. He (Brake 1985) defines subcultures as being:

> meaning systems, modes of expression or life styles developed by groups in subordinate structural positions in response to dominant meaning systems, and which reflect their attempt to solve structural contradictions arising from the wider societal context... Subcultures negotiate between the interpersonal world of the actor and the dynamics of the larger elements of social interaction.
>
> Brake 1985: 8-9

He discusses different approaches to the study of subcultures, including that of the Centre for Contemporary Cultural Studies (CCCS) at Birmingham University.

The approach of the CCCS has been to analyse the ways in which the relations between dominant and subordinate cultures are negotiated. They suggest that in order to analyse youth subculture, youth needs to be located

> in the dialectic between a 'hegemonic' dominant culture and the subordinate working class 'parent' culture of which youth is a fraction.
>
> Clarke et al. 1975: 38

Sociological thinking about youth and youth cultures in the past decade has developed mainly via ethnographic work combined with participant observation and a critical theoretical analysis. These youth culture studies endeavoured to start their analysis from the perspective of young people, by taking such perspectives seriously, although not necessarily at face value. Hall and Jefferson (1975) argued that the institution of education, for example, structures and imposes ideological boundaries on young people's lives; therefore, research was needed to explore these boundaries, and to shift the emphasis away from the earlier one in which young people were viewed as problems.

> The emphasis shifted away from fitting young people in with the demands of dominant institutions as a means of policing their entry to the labour market. The youth cultures approach aimed to identify young people's resistances to these demands, taking a particular interest in the collective cultural activities of white working class males in Britain's inner cities.
>
> Griffin 1986a: 21

One significant type of study has been the ethnographic cultural exploration of working-class male white youth in their transition from school to un/employment. Willis (1977) is one of the best known of these studies which is subtitled 'How working class kids get working class jobs'. Moving on from the CCCS analysis referred to above, Willis begins from a position that the domination of one class in capitalism is not simple and deterministic but a constant struggle. Thus the accommodation of the working class to the demands of capital can sometimes be a consequence of the resistances developed at school. Willis argues that while the anti-school culture may be conceptualised as resistance, its similarity to shop-floor culture, e.g. a rejection of official roles, a mistrust of official values, a desire to be non-conformist, is such that the counter-school culture, in reality, prepares 'the lads' for entry into routinised labour; thus they more easily tolerate an alienating experience.

> In the way in which it is actually effective in the world the half rejection and cultural penetration of the present social organisation by the counter school culture becomes an always provisional, bare, sceptical yet finally acceptive accommodation within the status quo.
>
> Willis 1977: 145

Whilst Willis's work is a study of considerable significance, in particular for its demonstration of how ethnography can provide valuable insights, a frustrating aspect of his examination of cultural reproduction is that he does not follow up instances where an accommodation to the *status quo* need not be the only possible interpretation of some of the statements made by 'the lads'. For example,

> Joey ... It's been this way too long ... You gotta help

yourself, how many revolutions have there been that really worked?

ibid.: 198

Clearly this could be interpreted as an accommodating statement. But to use Willis's words once again:

> [Counter school culture] contradictorily maintains a degree of conviction of movement... the most remarkable demonstration of this contradiction is that of a nascent cultural understanding of abstract labour and class solidarity among disaffected working class kids...
>
> ibid: 145

The use by Joey of 'revolution' as a means of shifting power relations within capitalism warrants further probing, in order to explore the 'nascent solidarity' referred to. Joey's statement may be understood not only as individualism exemplified. His implicit acknowledgement that there may be other means suggests not simply that he has totally rejected these other ways, i.e. revolution, but, owing to Joey demonstrating his knowledge that revolutions are one form of social and political change, it could be interpreted as Joey's attempt to explore a different 'analysis'. This can be seen more clearly if one couples this statement of Joey's with an earlier one:

> Joey ... we've been brought up too selfish... you see on the telly so many people fuckin' affluent, you just want to try and do that, make it, get money, you don't care about others, the working class
>
> ibid: 198

This youth's implicit and perhaps naive acknowledgement of 'socialisation' ('we've *been brought up* too selfish') warrants further analysis. There is a movement here: a recognition of the *creation* of consumerism and aspirations. If 'the cultural level is clearly partly disorganised from within (Willis 1977: 145), then Willis could have explored some of this disorganisation further. The implication of the above comments is that while ethnography is very important in gaining an understanding of 'how working-class kids get working-class jobs', it could also be used to explore the production of counter-hegemonic statements – and so begin to analyse whether some working-class youth reject dominant group values/norms/practices?

A related point is that given the complex ways in which masculinity and 'rebellion' interrelate, it is not surprising that Willis noted that the 'lads' concentrated on

> their *own* experience, and not that of the girl or their
> shared relationship... The girls are afforded no particular
> identity save that of their sexual attraction
>
> ibid: 43

It would have been interesting to see if all of that group would have responded in such a way if they had been discussing the issue of 'girlfriends' with a woman researcher, and individually rather than in group discussions. The implication of this comment is that Willis's analysis may be no more appropriate than one based on the 'lads' making very different types of statements, with a woman researcher, on the subject of relationships. Group norms and same sex perceptions could be such that there was no room for the 'lads' to demonstrate any sensitivity to the needs of their girlfriends, or sensitivity to the 'double standards' of masculine culture. The implication of these points is that one is not certain if Willis's analysis is incomplete due to a lack of definition of 'resistance' and 'accommodation', or due to the limitations of ethnography, or due to a combination of all of these.

Jenkins (1983a) looks at young Protestant working-class life styles in Belfast of both women and men. His study is an attempt to understand the move from adolescence to adulthood, and the move from school education to the labour market. He used a 'participant observation' methodology by basing himself in a youth club in which he had previously been employed as a youth worker.[6]

---

[6]   It is appropriate to comment on his methodological approach. In discussing the advantages and disadvantages of such an approach: 'one negotiates an identity and this identity necessarily colours the rest of the research. By its very nature, participant observation must lead to partial accounts' (Jenkins 1983a: 23). He also discusses the point raised by McRobbie (1982) that working-class girls are more difficult to investigate than male peers (Jenkins 1983: 19). However, he states: 'I did not feel my sex to be a major disadvantage'. Despite Jenkins's brief exploration of these points, his statement cited above seems naive and simplistic. It would perhaps be more accurate to indicate that the researcher cannot be *clear* as to how these power relationships will affect the research relationships and consequent analysis, rather than to present a 'defensive' statement, such as that quoted above. He also appears to be assuming that the impact of a researcher is synonymous with disadvantage. This is not necessarily so. What is needed, however, is, at the very least, an acknowledgement that the impact of the researcher has to be considered, as argued for example by McRobbie (1982), Oakley (1981), Griffin (1985a) and Bhavnani (1986). Given the arguments of the above writers, and the number of sophisticated analyses of power inequalities in general, it seems that Jenkins could have discussed more closely the possible implications of such inequalities when discussing his research.

Jenkins introduces his study with an attempt to assess critically work done in the sphere of cultural reproduction, i.e. the process through which the working class can be viewed as learning and supporting (and, for Jenkins, 'at times, resisting' p. 2) its position in a stratified and unequal society. He suggests that the work of both Willis and Bourdieu is overdeterministic despite their claims to avoid a simple causal model which starts with social structure:

> Social structure cannot produce the social reality to which it is held to refer. At best, concepts of social structure might explain the behaviour of sociologically-informed individuals or groups; generally speaking, however, they make sense of society and cannot be used as causal explanatory factors.
>
> Jenkins 1983a: 11

So Jenkins uses the term 'life style' in order to stress the practices of individuals in cultural reproduction, and tries to explore how life-style differences *within* a class can be analysed in the cultural reproduction framework. Jenkins identifies three groups who appear to subscribe to different life styles: the 'lads' (by definition, exclusively young men) the 'ordinary kids' and the 'citizens'. He rejects the more common two-pole model arguing that studies which indicated only two sides had been carried out in study-samples of only one school, with, consequently, a narrower social spectrum than the one he worked with. He included girls in his sample, and, he claims that this led to a requirement for a category ('the ordinary kids') 'which, while not rough, is certainly not respectable' (Jenkins 1983a: 11).

Jenkins presents both demographic and interview extracts to demonstrate the differences and the overlap between the groups in a challenging manner. However, it is important to examine his general conclusions in his final chapter where he tries to pull together many of the arguments used earlier to see how these differences between life styles are produced and reproduced. A key point raised by Jenkins is that the interviewees in his sample display an individualism in their world view and in their explanations for the present state of affairs. He accepts that such an 'individualistic analysis' is one which is continuously reinforced and is a 'dominant cultural principle of our [sic] society' (Jenkins 1983a: 131). However, he argues that this individualism combined with a localism is a barrier to developing 'working class collective political organisation' (Jenkins 1983a: 132). If one accepts this, together with Jenkins's interpretation that the labelling decisions of strategically placed individuals in the arenas of education and the labour market are central in producing and reproducing the divisions within the young working class, then an individualism appears to be an 'accurate' assessment of the location of power for these young people. To put it another way, Jenkins suggests that one aspect of cultural reproduction is consequent upon the decisions of certain key individuals; as a result the fact that 'one of the central ideological strands in the thinking of the young people of Ballyhightown is their individualism' (Jenkins 1983a: 131) is not surprising. But for Jenkins to generalise from this that such an ideological strand is present within all classes, including the working class, in British society, takes no account of those layers who clearly do not totally accept such a world view, for example, active trade unionists and political activists. In addition, for Jenkins to extrapolate from the restricted physical mobility of the working class, that 'the socially mapped area within which responsibility can be allocated is correspondingly restricted' (Jenkins 1983a: 132) appears unwarranted. That some of his sample held 'them pigs at the brue' responsible for how the DHSS deals with young people may be interpreted by suggesting that some of the sample is therefore implicitly suggesting a wider allocation of responsibility than simply individualism. It is this which could have been explored further.

There is also a certain conceptual ambiguity and confusion in both Willis's and Jenkins's work. Jenkins states:

> One of the central issues which must be grasped in the analysis of cultural reproduction is the manner by which power may be [seen to be] mobilised and legitimated simultaneously in consensus and legitimation on the one hand, and resistance, coercion and grudging accommodation on the other.
>
> Jenkins 1983a: 7

If the study of cultural reproduction permits an analysis of the hegemony of dominant values, then to include 'resistances' within the sphere of cultural reproduction rather than cultural non-reproduction is confusing. It seems that a definition of cultural reproduction which is so wide and all-embracing *prevents* researchers from analysing resistances as potentially counter-hegemonic strategies. That is, there is an implication of a monolithic ideological domination which can never be challenged. Thus, whilst some forms of resistances can be traced through to a legitimation of the inequalities in a social structure, such as Willis's demonstration that counter-school culture actually prepared the 'lads' for accommodation to shop-floor culture and practices, there may be others which may not have the same implications. There is a second consequence. The concept of cultural reproduction, as Jenkins defines it, forces any research study using the concept in this way to be functional in their analyses of resistances. Thus, in the very definition of the concept, it is not possible to explore alternative means of analysing resistances.

To summarise, a weakness in the 'cultural reproduction' analyses is the inclusion of 'resistances' within such an approach, such resistances being viewed only as examples of practice which lead to *'grudging accommodation'* (Jenkins 1983a: 8). The consequence of this is that, at best, any resistances which could be embryonic forms of political development amongst youth go unnoticed, or that such a political development is defined out of existence. Most of the research on youth 'subcultures' was carried out during periods of relatively low unemployment and focused on white, working-class men such as the work of Corrigan (1979), Hall and Jefferson (1975), and Robins and Cohen (1978). These studies, whilst relevant for my discussion, do not demonstrate the ways in which their analyses are about both young women *and* young men, black and white, and, presently, in a period of high youth unemployment.

There is some work of relevance on the cultures of young women. For example, Hudson (1984) has explored how images of femininity conflict with images of adolescence for young women. From interviews with 15-year-old young women, their teachers, and social workers in the same town, as well as through an analysis of magazines for young women, she argues that the notion of adolescence subverts that of femininity. She points out that amongst social workers, the dominant expectation is that of femininity: 'femininity, first of all, meant feminine appearance' (p. 38). In addition, femininity includes stereotypical personality characteristics following Deaux (1976), such as 'gentleness, caring for others, quietness and dependence' (p. 41). Adolescence, on the other hand, carries connotations of unruliness and immaturity and is also the dominant discourse used by the teachers in her study. Hudson, argues that these two discourses, those of femininity and adolescence, serve to make young women often view themselves as being in the wrong. A further point is that there appear to be no analyses of any cultures of resistance for young women. It is not being argued that such cultures are repositories of truth, nor that such cultures *necessarily* represent a potential for political activity, but it would be interesting to see if behaviours are developed in a systematic way in opposition to established or expected patterns. However, neither do I accept Willis's (1977) challenging analysis that some cultures of resistance can serve to reinforce existing social structures unconditionally.[7]

A number of writers have done work which is relevant to the argument about possible sources of variation. McRobbie (1982) and Griffin (1985b) have made some forceful points about the experiences of white young women which could have implications in any discussion of their political views. In addition, Parmar (1982), Stone (1983), and Dex (1983) have written about the interrelationship between gender and 'race'. Similarly, the work of Brah (1984) can be considered in which it is argued:

> [t]he experience of unemployment of young Asians is thus centrally mediated through racial and gender divisions in contemporary Britain. However, the young people are not passive victims of structural determinations. Despite... differences between young Asians, as well as between them and Afro-Caribbean youth, there is growing solidarity between different sections of black youth. Political consciousness about a common oppression is crystallised around their daily experience of growing up in the inner cities of Britain, and gives rise to *specific forms of political activity and struggle.*
>
> Brah 1984: 42 (my emphasis)

Thus, the specific context and experiences of young people inform the ways in which issues within the domain of the political are discussed by them. Such an argument has implications not only for the ways in which young people's discussions are analysed, but also for the ways in which such discussions are obtained.

2.3 Youth unemployment: psychological studies

Using a questionnaire, Gillies et al. (1985) explored how young people viewed their future in terms of the anxieties they have about it. They found that unemployment was the prime cause of anxiety for these young people in Nottingham, with 'war' being the second most cited source of anxiety. They

---

7   Johnson's (1979) argument that working-class culture may be conceptualised via the problematics of 'consciousness', 'culture', and 'ideology' can be noted here. 'Problematic may be defined as a definite theoretical structure, a field of concepts, which organises a particular science or individual text by making it possible to ask some kinds of questions and by suppressing others' (Johnson 1979: 201). One may also argue that a problematic organises a particular field of enquiry, not only a science or a text. He continues: 'One aspect of critique, then, is to render explicit what is implicit, and to consider the underlying propositions' (ibid.). As Hudson's work, mentioned above, has done, it is argued that empirical work may allow for further explorations of the issue of resistance by using the problematics discussed by Johnson.

acknowledge that the

> effects, if any, of these anxieties on the mental and physical health of adolescents are unknown, but the high prevalence of these anxieties suggests that the effects on health of unemployment may extend to those who are at risk of unemployment.
>
> Gillies et al. 1985: 384

Thus, not only do some studies indicate that unemployment can cause stress, but also the *fear* of unemployment can lead to anxiety. This reinforces the suggestion put forward by Farish mentioned earlier: she suggests, that:

> The social control of young people, *through the threat of unemployment*, is apparent in a youth training initiative with an explicit agenda to reinforce the work ethic.
>
> Farish 1984: 7 (my emphasis)

An explicit agenda of reinforcing the work ethic is based on the assumption that this ethic needs to be reinforced for young people.

Studies which examine the political views of young people are often also based on a number of commonly held, but not always cited, assumptions about working-class young people. Humphries (1981) argues that working-class youth have been associated with delinquent and anti-social behaviour, and that such behaviour is most often understood within the 'cultural' deprivation framework, namely, that there is a faulty family socialisation process, implying authoritarian and inconsistent patterns of discipline, restricted conceptual codes, and low expectations of achievement, all of which contribute to a culture of poverty. One implication of this is, he argues, that successive generations inherit an anti-intellectual culture of resignation, low expectations and immediate gratification. Thus, youth are viewed as being politically apathetic – as witnessed through low polling figures – or that they have passively internalised predominant ideologies, with the consequence that any resistances to the major institutions are suppressed or neutralised. It is this reactionary implication to which Fryer (1986a) is pointing when discussing his 'agency theory' (see chapter 1). If they are not viewed as being politically apathetic, the working class young may be presented as potential political activists. In particular, it is suggested by some writers that the experience of unemployment for young people (already defined as rebellious by virtue of the psychological constructions of adolescence) will lead them to develop activities outside of the parliamentary framework – and these activities may be defined as political, e.g. Kettle and Hodges (1982). This view still rests, however, on a 'deprivation' assumption, namely that a culture of poverty leads to discontent, rebellion and a wholesale rejection of major institutions. The experience of unemployment and its dramatic rise for youth is cited as a catalyst in the 1981 uprisings, for example.

It is often claimed that women do not participate in political activity. Pulzer's (1968) assertion that there is 'overwhelming evidence that women are more conservatively inclined than men' (p. 107) expresses an idea present in many writings. Goot and Reid (1984) argue that studies of voting behaviour have uncritically accepted this idea, either by only sampling men (e.g. Lane 1968; Abrams 1966), or by assuming that women are 'conditioned' differently:

> (G)irls are conditioned from the time they see pink to accept, for example, that politics is a man's world... Our own position is different. In terms of theory, we reject 'socialisation'... as the only possible account for the political consciousness of women.
>
> Goot and Reid 1984: 124-5

Siltanen and Stanworth (1984) also argue that political science, political sociology and industrial sociology have characterised women as participating less than men; where women are defined as being politically active, they argue that political activism is seen as 'less authentic' than the political activism of men, or, that it is 'based on a relatively unsophisticated political understanding' (p. 186) on the part of women. There seems to be little available empirical evidence for such notions or, indeed, discussion of the theoretical confusion they may represent as to what is considered political.[8]

The school curricula, practices and government policy are formulated on the basis of the assumptions discussed above, the clearest example being the ways in which youth are being encouraged to participate in the YTS, both as a means of keeping young men off the streets, and, by implication, away from rebellion, and as an attempt to discipline them into the work ethic at a time when *all* jobs, and the jobs they would hope to get, are either non-existent or not open to young people any longer. The view of youth as

---

[8]   Whilst it may be a truism to suggest that girls experience their social environment differently to boys, this does not mean that they are necessarily less inclined to consider or discuss political issues. What is defined as being in the domain of politics requires further consideration, therefore, bearing in mind the earlier discussion on political apathy, political cynicism, and anomie outlined in the previous chapter.

potential trouble-makers also rests on theories such as those of Erikson (1971), or on studies published within developmental psychology, that youth or adolescence is a period of confusion, storm and stress leading to a rebellious phase in the individual's life span.

The particular circumstances of the present decade, with its extremely high levels of youth unemployment, and the consequent development of a range of 'employment and training' schemes needs systematic examination in considerations on youth and politics. It could be argued, following Finn (1983), that these training schemes, and the consequent restructuring of the youth labour market constitute a particular set of events which could have an effect on the political socialisation of those experiencing this training transition in Britain in the mid 1980s (Niemi and Sobieszek 1977). Additionally, Niemi and Sobieszek suggest that teenagers are more trusting and less politically cynical than adults; they also point out that identification with a political party is one of the most long-lasting identifications for an individual. Stacey (1978) has also reviewed political socialisation from a life-span perspective, and Rose and McAllister (1986) suggest that the significance of primary socialisation in determining the division of the vote is relatively weak when compared to current forces in determining the vote.

2.4 Youth, unemployment, and politics: psychological studies

Certainly, issues of specific context, experiences and methodologies have not always been tackled in recent psychological studies of the unemployed. The psychological work on unemployment has been strongly influenced by Marie Jahoda's work with older, unemployed men in the 1930s; other studies have adopted individualised analyses based on clinical models (e.g. Stokes 1983). Some have combined quantitative and qualitative analyses (Breakwell 1982), to examine identities along with other aspects of psychological interest. The work of the MRC and Economic and Social Research Council unit at Sheffield (the Sheffield Applied Psychology Unit) is probably the most extensive in this area, although this too has been heavily biased towards quantitative methods (Warr, Jackson and Banks 1982; Warr, Banks and Ullah 1985; Ullah and Banks 1985; Ullah 1985; although see Ullah 1987 for an exception to these quantitative studies). The research programme of this unit began with an exploration of the mental health of 'less qualified young people' (Stafford, Jackson and Banks 1980), continued into an investigation of the job aspirations and job search behaviours (Stafford and Jackson 1983), and is now exploring both social support and psychological distress during unemployment (Ullah, Banks and Warr 1985). Furnham (1985) suggests that the studies of the psychological consequences of unemployment in young people tend to show that unemployment causes stress, a lowering of self esteem, and a change in expectations. However, in his review article, he has not specifically commented on studies which have investigated the political views of young people. Partly this is due to the fact that psychological work on the political views of the young has not been extensive. The work reported by Coffield, Borrill and Marshall (1983) has implied that the experience of unemployment is such that those who experience it are moved to participate in potentially radical activities, while the work of Bunker and Dewberry (1983) implies that all ages of unemployed tend to withdraw from social contact and retreat into their homes, that is, the unemployed become politically quiescent. How far this last is true for young people requires closer investigation.

Breakwell (1986) has conducted a study to explore the political responses of unemployed young people in Britain, while at the same time looking at how these young people explained their own unemployment, and unemployment in general. The method used was a structured interview schedule which lasted approximately an hour. There were five questions which explored explanations for unemployment, and the questions on political involvement were of three types: political affiliation, faith in politics, and anticipation of violent change.

> The results are easily summarised: these young unemployed were not involved with political or social movements, did not wish to join them, had no faith in political change though some thought a political party might quell unemployment, and a large majority expected violent changes would occur and an even greater number would support such attempts at change. It had been intended to examine attributional strategies in relation to political involvement; this proved impossible given the homogeneity in absence of such involvement.
>
> Breakwell 1986: 13

This apparent homogeneity of views may be misleading; a detailed open-ended interview could have provided instances of activity which the respondents may not have defined as 'political', but which could have been placed within the domain of politics (see previous discussion in chapter 1 of the work of Schlozman and Verba 1979).

A similar point may be made about the work of Lowe and colleagues (Lowe, Krahn, Hartnagel and Tanner 1985; Lowe 1986). Their research is also used to suggest the lack of a political response to unemployment on the part of young people (Lowe 1986). The same point, as made in relation to the Breakwell (1986) study may be directed at the Canadian work: to use the word 'politics' when discussing views of unemployment and society with young people may result in the topic being defined as one which requires detailed information of parliamentary processes, and thus be seen as 'irrelevant' by young people. Future studies could take this possibility into account.

The work done by Billig and Cochrane in the last few years is an interesting attempt to explore the political perspectives of 'adolescents' and is central to this discussion. Cochrane and Billig (1983) provide a summary of their study which involved two surveys of fifth formers in the West Midlands in comprehensive schools, each survey covering over 1,000 students. The survey questionnaire was designed to tap many factors in political identification and beliefs, including aspects such as class identification, party choice, attitudes towards the political system and knowledge of policies. The surveys were carried out in 1979 and in the winter of 1982. In addition, they engaged in participant observation of the meetings of the youth sections of the Conservative and Labour parties in the area. Not only are their findings of interest, as a general contribution to the study of the political perspectives of adolescents, but also, as they point out, unemployment levels in the region rose dramatically between the two surveys.

> Whereas in 1979/80 only 4% of the fathers of our respondents were unemployed, by 1981/2 this figure had grown to 15%. Employment prospects for school leavers deteriorated even faster and to such an extent that hardly any of the fifth formers who left several of the schools we studied obtained immediate employment.
> Cochrane and Billig 1983: 31

They also note that the Social Democratic Party (SDP) emerged in Britain in that period, and they discuss its possible impact on structuring the views of the school students they surveyed. They found that there was a substantial increase, within that sample, of support for the National Front. Such support had increased from 6% to 14%, and was accompanied by an increase in identification with the ideology of the National Front. This was 'often accompanied by unashamed racist opinions, openly expressed' (p. 33). They argue that what occurred in the intervening period led to a growth of pessimistic feelings for the future accompanied by a conviction on the part of their sample that no-one, including politicians, had any control over events. Cochrane and Billig suggest that these developments coincided with a large decline in support for the major political parties: for Conservatives, from 35% to almost 17%, and for the Labour Party, from 51.5% to approximately 43%. However, support went from 6.3% for the Liberals in the 1979/80 sample to almost 25% for the Liberal and the SDP together in 1982. The authors argue that the decline in support for the two main parties was accompanied by a lack of enthusiasm or conviction on the part of those who continued to support the parties, and that the issue of apparent lack of control created an acceptance of:

> apparently simple, often nationalist, sometimes authoritarian solutions to economic problems.
>
> Cochrane and Billig 1983: 32

The authors also demonstrate how such nationalist solutions were frequently stated by supporters of *all* parties, including the Labour Party.

In other papers, the authors analyse the reasons for the support for the SDP by their sample (Cochrane and Billig 1983), and they test three models of political extremism in relation to National Front identification (Cochrane and Billig 1982a). There are a number of avenues for discussion as a consequence of their research which used a number of differing and complementary methods, but two are especially pertinent for this project.

Firstly, Cochrane and Billig (1983) refer to a measure of Socialist Attitudes which they constructed. They found that 50% of those with high scores on this scale said they would not support the Labour Party, or, indeed, any grouping further to the left.

> Instead, it was the SDP, the NF and the BM [British Movement] who were picking up their support or, even more commonly, *there was a general rejection of any political involvement whatsoever.*
>
> Cochrane and Billig 1983: 33 (my emphasis)

In a significant concluding paragraph, the authors state:

> It is possible, of course, to overstate the significance of the political views of 15/16 year olds as indicators of future voting intentions or other forms of adult political activity. Indeed, the traditional view has been that while at school political opinions are unrestrained by reality and therefore tend towards the fantastic; the schoolboy or girl is therefore able to show off his or her daring, shocking or extreme views. When, however, the young person is exposed to the

reality of the workplace, then harder economic influences
take over, and the vast majority (of) people become
socialised into accepting one of the (up until now) two
main parties...

Cochrane and Billig 1983: 34

They conclude their article with:

[T]he traditional dismissive view of adolescent politics is
based on the assumption that school leavers will get jobs.
This assumption is clearly no longer viable in many areas.

ibid. (my emphasis)

Thus, in this final sentence there is an implication that the rapidly
changing context of employment prospects for young people, coupled with
the *fear* of unemployment (e.g. Gillies et al. 1985), could mean that further
investigations are necessary. Secondly, whilst the work of these two
researchers is instructive, one could argue that their suggestion that the
school students they surveyed rejected 'any political involvement
whatsoever' can not be accepted at face value. The main drawback of
surveys is that respondents' answers are dependent on their own perceptions
of the written questions, many of which had the word 'political' in them.[9]
Thus, a variety of linguistic interpretations of questions and answers are
possible in surveys. It may also be difficult, in self-completion
questionnaires, for researchers to be confident that the literacy skills of all
respondents are at a level where the subjects are able to comprehend every
question. Thus, such techniques may be of only limited help in sorting out
individuals' interpretations of key political concepts, a point made, and taken
note of by the authors, who also conducted group discussions to overcome
this limitation. This point has also been made by Billig (1978) in his study
entitled *Fascists*. Ethnographic and interview methods may be helpful in
tackling the issue of 'political involvement', and its significance for young
people in the context of their employment opportunities.

Taylor conducted a study in 1983 on the political views of young
unemployed people, using ethnographic and interview methods. The sample
comprised 42 women and 44 men, 30 being of Afro-Caribbean origin, 30 of
Indian subcontinental origin and 26 white. She interviewed and looked at
diaries (the exact methodology of her study is not available) of 86 young
people, between the ages of 17 and 20 years, 'poorly qualified' (Taylor

---

9   See Coffield, Borrill and Marshall (1986) for a brief discussion of how the word 'political'
    often silences working-class young people.

1983: 17), 42 of whom had not been involved with either the Youth Opportunities Programme or a job, 26 of whom had had one job, the other 18 being equally divided between having only YOP experience or temporary, unofficial and casual employment. Her section on 'Causes and Cures of Unemployment' is worth commenting on. She points out that only 4 of her sample blamed themselves when asked the general question of what were the causes of unemployment, with 54 blaming the present government and/or the present Prime Minister, 8 blaming the present government but viewing the situation as developing before the entry of the 1979 Conservative administration, and 8 (including one white person) blamed 'discrimination'. One person blamed the unions for not doing much about the situation, and one blamed strikes and too much expenditure. What is a little startling about this is Taylor's comment. She argues that media coverage of unemployment links unemployment with government policy, and says:

> it is not surprising that young people give this response. *How far it arises out of a heightened political consciousness,* however, is questionable.
> Taylor 1983: 40 (my emphasis)

Taylor's conclusion does not fit easily with other empirical evidence. Wober (1980) for example, shows that school leavers have relatively low levels of interest in news and current affairs television, and links this to the general finding that those who watch less news on television 'have less political knowledge'. Therefore, if Taylor's sample had knowledge of media coverage of unemployment, then, following Wober, they would have some political knowledge. While it is not possible to assume that greater political knowledge is synonymous with 'heightened political consciousness', it is clearly not accurate to make the assumption that Taylor does. It could be argued that a clearer definition of 'political' combined with some further probing of the responses may have led her to some very different conclusions. For example, one issue which might have been discussed concerns the extent to which the young people in her sample define themselves as being disenfranchised, and thus place themselves outside the domain of conventional politics.

The latter is a question which Cohen (1983) raises. He points out that many of the unemployed youth he interviewed had specific, radical demands,

> but I was left with an over-riding impression of cynicism about politicians of every kind, and a general disbelief in the solutions to the crisis put forward by socialists.
> Cohen 1983: 28

His overall argument seems to be that the traditional strategies of radical groups of the left are, at best rigid, at worst, off-putting, through their emphasis on 'serious' politics which connects hardly at all with present youth cultures. He says it is necessary to shift

> the grounds of common sense towards a more open space where socialist ideas can be set against the revalued experience of a new working class generation, and tried and tested for their realism and relevance.
>
> ibid.: 36

Thus, when Hall (1984) argues that:

> Politics are rooted in *social relations,* not just in a programme of political targets
>
> p. 18 (my emphasis)

it is this dimension of social relations which many of the studies of youth and politics have missed out. It seems that Cohen may be working with Hall's (1984) conception of the projects of socialism, namely, that these projects have to be rooted in a struggle to command the 'common sense' of the age.

The writings of Billig and Cochrane which present their analysis of political meetings of the youth wings of the Conservative and Labour Parties appear to bear out the points raised by Cohen and Hall. In their papers, the writers point out there is a distinction drawn between 'fun' and 'boring politics' in the organisation and events of the Young Conservatives. In contrast, the Young Socialists saw 'politics' as the dominant motif for their meetings. Billig and Cochrane say:

> a radical group, opposed to the dominant culture has particular problems in choosing politically acceptable, yet genuinely attractive forms of fun.
>
> Billig and Cochrane 1982: 39

Billig (1986) continues this earlier analysis in a recent piece. In this article, he presents a powerful argument for studying a group 'characterised by ordinariness' (Billig 1986: 71) and explores how the study of the Young Conservatives can reveal much about:

> ordinary ideology... They [the Young Conservatives] had no need to empty their minds of conventional images in order to build a purer system of thought, but insisted that they

were perfectly at home with the conventional. However, because this ordinary outlook was brought into contact with the extraordinary world of organised power politics, certain aspects are thrown into sharper focus.

Billig 1986: 69/72

Through a careful ethnographic analysis of these interviews and discussions Billig succeeds in demonstrating that embedded in the notion of being a member of the Young Conservatives is a requirement to eschew party political discussions in meetings and social events – evidence of Giddens's (1979) argument that one characteristic of ideology is that it makes the present appear natural. Instead, the emphasis is on the 'naturalness' of a common aim: to help in the election of future Conservative governments and to 'have fun' in the intervening periods. In the earlier work of Cochrane and Billig (1983), this approach is contrasted with that of members of the youth section of the Labour Party who demonstrated considerable, consistent and frequent interest in parliamentary party politics.

2.5   The domain of politics

It has been suggested in previous sections that although youth cultures may represent only a fraction within other cultures, they provide an appropriate starting point for an exploration of the political awareness of young people. However, the cultural reproduction thesis is weak because of its over-inclusivity: resistances are analysed within the cultural reproduction framework rather than being used to analyse potential cultural non-reproduction. When 'cynicism' and 'apathy' are used as descriptive terms, they have the effect of making any 'resistance' invisible. For example, if 'common sense' is being challenged, it does not seem to be adequate to examine only whether youth are entering political parties and trade unions, and to use this as a criterion for defining political awareness. The development and visibility of youth cultures in the last two decades along with a change in the working-class 'rhythm of gratitude and deference' (Hall 1984: 19) requires different approaches.

The late Raymond Williams discusses this issue and says:

> I would say that we have to distinguish between areas of consciousness which are genuinely open to recognition of real situations (thus allowing some real possibility of choice) and these different real pressures in which people are truly conscious of the determinations on their lives... [T]here are disciplines of capitalism [which] exert a control on people based not so much upon positive assent as upon

the absence of immediate alternatives.

Williams 1983: 15

The concept of hegemony may be useful in the analysis and definitions utilised to explore the political conceptions and views of the young unemployed.

Hegemony may be viewed as being an order in which a certain way of life and thought is dominant in which one concept of reality is diffused throughout society in all its institutional and private manifestations, informing with its spirit all taste, morality, customs, religions, and political principles, and all social relations, particularly in their intellectual and moral connotations.

Williams: quoted in Kolakowski 1978

There is a further point. As Clarke et al. (1975) stress, there is a constant struggle for such hegemonic ascendancy with the consequence that there are competing candidates for hegemony. It is these latter which need to be investigated in relation to the young unemployed. Femia's (1975) comments on hegemony and consciousness are pertinent here. He states:

In his [Gramsci's] schema, members of subordinate classes come to accept the dominant network of beliefs as an abstract version of reality, *but their life conditions weaken its binding force* in the actual conduct of affairs.

Femia 1975: 46

If hegemonic rule is rule through consent, then cognitive and affective aspects of individuals may be shaped by the institutions of civil society to obtain this 'consent'. Thus Femia argues 'consent becomes essentially passive' (p. 33). However, there also exists a contradictory consciousness, necessitating a struggle for hegemony:

Lurking below the usually conforming surface are subversive beliefs and values, latent instincts of rebellion...

Femia 1975: 43

Femia suggests, from an examination of Rodman's (1963) review of the literature on delinquency, that what occurs is not a 'flouting of the middle class ethos', but a 'stretched value system', with a low degree of commitment to *all* values.

This issue of whether a value consensus exists has been carefully considered by Mann (1982). By re-analysing empirical studies which explored value commitment in Britain and the United States, Mann considers the notion whether there is a 'social cohesion of liberal democracy'.

> In this paper, I will attempt empirical testing of the theories
> of both 'consensus' and 'false consciousness' sociologists.
>
> Mann 1982: 375

Certain of his comments are worth noting here. He points out, from his consideration of Free and Cantril's (1967) study of American political attitudes that a substantial proportion of the electorate are operationally liberal, but ideologically conservative. Later he argues, using McClosky's (1964) work, that the political values of those who are politically active are far more likely to be internally consistent than those of the population at large. A theme which is strong throughout Mann's paper is the necessity for empirical work to explore questions such as commitment to political values:

> The crucial questions are empirical: *to what extent do the
> various classes in society internalise norms, values, and
> beliefs which legitimate the social order?*
>
> Mann 1982: 376

He concludes his paper with:

> The central argument of this paper is that the debate...must
> be an empirical one. The way is open to further empirical
> investigations.
>
> Mann 1982: 392

Following from the argument in this chapter, it seems appropriate to investigate the point above in the present economic context. The need for empirical work is also argued by Willis:

> Empirical work on change...is very important. [Culture and
> consciousness must] *start the analysis*. The point is to see
> how material change and developing contradictions affect,
> and are affected by modes of *living* them, and by
> *understanding* them, and by what capacities they are either
> resisted or accommodated.
>
> Willis 1984a: 18

From the earlier sections, it can be seen that there are a number of issues which are worthy of exploration in relation to views of politics in the context of unemployment. Some of these were summarised at the end of chapter 1. In addition, however, it seems that possible political responses have been missed, due to either the methodology used, or to the inadequacy of the theoretical framework. Thus, in concentrating on the political arguments, conceptions and views of young people it may be possible to explore further the doubts which have been raised as to the limitations of the more conventional indicators of political responsiveness; for example, should, or could political cynicism be viewed as an embryonic political response rather than as an indication of political apathy? For Raphael (1970)

> Power and conflict are indeed key ideas for the understanding of political activity but they cannot be used as defining terms in order to distinguish political from other social relationships. I therefore prefer the old method of defining the scope of politics in terms of the State.
>
> Raphael 1970: 34

This definition is helpful, if limited, bearing in mind that the notion of the State necessitates an inclusion of the Local State (Cockburn 1977).

However, Hall's (1983) argument that politics are rooted in *social* relations and not simply in programmes of political targets must also be considered. In addition, Newby and Vogler (1983) cite Alt's suggestion that the present persistent economic problems in Britain and their apparent intractability have led to a greater fatalism about their solution which could be examined with specific reference to the experience of unemployment. The research to be conducted will attempt to take on board the points raised in the previous discussion.

> My own belief is that the deviant/conformist distinction that sub-culturalists took from delinquency theory (it is used by Willis too) may not be the best way of understanding youth politics. 'naughty' teenagers are not the same as 'rebellious' teenagers. Sub-culturalists followed the mass media in focusing on *spectacular* youth, but in doing so, they missed the subtler ways in which young people resist and seek to *change* their situation.
>
> Frith 1984: 57

The term 'politics' can appear too broad or too narrow. From the earlier discussions of youth cultures, one conclusion which may be drawn is the difficulty in understanding everyday social life, because such life is fragmented. In particular, there is a distinct fragmentation between the economic and political: that this is not satisfactory can be seen if, following

Meiksins Wood (1981), we understand the economy not as a 'network of disembodied forces' but as a set of social relations. She bases her argument upon the notion that economic categories (such as employed, unemployed) express determinate social relations. However, she points out that modes of production are not abstract structures but are relations of domination which confront people, who then have to act in relation to these modes of production. So, she argues as modes of production are contested in the political sphere, they are part of it. Therefore, economic and social relations both help to comprise the domain of politics. This argument provides a definition of politics: politics can be defined as being the means by which human beings regulate, attempt to regulate and challenge with a view to changing unequal power relationships.[10]

2.6 The research issues

The central question of the study, is, therefore, an empirical one: how do young people discuss political views and political arguments in the current context of unemployment.

Given the dominance of discussions about employment prospects for young people, and a definition of politics which includes daily experience, any exploration of the ways in which young people discuss political issues requires a knowledge of how the young people view employment, unemployment and training schemes. This can best be explored by conducting at least part of the study at a time when the young people are part of the labour market, or, eligible to be part of it.

In order to be able to explore views of politics, including views about un/employment, it is necessary to develop a relationship with young people within a period of confidence for them. The final year of school, despite anxieties about future employment prospects, is a period when they are likely to have such a confidence in the sense that they are the oldest group in the school, and shortly able to define themselves as closer to adulthood than childhood.

Given the earlier argument that youth is not a unitary category, a related issue is to understand how racial structuring and patriarchal relationships both inform, and are informed by such views.

---

[10] I am grateful to Quentin Hoare and Branca Magas for discussing this definition of political with me.

2.7 Summary

This chapter has argued that contemporary levels of youth unemployme
provide a changed context for young people. It has been demonstrated tha
subcultural approaches to the study of youth have been limited in two
senses. Firstly, because the subculturalist approaches have not looked at
explicit or conscious views, and secondly because these studies tended to
look only at young white men, as well as often having been conducted in
periods of substantially lower youth unemployment. The more recent survey
and ethnographic work of the social psychologists Billig and Cochrane has
directly tackled political views, but the limitations of the survey method
have meant that detailed explorations of the meanings of political issues
could not be explored by only using their survey data.

Section 2.5 takes into account the implications of the previous discussions
and points to the necessity for studies which begin by establishing the arena
of 'political' in a wider sense than in previous studies. For example, this
arena should include the relationship of young people to the economy. It is
further suggested that whilst there is some ambiguity surrounding some of
the theoretical analyses of politics, there is also a need for empirical work
which can incorporate some of the points raised in this chapter and which
may also aid the process of clarifying theoretical confusions. The research
issues for this study, outlined in section 2.6, are organised around the central
question: what are the ways in which young people discuss political issues
in the current context of unemployment.

3 Theoretical and methodological frameworks

We, the older generation, did not understand, as most men do, and as young women are learning today, that work and the longing for love can be harmoniously combined, so that work remains as the main goal of existence.

Alexandra Kollontai   *Autobiography of a Sexually Emancipated Woman*

3.1 Introduction

> The study of attitudes, and opinions of individuals has begun to give way to research on social representations of social reality. It has become more and more clear that such representations are not just expressions of acquired behavioural dispositions, but are important reflections of the social reality in which we live and have a shared and collective nature.
>
> Tajfel, Jaspars and Fraser 1984: 2

The question raised at the end of the previous chapter expresses the central aim of the study: what are the ways in which young people discuss political issues in the current context of unemployment? The argument, in general, has concentrated on the approaches to theorising about youth. One approach may be viewed as the 'adolescence' approach whose *raison d'être* is that there is something particular about people in their teens, this particularity being rooted in the biology and the psychology of the individual as suggested by Erikson (1971). The other main approach may be seen as the one developed by Hall and Jefferson (1975) which argues that youth are a fraction of the class from which they originate. Thus, in their concentration on working-class young people, Hall and Jefferson argue that the responses, behaviours, and cultures of youth are to be viewed as part of a general working-class culture, mediated through age. Both positions appear to have considerable strengths. Clearly, the class position and location of individuals structure their behaviour, but do not necessarily determine it.

A plethora of historical and social anthropological work informs us that 'teenage' and 'adolescence' are not biological givens and that age is a social construct. Aries's (1973) challenging work on the history of childhood appears to demonstrate that the way in which children have been defined is a consequence of the spatial and temporal cultures which they inhabit. Despite Pollock's (1983) reassessment of the argument presented by Aries (1973), the general point seems to be accepted, namely that the way in which chronological ages and the changes associated with a particular age are understood is mainly a function of the *culture* in which the ages are being interpreted rather than a function of apparent biological 'givens' which unfold at specific ages. Demos and Demos (1969) have argued that adolescence, similarly, is an historical construct which arose in the period of the Industrial Revolution. In spite of these points, age is often used as a major means of ascribing people to different groups, as for example within legal and educational institutions. Similarly, there is a series of beliefs and stereotypes associated with differing age groups. Thus, whilst chronological age may not be indicative of a definite biological 'given', it does have a social reality and dynamic.

So, the weakness of the 'adolescence' approach is in its implicit acceptance of a biologism about teenagers, whilst the danger of the arguments put forward by Hall and Jefferson (1975) is that the cultural specificity associated with age could be lost through an overemphasis on class position.

3.2 The theoretical framework

The tension, between the two main approaches discussed earlier, may be understood as the distinction between psychological and sociological approaches towards young people. Doise (1978) has argued, as a social psychologist, that the contact between psychology and sociology is at the level of cognitive structures. However, his view of cognitive structures is that while the psychological and sociological universes of discourse are not reducible to each other, they do have a mutual relevance. Doise, in general, argues that social psychology is able to construct models of cognitive processes which can take into account the active way in which human beings structure their social environment.

> Social psychology has no bearing on micro-sociology (i.e. the study of the family, a trade union etc.). It is concerned with the *integration* between the individual and the social, most frequently by studying the interaction of a limited number of individuals. Such interaction enables us to cast light on the processes which constitute the individual, from the social standpoint, and the social from the individual standpoint
>
> Doise 1978: 65 (my emphasis)

In order to cast light on the processes mentioned by Doise, a social psychological study has to avoid the pitfalls of over-sociologising or overbiologising – both of which can lead to overly deterministic views of individuals. The issue of which concepts are used, as well as which methods are appropriate for the investigation of the cognitive structuring of social reality need to be discussed here.

In the past decade, the theoretical framework of social representations appears to have dealt with a number of the issues discussed above. Moscovici (1976), whilst distancing himself from Durkheim, argues that Durkheim's notion of 'collective representations' – that is that all human life centres around the notion of the shared symbol – can be understood as implying that the task of social psychology is to define social representations of individuals. Despite Moscovici's reservations about Durkheim's functional approach, he is clear on the value of 'social representations' for psychology. Moscovici argues that within sociology, representations were considered as 'givens': they were known to exist, but little interest was displayed in their structures or internal dynamics. He argues that social psychology can explore such dynamics and internal structures: in other words, that social representations be considered as phenomena, and not as concepts (Moscovici 1981). The position of Durkheim in relation to collective representations was that they embrace a large range of intellectual forms including myths, science, religion as well as the categories of time and space. However, Moscovici argues, that

> In his [Durkheim's] theory, social representations assume the function of concentrating and stabilising masses of words or ideas, as though he were dealing with stagnant layers of air in the atmosphere of society. This is not completely misleading, but in our times, what strikes the observer is rather their mobile and circulating character, in short their plasticity. They remind one more of dynamic forms, which are capable of influencing an aggregate of relations and behaviours, emerging and disappearing together with these representations.
>
> Moscovici 1981: 185

For Moscovici, social representations are dynamic because they both communicate and create knowledge. He argues that there is a need for the collection of data which could illuminate the transmission of the social images carried by human beings. In the collection of such data, social psychologists need to consider how such imagery is generated, how it evolves, and how it is maintained as a shared representation.

Whilst these representations, which are shared by many,

enter into and influence the mind of each, they are not thought by them; rather, to be more precise, they are re-thought, re-cited and re-presented.

Moscovici 1984: 9

He argues that social representations are autonomous because they are usually envisaged as unquestioned realities. In addition, they exert constraints.[1] However, human beings are not passive in the manner in which they deal with ideas:

> So, what we are suggesting is that individuals and groups, far from being passive receptors, think for themselves, produce and ceaselessly communicate their own specific representations and solutions to the questions they set themselves...(P)eople analyse, comment, concoct spontaneous, unofficial philosophies which have a decisive impact on their social relations...
>
> Moscovici 1984: 16

Furthermore, he argues that ideas, once released amongst people behave, and are, like material forces. Thus, social representations are means of both constructing and communicating knowledge, whose dynamics and internal structures social psychology can explore. In thinking of them as re-presentations, Moscovici stresses agency in relation to individuals. While he accepts that ideas can develop an autonomy of their own, Moscovici argues that the study of social representations does not imply that individuals are passively 'socialised' into holding such ideas.

He continues by outlining how social representations are generated psychologically. Social representations, he suggests, *anchor* the familiar to the unfamiliar; in so doing, social representations *objectify* ideas. This latter is a mechanism by which social representations are then reproduced from the abstract to the concrete; they are reformulated into the sphere of things which can be seen, touched, and therefore controlled.

> Anchoring and objectifying are therefore ways of handling memory. The former keeps it in motion... The second... draws concepts and images from it to mingle and reproduce (social representations) with the outside world.
>
> Moscovici 1984: 43

---

[1] It may be more appropriate to view social representations as also enabling, rather than as simply being constraining.

Thus, Moscovici's presentation of social representations suggests a social psychological means of exploring both large-scale social processes, and the psychological means of the interpretation and communication, and so, the reconstruction of these representations.

Moscovici's influential discussion has not escaped controversy. Potter and Litton (1985b) have argued that the ambiguities in the outline of the phenomena mean give cause for concern as to the precise nature and identification of social representations. The central point of their argument appears to be that Moscovici's conceptualisation of social representations necessitates a set of social representations, about the social representations to be studied. Thus, they argue, a study of public schoolboys and comprehensive schoolboys and their social representations (Hewstone, Jaspars and Lalljee 1982) presumed that the schoolboys themselves identified with the categories of comprehensive and public education to which they were assigned. Potter and Litton argue convincingly that the project of identifying different social representations with different groups and then defining groups in terms of the different social representations they hold is a circular one.

Secondly, Potter and Litton examine the notion of consensus in social representations, and suggest that consensus may be considered at three levels: mention of a social representation, availability of a social representation and use of a social representation in practice. They suggest that confusions will occur if these different aspects of social representations are collapsed together. Their third main point is that from the empirical work they examine (work which has been published in English such as that of Herzlich (1973), di Giacomo (1980) and Hewstone et al. (1982)), those researchers have characterised social representations as single and mainly static entities. Potter and Litton argue that there is an assumption of consensus within the theory of social representations which leads, in these empirical studies, to the use of analytic techniques which average the responses of participants and thus smooth over any diversity. They conclude their article with the suggestion that owing to the weakness in the empirical work they cite, social representations should be replaced by 'the more clearly defined idea of linguistic repertoire' (Potter and Litton 1985b: 89), which they state are 'recurrently used systems of terms for characterising actions, events and other phenomena' (ibid.).

Moscovici's reply to this piece is illuminating. He claims that this lack of definition of social representations is not a weakness:

The so-called vagueness that afflicts social representations arises by design, and here is the reason for it. One problem in social psychology – and perhaps in cognitive science as well!- is the compulsion to produce predictive theories concerning an isolated mechanism...Once stated, these theories are put into concrete forms in hundreds of experiments which are begun in enthusiasm and end up in disappointment. Then, they disappear without anyone knowing why. Thus social psychology has become an archipelago of lonely paradigms, unrelated to one another and without any common object. One might therefore conclude that we should abandon the quest for predictive theories, on the one hand, and do away with an epidermic view of man [sic] on the other. Instead, let us now try to build some descriptive and explicative theories that have a wider range and a deeper grasp of phenomena, such as social representations. Let us also breed a line of thinkers who are not head shrinkers, but head enlargers. In this sense, 'vagueness' has a positive role to play. *Clarity and definition will be an outcome of research instead of being its prerequisite.*

Moscovici 1985: 91 (my emphasis)

This long extract from Moscovici's reply gives some depth and texture to his ideas. Potter and Litton's attempt to refine the phenomenon of social representations by using linguistic repertoires is rejected by Moscovici. He concludes:

Social representations are not a concept in search of a theory, but rather a phenomenon in need of data and theories...The road I am advocating is certainly longer and slower. But how else should one proceed if one wants to reach something meaningful and of lasting value?

Moscovici 1985: 92

Moscovici (1984) also argues, from empirical studies, that notions of personal and situational attribution, which appear as neutral categories within the sphere of Attribution Theory are not neutral. He cites empirical work to demonstrate that when the proposition 'people only get what they deserve' is studied among different groups, such an attitude was expressed mainly by people belonging to a majority or to a ruling class. Thus, this 'personal attribution' approach is present amongst dominating groups, and situational explanations are present within dominated groups. He suggests that from the societies which are under consideration, personal causality is a right-wing explanation and situational causality is a left-wing one. Thus:

> Dominating and dominated classes do not have a similar representation of the world they share but see it with different eyes, judge it according to specific categories and each does so according to their own categories. For the former, it is the individual who is responsible for that befalls him [sic] and especially his failures. For the latter, failures are always due to the circumstances which society creates for the individual.
>
> Moscovici 1984: 51

Potter and Wetherell (1987) further develop the arguments in Potter and Litton's paper. They outline (pp. 139ff) how they understand Moscovici's theoretical writings about social representations: social representations are mental entities and are the means by which people understand and evaluate their worlds. In Moscovici's writings, they see him as saying, firstly, that social representations, being intrinsically linked to communication processes, are social because they originate in social interaction. Secondly, they suggest that Moscovici has argued that social representations provide an agreed code for communication; therefore, 'disagreement in representations will lead to conflict, dispute and misunderstanding; the conversationalists will be stymied in their attempt to communicate' (Potter and Wetherell 1987: 141). Thirdly, they suggest that Moscovici claims social representations are social because they are a theoretically coherent way of distinguishing between social groups. Potter and Wetherell, by expressing three main reservations similar to those presented by Potter and Litton (1985b) about the theory, suggest that the utilisation of 'interpretive repertoires' provides a way out of the difficulties which are present in Moscovici's arguments.

Jaspars and Fraser (1984) have entered the discussions by commenting on the relationship between social representations and a different theoretical tradition, that of the study of attitudes. Tracing the history of social attitudes as studied by Thomas and Znaniecki (1918–1920), they point out that their notion of attitude was social from its inception. Under the influence of Allport, however, 'attitude' became more closely allied to a paradigm of the individual, and, that in the mid 1980s, has:

> become more and more individualised, and is currently interpreted as an individual response disposition sometimes combined with an individual cognitive representation.
>
> Jaspars and Fraser 1984: 123

Their plea for social psychology to consider attitudes as social representations is well timed. Fraser's (1986) paper continues the analysis begun in the 1984 article mentioned above. He argues that there has been no attempt to study the structuring of widespread attitudes:

> I suggest that we should study structured sets of attitudes that are widely shared, and in doing that we will be studying social representations.
>
> Fraser 1986: 7

The implication of this, for Fraser, is that such a rethinking could provide a means of developing strategies for empirical research into social representations. He is anxious that there is clarity that what is being studied are social representations and not merely a 'jumble of attitudes' (Fraser 1986: 10). He uses the example of attitude studies which have looked at popular perceptions of the determinants of high unemployment, pointing out that in Britain, results such as 35% of the electorate feeling that the present government's policies have had nothing to do with the level of unemployment, 60% believing that a world recession is the major determinant, 40% expressing a willingness to join in demonstrations if unemployment continues to rise and 55% believing that many unemployed individuals lack motivation or skills, do not demonstrate the existence of one or more social representations. From this, he argues that the data:

> can be seen as a jumble or mish-mash of attitudes and attitude differences...I wish to stress that I am not claiming that there are no such things as social representations...I am suggesting the existence of social representations has not been convincingly demonstrated.
>
> Fraser 1986: 11–12

Fraser points to two problems. Firstly, is it possible to demonstrate that individuals operate with organised systems of belief? Secondly, can it be shown that there is a substantial number of individuals who 'are sustaining essentially the same coherent outlook to justify the invoking of a social representation' (Fraser 1986: 13)? It is at this point that some observations may be made in relation to both Moscovici and, firstly, Fraser.

Mann's (1982) paper in which he deconstructs the consensus of consensus theorists is illuminating here. He demonstrates that most values are stated so vaguely that they may legitimate any social structure. Because values embody absolute standards such as those of achievement and equality in Western societies, it can be difficult for them to co-exist without conflict; thus, he argues, they are insulated from each other. It is because of this insulation that liberal democracies achieve cohesion because there is no commitment to core values which are necessarily in concordance with each other. Given that Mann states that there is a disjunction between general abstract values and concrete experiences, it would not then be surprising to discover that empirical studies of attitudes about the causes of unemployment appear contradictory, lacking in clarity and are sometimes confusing – that is, they are disjunctive in Mann's usage. However, it does not necessarily mean that there are not social representations about unemployment; rather, it could be argued that the social representations themselves consist of contradictory sets of attitudes which are 'insulated' from each other, but that these attitudes may (following Mann) still co-exist within a social representation. Therefore, whilst social representations may involve attitudes or belief systems which are consistently associated with each other, there is no essential requirement in Moscovici's thesis that these attitudes/belief systems must be logically coherent. It may, indeed, be more appropriate to argue that all social representations are sustained by the absolute values discussed by Mann; if so, then these values, being in conflict with each other, will necessarily give rise to contradictory attitude/belief systems within a social representation.

There is, also, another way in which it is possible to consider Fraser's argument. Billig (1984a) in his paper entitled 'Political Ideology: Social Psychological Aspects' suggests that psychology could consider itself to be in the business of understanding how the contradictions of capitalism are reproduced socio-psychologically. If so, then contemporary capitalist society, he argues, is characterised by both free enterprise and state intervention. A rhetoric of traditional capitalist individualism will therefore exist alongside the rhetoric of socialist intervention. Thus, using Billig's point, we can see that there may be a number of competing arguments. These arguments will then give rise to differing attitudes towards the same issue, and thus, Fraser's example does not necessarily preclude the existence of social representations.

For example, discussions (e.g. Hall 1984) as to how politics should be discussed, debated and dealt with could be viewed as discussions about the 'cognitive style of politics'. Those who see Communists as 'red fascists' are using the ideas about *style* of political discussions as their main categorising scheme, rather than paying particular attention to the content of the utterances from Communists. Those, however, who reject this categorisation of Communists as 'red fascists' argue that it is the content of the statements which needs to be attended to, not the manner in which they are presented. Both of these approaches may be seen as being based on social representations of politics, with one representation stressing style as its central organising feature, and the other, content.

In outlining Moscovici, and the reservations expressed by Potter and Litton, and Potter and Wetherell, and Fraser, I have attempted to remain faithful to the language and spirit of their arguments in order to explain my position in this discussion.

3.3 Ideologies and social representations

I shall approach social representations differently. Moscovici has been quoted above as asserting that social representations are phenomena in need of data and theory. Let us take the theory first. Social representations may be considered to be elements or themes (Billig 1984b) within ideologies. It is not appropriate to enter into a detailed discussion of the scholarly and stimulating writings on the nature of ideologies, except to point out that ideologies are often understood as shared systems of belief. When conceptualised in this way, elements within ideologies do require to be seen as consensual, as being shared, as implicitly delimiting groups and as being very similar to, if not identical with, attitudes. However, if ideologies are understood from within their historical development, the concept, from its inception, has clear negative and critical connotations. That is (as for example Billig (1982) points out), the term developed from post-Revolutionary France with negative connotations, and in retaining these negative connotations, it is possible to retain its original critical aspects.

Thompson (1984) has 'offer(ed) a plea for, as well as a reformulation and defence of, a critical conception of ideology' (Thompson 1984: 4). His book, in examining the writings of Bourdieu, Gouldner, Giddens, Ricoeur, and Habermas, amongst others, is predicated on the idea that

> We cannot study ideology without studying relations of domination and the ways in which these relations are sustained by meaningful expressions.
>
> Thompson 1984: 11

It is within the sociological and political universes of discourse where the debates and arguments around the specific implications of such a definition exist. For psychologists, an understanding of ideology which preserves this critical conception will allow a better grasp on the ways in which individuals cognitively structure their social reality.

Clearly, Moscovici's conception of social representations is ambiguous in many ways. That he discusses social representations as images is not only limiting of the concept as a visual one, but also there are implications that individuals *hold* social representations, that individuals *carry* social representations – that is, that social representations are entities or analytic categories which are located within individuals. This follows from Moscovici arguing that they are phenomena. However, he simultaneously argues that social representations are *processes* although he does not wish to make an explicit distinction between phenomena and processes.[2]

> After all, how we think is not distinct from what we think. Thus, we cannot make a clear distinction between regularities in representations and those in the processes that create them.
>
> Moscovici 1984: 67

Despite Moscovici's refusal of a clear distinction between the phenomena and the processes, some of the empirical work which has been developed from his theoretical writings (e.g. Hewstone et al. 1982; di Giacomo 1980) has not always demonstrated its awareness of his refusal. Thus, when Potter and Wetherell (1987) rightly state their unease with the averaging, analytic techniques used in many empirical studies of social representations,[3] basing their criticism on Moscovici's suggestion that social representations are consensual, these criticisms may also be directed not only at the ambiguities in Moscovici's writings, but also at the *type* of empirical work generated by other researchers who identify themselves as examining and therefore *interpreting* Moscovici's writings on social representations.

For Moscovici does suggest that social representations are consensual. However, he also comments rather deprecatingly on the project of social psychology which focusses upon and decontextualises single mechanisms, or pseudo mechanisms and 'ascribe[s] a general value to it' (1984: 66). In the preceding paragraph he notes:

> By saying that representations are social we are mainly saying that they are symbolic and possess as many perceptual, as so-called cognitive, elements. And that is why we consider their *content* to be so important and why we refuse to distinguish them from psychological mechanisms as such.
>
> Moscovici 1984: 66

---

[2]   I am grateful to Elinor Scarborough for suggesting this point to me, which she also discusses in Scarborough (1988).

[3]   See their discussion on p. 144 of Potter and Wetherell (1987).

Moscovici's overarching aim in his recent writings about social representations has been to transform the current projects of social psychology. However, I would suggest that such a transformation may only be possible if the relationship between social representations and ideologies is systematically debated.[4] Such a systematic and detailed examination of the arguments is beyond the scope of this study. However, some preliminary comments may be made at this stage. To recap: a critical conception of ideology allows for the argument that elements or themes within ideologies may be considered as social representations.[5]

While Moscovici does touch on the possible relationships between social representations and ideologies, Scarborough (1988) implies that he argues that social representations are to be located in informal, inter-individual communication while ideologies are located within formal groups:

> But this account suggests a deep ambiguity in Moscovici's position... [and we end up with] social representations [being] a function of the institutional structures of a society – leaving us the problem of accounting for social structures.
>
> Scarborough 1988: 27

Again, it is necessary to approach the issue in a slightly different way. When considering ideologies and themes within ideologies, it is essential to grasp that the communication of ideas is heavily mediated through language. That point is not new. The consequence of this is that any attempt to consider the communication and reproduction of ideologies must take this into account. It could be argued that Potter and Wetherell (1987) aim to do this in their arguments about discourse and social psychology. However, they define discourse 'to cover all forms of spoken texts... and written texts of all kinds' (1987: 7). The problem with this is that any consequent analysis will remain at the semantic level, and thus, make invisible the relationships of domination and subordination discussed by Thompson (1984) in relation to

---

4   Scarborough (1988) is a recent example of an explicit examination of this relationship. Her paper is entitled 'Attitudes, social representations and ideology'.

5   While this may be an extremely significant re-location of Moscovici's concept of social representations, given his concern to distance himself from Durkheim and the ambiguities in Moscovici's writings, I would suggest that it is very unlikely that he would be hostile to such a re-casting of the term.

ideology.[6]

Thus both the Moscovici and the Potter and Wetherell arguments ignore the relations of domination and subordination within communication. And that is why there is such a frustrating and unproductive discussion between them. For if we work with a critical conception of ideology, we can see that social representations are not 'mental entities', but ideological elements which derive their force both from their relationship with the material world, as well as having an autonomy of their own. Again, the nature and forms of this relationship are properly the subject matter of political and sociological theory; however psychologists can start from the notion, not that ideologies provide a social cement (and Mann's paper cited above demonstrates the lack of consensus), but that they are better understood as being regulatory in the processes of domination and subordination. To understand ideologies as regulatory does not mean that we should ignore what Miliband (1977) points out is 'the many-sided and permanent challenge which is directed at the ideological predominance' (Miliband 1977: 53) of dominating groups – rather it is to understand that this challenge may still occur within the framework of the prevailing ideas.

Before dealing specifically with the implications of this approach for both the Moscovici and the Potter et al. arguments, an example may help to clarify the above. There are a number of ideologies of racism, but within contemporary Britain, it could be argued that the immigration and nationality legislation forms one element or theme. Some people will argue that this legislation on immigration is necessary in order to eliminate racism, while others will argue that the legislation itself maintains and perpetuates racism. Both groups are calling forth the immigration and nationality legislation, but suggesting opposing forms of action. This element, theme, or social representation, is common to the two groups, but to understand the regulatory nature of the consequent arguments and actions necessitates examining other social representations which are utilised simultaneously. For example, the former group relates its argument to the theme of black people being the problem, while the latter relates its argument to the theme of how labour is organised within capitalism.

---

[6]   In their book, Potter and Wetherell (1987) have four indexed references to ideology: these references all use the term in different ways. For example, they point to ideologies as distorting processes (p. 118), and as a shared system of beliefs (p. 140); they also use the term as an adjective when suggesting that *Hansard* be examined for documentary research for it provides 'an ideologically powerful form of spoken material' (p. 163). Their final reference to the concept is on the last page of their book, in paragraph of their book that they consider a critical notion of ideology using Thompson (1984).

To return to the arguments of the psychologists, we can then see that social representations are most helpfully defined, not as mental entities which originate in social interaction but as ideological elements which are rooted within political, economic and social relations. Thus, social representations *per se* do not define groups; rather, the configurations of different social representations, and different aspects of a social representation which will be foregrounded by different subjects, may provide a basis for an initial insight into how meanings of domination are mediated by language. Further, Moscovici, in discussing social representation theory, opposes common sense and science. If social representations are understood as ideological elements, then it can be seen that this opposition (for science must also be part of the ideological framework), in itself, is a false one.[7] Potter and Litton (1985) argue that social representations are viewed as single and static, despite Moscovici's description of their plasticity – but if social representations are understood in terms of the reproduction of the *processes* (and hence a constant movement) of domination and subordination, this misunderstanding will not develop. Potter and Wetherell's (1987) pleas for interpretive repertoires and discourse analysis – a 'repertoire is one component in a systematic approach to the study of discourse' (Potter and Wetherell 1987: 157) – can now be seen to be misplaced.[8]

They begin by arguing that interpretive repertoires are not *intrinsically* linked to social groups, then slip into viewing interpretive repertoires as synonymous with discourse analysis (p. 156) and then argue that the concern

---

[7] For Moscovici the common sense deals with the 'consensual' universe and science with the 'reified' universe of 'factual knowledge'. It may be noted that this opposition confuses his arguments: following Doise (1978), whilst representations of social reality ('common sense') are not scientific, they may make possible the scientific activity to which they are subject: 'Scientific activity is virtually an operation by which ideological realities are transformed' (Doise 1978: 49).

[8] From the introduction to their recent book, it can be seen how Potter and Wetherell (1987) define 'discourse': 'We will use discourse in its most open sense... to cover all forms of spoken interaction, formal and informal, and written texts of all kinds... For the moment, it is important to emphasise that our concern is not purely with discourse *per se*; that is, we are not linguists attempting to add social awareness to linguistics through the addition of the study of pragmatics. We are social psychologists expecting to gain a better understanding of social life and social interaction from our study of social texts' (Potter and Wetherell 1987: 7).

Despite their concern to be seen as social psychologists rather than linguists, the writers do not explicitly include a discussion of the relationships between discourses and the processes of domination and subordination. It is of course entirely appropriate to study how discourses operate within ideologies; but such a study must have built into it a means of interpretation to demonstrate how discourses serve to sustain relations of domination, and how language then becomes a medium of power and control. This critical aspect of ideologies is in general not present in their book.

of discourse analysis is with language use (p. 157). The plea is misplaced for, in their discussions of discourse, they do not discuss unequal power relations; and if the idea of discourse is to be removed from the solely linguistic (which they want to do), then it is imperative to include within the notion of discourse as communication the power relationships within which meanings are expressed.[9] Finally, Moscovici's argument is very strong when he states his desire that his view of social representations has built into it the starting point that human beings are active in the ways in which ideas are dealt with.

Therefore, it is being argued that the above comments indicate a considerably greater analytic flexibility when social representations are conceptualised as ideological elements which occur in different configurations, with different aspects foregrounded in different contexts or discussions, and that they both shape and are shaped by the relationships of domination and subordination in which they are embedded. Without wanting to imply a significance which is not present, the above arguments suggest a starting point for a theory for the 'phenomenon' of social representations. The next section will discuss the 'data collection' for this phenomenon.

3.4   The methodological framework

In the previous section it was argued that Moscovici's outline of a theory of social representations suggests a distinct and demanding project for social psychology. Social representations are conceptualised as elements of ideologies, the study of which begins by viewing human beings as active in understandings of social reality.[10] A critical conception of ideology is being used here; that is, that ideology is understood as the means by which meanings serve to regulate, and can also serve to contest relations of domination and subordination.

Moscovici has unequivocally stated that social representations are phenomena in need of theory and data. This section will consider how social representations can be described, and analysed. Billig's (1984a) argument that psychology could be in the business of understanding contradictions becomes the starting point. When considering the domain of politics, it is

---

9   For this conception of discourse I am, of course, indebted to the work of Michel Foucault, e.g. 1977 and 1980.

10   '[Another] implication – and one which could have been foreseen – can be expressed in a few words: the study of social representations requires that we revert to methods of observation... A return to observation would involve reverting to the humane sciences... Only a careful description of social representations... will enable us to understand them' (Moscovici 1984: 67-8).

necessary to move away from the general psychological assumption that people search for and then create a consistency in their belief systems. Rather, it is necessary to analyse the ways in which the domain of politics is ideologically reproduced – and how contradictions within these ideologies serve to sustain and contest relations of domination. To be more specific, the ways in which ideas about politics in contemporary Britain are presented is pertinent. Hall (1985) in his discussion of the hegemonic[11] project of Thatcherism notes that a simple characterisation of this political ideology as 'anti-statist' is incorrect. Whilst it is clear that the dismantling of the welfare state is anti-statist, he also points out that Thatcherism is highly state centralist in many of its strategic operations. Thatcherism, he argues has tried:

> to 'unify' the *contradictory strands in its discourse* – the resonant themes of organic Toryism: nation, family, duty, authority, standards, traditionalism, patriarchalism – with the aggressive themes of a revived neo-liberalism: self interest, competitive individualism, anti-statism.
>
> Hall 1985: 122 (my emphasis)

This specific example thus elucidates the argument that rhetorics of traditional capitalist individualism will exist alongside rhetorics of socialist intervention. The empirical question is how these may be best explored, described and analysed.

Billig (1984a) concludes by suggesting that psychologists should utilise 'naturalistic' methods when studying ideologies of politics; further, all of Moscovici's writings about social representations demonstrate that they must be *described* in detail. Thus, it will be argued that a qualitative (as distinct from quantitative) analysis, which implies the use of 'naturalistic' methods, is the most appropriate way to use the theory of social representations as a means of understanding and analysing the ways in which young people discuss political issues. There are two main reasons for this, in conjunction with the reservations outlined about large-scale survey work in chapter 1. Firstly, the present study is an early attempt in Britain to describe young working-class people's ways of organising their arguments about political

---

[11] This concept, from Gramsci, has been discussed briefly in the preceding chapter. It is not within the scope of this book to outline the discussions and debates about 'hegemony' and contemporary British politics. Nor, indeed, although the task is an interesting and challenging one, is it appropriate to detail Gramsci's view of 'common sense'. As Roiser (1987) has also pointed out, there are clear suggestions for examining the theoretical linkages between the Gramscian notion of 'common sense' and its use by Moscovici: but that would form the basis of a different study.

issues. Secondly, as has also been noted earlier, studies of 'politics' have been narrow in their definitions of the realm of politics, and the possibilities which such studies claim for generalisability in relation to the domain of politics are not always sustained.

The first reason reminds us of C. Wright Mills's injunction:

> Be a good craftsman [sic]. Avoid any rigid set of procedures. Above all, seek to develop and use the sociological imagination. Avoid the fetishism of method and technique.
>
> Mills 1959: 217

The aim of this study is to describe how young people discuss issues within the domain of the political, and therefore, it is necessary to have some understanding of the ways in which political issues are discussed. That is, any such description requires a close analysis of their arguments and views.[12]

Detailed research which attempts to look closely at processes is often referred to as ethnography. Malinowski's approach to ethnography still remains the strongest interpretation of ethnography within social anthropology, namely, that it is a series of methods which can:

> grasp the native's [sic] point of view, his relation to life, to realise his vision of the world.
>
> Malinowski 1922; quoted in Spradley 1979

Grimshaw, Hobson and Willis (1980) suggest that:

> Historically, ethnographic work has arisen from an awareness of the benefits of political participation in, and communication with a characteristic way of life or cultural form...
>
> Grimshaw et al. 1980: 73

It is clear, as argued by Connell (1983), that open-ended interviewing and

---

[12] Frankenberg's (1979) distinction between *savoir* (what someone knows) and *connaisance* (what someone knows about) and the methodological implications of this distinction is a relevant, but not central, point here. He argues that the former implies the possibility of understanding and change, 'knowing about does not' (Frankenberg 1979: 14). It is the methodological implications of this distinction which are relevant: 'How then is the relationship knowing about/knowing to be explored? I would argue by detailed studies which are usually small scale in nature. I am not arguing that large scale, comparative statistical studies are not useful, merely that they are often less useful either than their authors suppose, or their small scale opposites' (Frankenberg 1979: 15).

field observation do not necessarily constitute an ethnography. Connell's clear and systematic documentation of his reservations allow us to realise that an ethnography requires total immersion into the participants' way of life, to the extent that the researcher is identified as part of the community in which s/he is located. But it is rarely possible to assume that this is the case in field studies. It is not possible to be certain that the researcher is viewed by the participants as 'one of them' if the participants are aware that the researcher is present to carry out a study. If however that researcher does not reveal that s/he is conducting research, this denies the participants the right to information and is unethical. But Connell's critique of the ethnographic studies carried out by members of the Centre for Contemporary Cultural Studies at Birmingham University (for example, Hobson 1978; Willis 1977) is not destructive. It allows for the understanding that even though many studies claiming to be ethnographies are not, as such, it is still possible using a combination of methods such as, field observation for limited periods with open-ended interviewing, to explore the processes and dynamics with which social actors experience and interpret the world.

A frequently cited reservation towards the use of such methods within psychology is that they are not rigorous and are subjective. We may turn to Frankenberg (1979) again for his assertion that 'objectivity comes from living through and then transcending the subjective' (Frankenberg 1979: 14). He concludes:

> the most generalisable, objective conclusions can only be obtained from the most detailed subjective immersion of the researcher into the particular. Such researchers... develop gradually, but discontinuously, out of struggle to comprehend social processes within theoretical understanding.
>
> Frankenberg 1979: 19

From the above series of quotations, it can be seen that issues of understanding, meaning, and objectivity are not always able to be adequately tackled within methods which depend upon quantitative analysis. However, rather than set up a simplistic and apparently irreconcilable competition between field and experimental methods, and therefore between qualitative and quantitative analysis, it is more appropriate to tackle these points in relation to the aims of this particular study. In order to understand the themes within which young people discuss political issues, it is necessary to conduct an in-depth and therefore, small-scale study. This is not to run away from some of the reservations about small-scale work which utilises qualitative analysis:

> We are still in need of a method which respects evidence,
> seeks corroboration, and minimises distortion, but which is
> without rationalist, natural-science-like pretence.[13]
>
> Willis 1980: 91

A positivistic approach within psychology may well argue that it is philosophically impossible to understand scientifically the mental life of the individual. However, the limits of behaviouristic psychology, which is conducted within a positivistic framework *par excellence*, have demonstrated that a stimulus-response paradigm may often be unable to provide an understanding of human behaviour. When considering the domain of politics, in particular, it is clearly not possible to explore the central research question of this study, using methods derived from the natural sciences. For the study is based on the notion that human beings are social actors who are active in the understandings and re-presentations of ideas. Passerini (1979) captures one aspect of the present proposed study in her discussion of the use of oral sources in historical research.

> Even if we accept that coercion always has a material
> basis, what is it that leads the oppressed to accept their
> oppression in cultural and psychological terms, even to the
> point of praising it and preferring it to any struggle for
> change?
>
> Passerini 1979: 85

Passerini's question is helpful because it demonstrates her acknowledgement that the notion of human agency is important in social investigations, and she cites Shils to reinforce this point:

> No adult member of society is outside the system of
> education of scarce roles, facilities and rewards, and as a
> result, no adult – unless he [sic] is utterly, indeed almost
> catatonically apathetic – can entirely avoid rendering
> judgments at least about that sector of the distribution
> which he perceives immediately around him.
>
> Shils quoted in Passerini 1979: 86

---

[13]   It is necessary, however, to begin from a different starting point than that of positivism (see Heather 1976, for a critique of positivism; in addition, Grimshaw, Hobson and Willis 1980, deal with this in their book).

For social analysts, the issue then becomes one of how such judgements may be examined. Butters (1975) has suggested that alternative methods – alternative, that is, to the more frequent positivistic approaches – can develop and use ideas of 'appreciative understanding', 'analytic induction' and 'constant comparisons' without losing sight of the human agency which is present in any social research. The first of these is one which is familiar to many social anthropologists, whilst the last appears to have been developed from Glaser and Strauss's (1967) ideas of theoretical sampling and grounded theory. These will be considered more carefully later. Butters's paper is a helpful beginning, especially when he outlines the general principles of naturalistic field research. In addition, his clear presentation of the psychological dynamics between researched and researcher is helpful when considering the design of all social research.[14] However, Butters rejects 'appreciative understanding' because, he asserts, this notion relies on 'intuitive elements'. A phrase such as 'appreciative understanding' contains many potential difficulties in how it is used, and how it is understood. But it would seem that the main weakness of the concept appears when researchers are less than rigorous in reporting the development of their own theoretical insights. If such a development is not specified, the process of theorising in social research may be viewed as natural and coherent.

Butters also expresses clear reservations in relation to the idea of 'analytic induction', basing these reservations on his view that universals of human behaviour cannot be generated in this way. However, he seems to accept that there are some universals in human behaviour which could be tapped or 'discovered if the appropriate theoretical frameworks and methodologies are used. But Butters's reservations about analytic induction may be misplaced, if one does not accept the assertion that there are universals in human social behaviour. All behaviour is carried out in a specific context, and the way in which behaviour is interpreted is also constructed by context. For example, in a classroom, the raising of an arm by a child may be interpreted as the child wishing to ask/answer a question. In a home, the raising of an arm by a man in the presence of a woman could be interpreted as a threat of violence. Thus, even though the behaviour itself may be identical in both cases, the context in which it is carried out, as well as the interpretation

---

[14] Roberts (1975) has also pointed to the possible pitfalls for smaller scale studies which use non-statistical analyses. He poses the sympathetic but critical question: 'How can one describe and define a field without taking into account the impact of the researcher's participation on it (his [sic] 'Hawthorne Effect' so to speak)? What are the ethical rules which allow him to distinguish between observation and intervention?...And can the results of his closeness – a qualitatively full description – get beyond description to the level of science?' (Roberts 1975: 245).

placed on it is a feature of the culture – using culture in its widest sense to include time. Thus, Butters's arguments against analytic induction are based on an inappropriate notion of the task of the human sciences – namely, that the human sciences should seek out universals of human behaviour.

At the beginning of this section, Moscovici's request for data and theory which will allow some insight into social representations was pointed out. In tracing the content of social representations of politics, the question of relationship between 'data' and theory assumes a primacy.

Glaser and Strauss (1967) discuss the relationship of theorising and data collection for social research by using the idea of 'grounded theory'. They argue that as theorising is central to the research process, it will structure the methods used, the data which is collected, the analysis, and the report of the project.

> Grounded theory is based on the systematic generating of theory from data that itself is systematically obtained from social research.
>
> Glaser and Strauss 1967: 2

Thus, they take their argument further by suggesting that as the data is collected, so the theoretical formulations become refined, and so the further collection of data becomes modified.[15] They suggest that social research must, therefore, use theoretical sampling alongside the notion of grounded theory:

> Theoretical sampling is the process of data collection for generating theory whereby the analyst jointly collects, codes and analyses his [sic] data and decides what data to collect next and where to find them in order to develop his theory as it emerges.
>
> Glaser and Strauss 1967: 45

So, theoretical sampling forces researchers to consider what groups to observe, when and where to observe them, when to stop observing and what data to collect.

---

[15] I am grateful to Stephen Reicher for pointing out that Grounded theory contains an implicit assumption 'that there exists *a* unitary and internally consistent set of categories' (Reicher 1989, personal communication) which are waiting to be discovered by the empirical work. That is not an assumption consistent with the aims of this project. However, the kernel of grounded theory is that as empirical work proceeds, the categories used to obtain 'data' need to be constantly re-examined. It is that aspect which will be used in this project.

3.5 Summary and conclusions

This chapter has considered the theory of social representations with a view to utilising this approach for a study aimed at exploring the domain of politics with young working-class people. It has been argued that social representations are elements within ideologies which can best be analysed using a critical notion of 'ideology'. The fourth section of this chapter has considered how best to obtain and describe these social representations, and argued that field research combined with qualitative analysis is most appropriate.

Although there are assertions that qualitative methodologies lack rigour, it is clear that the study of social representations may gain some insights from ethnographic approaches. Spradley (1979) makes the point that one strength of an ethnographic approach is that concepts develop from the meanings particular to the context of the research, rather than only from the mind of the researcher. Grimshaw, Hobson and Willis (1980) complement this point by stating that there is a capacity in ethnographic projects to challenge, negate or force revision in existing accounts, and, perhaps, to develop other accounts. They argue that ethnographic work does not merely provide a description, but provides the possibility of going beyond 'experience' for its own sake in order to examine theoretical questions.

One way of doing this could be to use open-ended interviewing methods when a wholesale ethnography is inappropriate. Burgess (1984) discusses such interviewing, calling it 'conversations with a purpose'. Such conversations can be very useful in allowing a researcher to develop some insight into the dynamics of, for example, ways in which political issues are being considered, and negotiated by the interviewee. That this is not simply a collection of 'information' from the interviewee can be seen from the following quotation from Passerini:

> We should not ignore that raw material ... consists not just in factual statements, but is preeminently an expression and representation of culture, and therefore includes not only literal narrations, but also the dimensions of memory, *ideology* and subconscious desires.
>   Passerini 1979: 84 (my emphasis)

This is because, to explore the ways in which young people discuss political issues in the context of unemployment, it is appropriate to describe initially these themes based on the discussions outlined above of social representations. In order to do that, open-ended interviewing and group discussions seem to be the methods most helpful in constructing this description. Open-ended interviewing necessitates a relationship between interviewer and those interviewed which permits easy expression and communication. Therefore, such a study would also require more than one meeting between interviewer and interviewee in order to facilitate best such communication, within of course the constraint of financial and human resources.

4 The research study

In activity there is good fortune.

Arab Proverb

4.1 Introduction

The study was aimed at exploring the ways in which young people discuss politics. It has been argued that much of the research discussed in chapters 1 and 2 either considered a very narrow definition of politics, or remained solely within the area of cultural and everyday life. Politics has been defined as the means by which human beings regulate, attempt to regulate and contest unequal power relationships. Thus, issues within the domain of the political could include not only parliamentary politics, but also views of employment, unemployment and training schemes as well as concerns of everyday life. Therefore, the central question of the study may be considered as three subquestions:

(a) What themes are present in young people's discussions of employment, unemployment and training schemes?

(b) What themes are present in their discussions of voting and parliamentary politics?

(c) What themes are present in their discussions of everyday life?

Further, each of these subquestions needs to consider how the racialised and patriarchal structuring of the lives of young working-class people in Britain both are expressed within, and organise the themes to be explored.

Following the argument of chapter 3, it was decided that a pilot study involving interviewing – both semi-structured and open-ended – be conducted. After an outline of the pilot work is presented, the development and conduct of the fieldwork will be described. Finally, the characteristics of the sample and some general issues related to the interviews will be presented.

4.2 The pilot study and preliminary preparations

The main study was carried out in Middington, England, with the pilot study being conducted in Oakington. The pilot work, and the preliminary preparations occurred between October and early December 1984.

4.2.1   Preliminary preparations

Owing to my close contact with the Middington City Youth and Educational Services in the eight years before conducting the study, I was able to discuss both the conceptual basis of the research, as well as possible research strategies with a number of workers employed in the above services. These one-to-one discussions lasted between one and four hours, and detailed notes were taken by myself during these discussions. The individuals with whom I discussed my study included two members of the Middington Local Education Authority Inspectorate, careers officers, community and youth workers, and teachers based in both schools and the Further Education sector of the city. From these discussions, I decided that the most appropriate way to begin the research was to spend some time 'hanging around' in youth and community centres, as well as in a shopping centre in central Middington where, I was informed in all the discussions, many young people spent their time.

4.2.2 The pilot study

Parallel with my discussions in Middington, I considered it necessary to try out some interview schedules and questionnaires. In order that I could try a variety of interviews, I decided to conduct the 'pilot' in Oakington, a town about 40 miles from Middington. This was because I had not yet decided which area of Middington would be most suitable for the study, and did not want possibly inaccurate rumours and informal discussions based on my pilot work to occur in Middington.

My employment as an Educational Psychologist in 1978 and 1979, coupled with some close contacts developed in the following years with Oakington Youth Service, provided an initial starting point for the Oakington based pilot work. I had developed a structured interview schedule using the questionnaire of Billig and Cochrane (1982) including their 'Socialist Attitudes Inventory', along with other questions used in other studies. This structured interview schedule, which also contained a short self-completion questionnaire, was tried out with two 17-year-olds, both white, one woman and one man. The interview was tape recorded and lasted approximately 30 minutes.

From the comments of these two pilot interviewees, two points were clarified. Firstly, that the structured interview schedule, coupled with a self-completion questionnaire had the effect of producing short, one-sentence answers. In addition, any self-completion questionnaire has to assume a certain level of literacy and comprehension, and it was glaringly obvious that certain questions could not be presented for it was not clear how many 17-

year-old working-class young people would feel confident in their own ability to read and understand these questions. This emerged from both pilot interviews, as well as from the two post interview discussions. Secondly, the words 'politics' and 'political' produced responses such as 'Oh, I don't know anything about that' and 'That's boring' coupled with a very clear lowering of confidence among the interviewees. These two aspects showed that the closed, structured interview was likely to be viewed as a 'test', to which there were correct and incorrect answers, with the concomitant implication that an individual could perform badly, despite my reassurances to the contrary.

The semi-structured interview schedule, developed as a much looser schedule, and based not only on questionnaires and schedules such as those of Billig and Cochrane, but also using some of the arguments and issues raised in the 'youth subculture' work was conducted with four young people who had left school, and all between the ages of 16 and 17 years. Three were women, two black and one white, and the fourth interviewee was a white man. Again, these interviews were tape recorded, and lasted for approximately 40 minutes. Whilst these semi-structured interviews encouraged more relaxation, and therefore led to slightly more detailed responses, it was clear that the interviewees wanted the 'space' for more discussion of many of the questions: they indicated that because they could not see why some issues were included (and each interviewee pointed to different issues), they felt that they had nothing to say on some points. If these 'nothing-to-say-points' were consecutive within the interview, the consequent silences produced a rupture in the rapport which had been developing.

With hindsight, it was clear that open-ended interviews were also not appropriate in a situation where the interviewees had had no opportunity to observe me or talk with me prior to the one-to-one interview. The interviewees were clearly embarrassed and made uncomfortable both by probes and the use of reflection techniques as well as by some of the silences.

From this pilot work, it appeared that any one-to-one exploration of the central research questions required an informal agenda for the interview, coupled with a flexible approach which could allow interviewees to discuss particular issues at length, if they wished to do so. It was also clear that any interview which incorporated a relatively open-ended approach had to have been preceded by the interviewees being allowed to get a 'sense' of me, in a context where their confidence was high. That is, prior to one-to-one interviewing, potential interviewees had to have had opportunities to meet with me in groups.

4.3   The field work

From the insights gained from the pilot work, I decided that the next strategy for data collection required some careful observation and quasi-ethnographic strategies.

4.3.1   'Hanging around'

I therefore decided that I would spend some time 'hanging around' in the Norgate Centre, a vast indoor shopping centre in central Middington. The purpose of this was to gain specific insights into the way in which some young people spent their time. I had been told that many unemployed young people spent substantial parts of the day in the Centre, mainly congregating around a square, known as Halle Square. In order to have some idea of the places and people that the potential interviewees may talk about, it was clearly a good place to begin the study. I spent three weeks, six days a week there from mid November to early December 1984. The first day I arrived at 11 a.m., and, having located the square (which also functions as a gallery above a cafeteria), sat down on some benches from which I could survey all four sides of the square, being careful not to settle down on a bench where it might appear as if I was intruding.

In the first three days, while being careful not to stare at any of the young people in the square, I had been registering, and later noting the friendship groups, the movements of individuals between these groups, including their racial and gendered composition, the patterns of arrival and the lengths of time spent by individuals with their peers. With no direct indication from any one individual who came regularly to the square, I was aware, however, that I had been noted as someone who was not a Christmas shopper, nor as someone who could be defined as a 'meths drinker' – the two main groups of people in the square apart from the young regulars.

There were between twenty and sixty-five young people who were standing in the square at any one time, mainly young men, ranging in age from approximately 14 years to their late twenties. Most of the young people arrived between 2 and 4 p.m. on the weekdays, and between 12 and 2 p.m. on Saturdays. The white young men who were present regularly in the square appeared to be in fairly close-knit groups. They also spent a considerable part of their time going in and out of some of the shops as a group. There appeared to be little interaction between them and the groups of black young men, with occasional brief conversations between them and the groups of young women. Unlike the young men's groups the groups of young women included both black and white. Usually, there were approximately ten to twelve young women present in the square at any one time, with the number increasing to twenty-five on Saturdays, when the square, and the Centre, were busiest. The membership of the groups of young women seemed to be consistent – any young woman who came into the square would first establish her presence with a group of young women, before deciding where she would stand, who she would talk to and which young men she would acknowledge. Both black and white young women did this, although often the women would then leave the group in pairs and stand somewhere else around the square.

After three days of sitting in the same seat, smoking cigarettes, and watching all the people in the square, not just the young people who were 'hanging around', I approached a man in his late-teens. The man I approached was someone whom everyone had acknowledged – either when they arrived in the square, or when he did, which was usually at about 3 p.m. I knew that my presence had been noted by him, mainly because when the young people standing in the square had been 'moved on' by either police officers or security guards, so had I. Further, I had returned to my seat – just as they had returned – and not been 'frightened away'.

The black young man I approached turned out to be studying at a Further Education College in Middington - spasmodically, as he informed me. My initial contact had to be appropriate – I knew I had to present a manner which was humble without being ingratiating, confident without being arrogant, and relaxed without being too 'laid-back'. It was here that I made a *faux pas* which could have ended any further research period in the square. I began my conversation with him by saying 'I know you've noticed me sitting here for the last three days, so I thought I'd come and tell you what I was doing.' My explicit acknowledgement and stated assumption that he may want to know more about me was the blunder. 'No, I haven't noticed you', was his reply. Thinking fast, I merely responded with 'Oh come on – of course you have - don't be so snotty'; the written words are unable to convey the lightness of tone, the hint of laughter, and the naturalness in my voice, which were all fortunately present. After a ten-second pause, he invited me to tell him what I *was* doing. Having explained I wanted to write a book about what young people thought of society, and clarified I was not a detached youth worker but a student on a grant of £70 per week, he visibly relaxed, made a joke, and began to tell me what he thought. The lively conversation lasted two and a half hours, during the course of which two other young men joined us. Once I had been seen to have been 'passed' by him, most of the other young men who came regularly to the Norgate Centre would come and talk to me daily, albeit sometimes very briefly, about political and related issues.

I have described this in some detail in order to comment on the issues of reliability and validity in social research. Reliability refers to the idea that measures must be repeatable and consistent. Whilst Kidder (1981) in a discussion of inductive research states:

> The technique, in fact, requires changing the question to take account of the unanticipated answers and observations which come along
>
> Kidder 1981: 105

and argues unequivocally that 'numbers alone do not ward off bias' (p. 110), she is more reticent on the issue of reliability of unstructured interviews:

> As a measurement device, such an interview procedure is inadequate, for its flexibility results in lack of comparability of one interview with another. There can be little doubt of the usefulness...of such interviews as a source of hypotheses that can later be submitted to a systematic test by more quantitative methods.
>
> Kidder 1981: 188

Clearly, comparability of interviews or discussions when conducted in a large shopping centre in the pre-Christmas season is difficult to control. However, my decision to not carry out all of my research at this location was not based only on the apparent lack of repeatability of the discussions. The high face validity of the discussions was apparent.

I also learnt a considerable amount about the ways in which the research could proceed. Firstly, it was clear that the young people were prepared, and anxious to discuss 'society', once they had been able to test me out. This testing took the form of questions as to why I should be interested in their views; my replies appeared to be assessed not only by their content, but by the manner in which I spoke. Secondly, the discussions covered a wide range of topics, including a comparison of Cuba and China on one day, but always excluded comments by the young people about their own households. In addition, issues of sexual orientation and sexual practices were rarely introduced by the discussants. Thirdly, I realised that admitting a lack of knowledge about popular music or contemporary styles of clothing did not lead to their refusing to talk with me. In fact, such a lack of knowledge was used by them to teach me about these aspects of their lives, and this teaching allowed them to retain control over the discussions. Finally, it was clear that my disagreeing with their tastes in music or clothing did not prevent their being prepared to talk with me. For example, they would sometimes play a short piece of music on a portable cassette player and ask for my opinion. If I did not like or understand it, I would say so and some would laugh whilst others would urge me to buy it so that I could listen to it at leisure.

However, three aspects of the situation forced me to reformulate the research procedures. Firstly, as has been noted above, there were far fewer young women than young men present and 'hanging around'. In addition, the reasons for the presence of most of the young women appeared to be to both talk and laugh with other young women, while keeping track of the activities of particular young men. Given the overwhelmingly heterosexual ethos present within the young people in Halle Square, whilst it was 'cool' for the young men to be seen talking with me, and to be intrigued and interested in the research, the time spent by the young women in conversation with me was time taken away from talking with their peers. This heterosexual ethos was later confirmed by other participants in the study. With time, it could have been possible to create more appropriate times to talk with the young women. However, the second reason for changing the location was that only some young people would spend their time regularly in the Norgate Centre. The aim of my study, however, was to explore the notions of politics and unemployment present amongst young working-class people. Thus, it seemed inappropriate to only talk with the young people who chose to come to the Norgate Centre. The third reason for changing the location of the study was that the age range of the people I spoke with was 14 to 29; this age range and the concomitant very wide range of experiences militated against the development of systematic insights into the way in which politics was discussed.

The next part of the study involved my spending substantial lengths of time in centres for the unemployed and youth centres. This was done in January and February 1985, and involved spending parts of every weekday as well as weekends at the youth centres. The youth centres in Middington operate such that youth of 'Asian' origin attended at particular times, with the girls going on Sunday afternoons. Young people of Afro-Caribbean origin attended centres which had very few other black young people, and virtually no white young people present. The young white people went to centres often for specific classes, such as weight training and badminton. Again, quasi-ethnographic techniques of observation, 'being around', group discussions, and semi-focussed interviews were carried out, and copious field notes kept. In the youth centres, the young people accepted my lack of coordination in playing pool and table-tennis and tried to teach me to improve my game. In some sessions, they also attempted to teach me to write Urdu. However, the presence of loud music, and their disinclination to talk with me in a room outside the main halls militated against having detailed discussions in these centres. In addition, similar reservations to those reported above in relation to the Norgate Centre were developed, and I decided that to base the study only in such centres was inappropriate in view of the aim of the study. Field research often makes the choice of sampling strategies as presented in textbooks difficult to follow:

> For, in practice, the researcher has to apply sampling strategies to particular research problems as it is rarely possible to follow the ideal strategies outlined.
>
> Burgess 1982b: 78

4.3.2   Group discussions

One of the aims of the study was that there should be approximately equal numbers of young women and men. In addition, it was also necessary to have adequate ethnic variation in the sample. The final constraint was the necessity to interview people of a very similar age; the experiences of school and the labour market can be remembered very differently at different ages, and this variation may be important when discussing political views and arguments with young people. Thus, because it has been argued that the group should be fairly homogeneous in respect of age and social class background, with adequate variation in terms of ethnic origins and sex, it seemed appropriate to begin the study in a school in the locality in which I had based the study.

Three schools were used in all: one comprehensive school in the centre of the south/central area of Middington provided the majority of the respondents. The other two schools were also comprehensives, one situated approximately one mile away from the main school, and serving a very similar catchment area. The third school, a girls' comprehensive school, was approximately two miles away. Middington Local Education Authority has some single-sex schools, in order to be able to cater to demands for either single-sex or two-sex schools. Thus, the range of backgrounds of girls in this third school was much greater than the backgrounds of the students in the other two schools. However, very few girls of 'Asian' origin attended the first or second schools – so, in order to ensure ethnic and sex balance in the sample, it was necessary to base myself for some time in this girls' school from which potential respondents could be drawn.

There were eighty-seven fifth formers in the main school, of whom approximately 65% were present at any one time – the rest being out on Work Experience schemes, avoiding lessons, playing truant, or were suspended. The school had 500 school students on its register – 40% of these were girls, a quarter of the students were of South Asian origin, the rest being divided between those of Afro-Caribbean origin (45%) and white school students (30%). These percentages are approximate as the proportions were obtained from discussions with the headteacher. The numbers on the school roll have decreased substantially in the past decade, from 1,200 in the mid 1970s, to 500 at present.[1]

In all three schools I organised discussion groups with the fifth formers. Thus, all those students who were later interviewed on a one-to-one basis (see section 4.2.3) had been in a discussion group with me at least twice. There were a number of reasons for organising single-sex discussion groups. Firstly, it was necessary that all potential interviewees should have a sense of me and the issues to be covered in any one-to-one interview. Development of rapport could only be facilitated by the school students acquiring this sense in a context where they could assess me, without their feeling embarrassed. Group discussions with their contemporaries seemed an appropriate way to set up such an assessment. Secondly, as has been mentioned in the section on the pilot study, this age group are interested in discussing, but appeared to have little confidence in their views about society, this lack of confidence sometimes being expressed as 'politics is boring [yawn]'. To demonstrate to them that they *did* have views required group discussions. This is because even if an individual feels they have little or nothing to say on a particular topic, they may burst out with a comment when they hear views of their contemporaries, and so realise they *do* have something to say. Thirdly, if 'politics' is boring, it is unlikely that such issues will have been discussed at all outside the classroom. It was therefore necessary that potential interviewees had had a chance to consider the issues which would arise in the interviews, and group discussions are an

---

[1] I shall describe, in detail, the school in which 65% of the interviewees were based. The general pattern of the study was the same in all schools; I shall comment on differences in ways in which the study was run when these differences affected the study itself, and ignore procedural variations due to the differences in organisation in the schools.

appropriate way of permitting such consideration.[2] Fourthly, I felt it necessary that potential interviewees realise that the one-to-one interviews would be about social issues, as distinct from an exploration into the personal lives of the school students. The study was not about relationships with parents or about 'sex and drugs and rock 'n roll' unless they wanted it to be so. Hence my explanation that I wanted to know their views, and what interested them about society. The informal agenda for the individual interviews was to be structured by the topics which the school students considered relevant, and group discussions were the optimal means of finding out what those topics were. Fifthly, the discussion groups were single-sex. My 'hanging around' in the Norgate and youth centres indicated that young women often said much less in mixed-sex discussion groups than in single-sex ones. In addition, both young women and young men are often very aware of possible sexual connotations of words, phrases and sentences, so that mixed-sex discussion groups were likely to involve too much 'messing around', and thus require controlling behaviour from myself – a totally inappropriate requirement for a researcher. Finally, the group discussions as well as later individual interviews were voluntary – it was clear to the students that I had no authority within the school, and no comments, either from staff members or myself ever suggested otherwise.[3] Thus, the rationale was that the school students could 'try-out' the discussions, come to a second one, and then decide if they wanted to come to individual interviews. The lists allocating students to a group were drawn up by me, working through the school register (i.e. alphabetically) as well as according to the strictures of the timetable.

The tape-recorded discussions took place, mostly in the school library, with no-one else present, or able to hear the discussion. To each group I explained that young people had not often been asked what they thought about 'society', and that I was interested in finding out what they thought. I explained that I was conducting the research as a student – and concretised

---

[2]   It could be argued that the experience of the group interviews 'created' the views expressed in the individual interviews. This argument rests, however, on a notion of individuals which the theory of social representations and the rhetorical approach are challenging: individuals do not possess one view (or attitude?) which psychologists should then obtain. To conceptualise group discussions as 'contaminating' the content of individual interviews is misplaced and mistaken (see extract from Tajfel, Jaspars and Fraser 1984 cited at the beginning of chapter 3).

[3]   I am extremely grateful to the staff and headteachers of the schools for respecting the requirement that I demonstrate my distance from teachers by never discussing either individual students or issues which arose in the discussions. I also sat separately in staff rooms so that if a school student came to the door of the staffroom, they would see that I was not socialising with the teachers.

this by saying that I was writing a book about their views. Issues of confidentiality were discussed; I then restressed that these discussions were voluntary - that I was not a school teacher, nor 'from the Council', who would report back to others, and that I lived in Cambridge, although I did have a large number of friends, contacts and acquaintances in Middington. The most common questions from the school students were about the income I was receiving for doing such work.

Each session began with my asking everyone in the group to state, in turn, what they thought they would be doing on leaving school. There were two reasons for this. The first was that if anyone was a little nervous or reticent about speaking in a group, the first time one speaks in a group can be difficult. By asking each individual to say what they thought they would be doing in March or May 1986, this initial non-speaking in a group had been overcome. Secondly, in every group, at least one person would mention either potential unemployment, or the Youth Training Scheme (YTS). This mention of unemployment or YTS had occurred in the pilot work. Thus, the second reason for asking potential interviewees to state what they would be doing on leaving school was to pick up on this aspect of their futures in order to get the group discussion going. It was from this cue that I would ask either about unemployment, or the YTS, and in this way, the group discussions began. My role in these always lively discussions was to act as a chairperson, and to request them not to speak at the same time, as the tape recording was then unclear. Each discussion lasted approximately 50-60 minutes; the issues which emerge spontaneously from these discussions ranged from discussions on unemployment, nuclear war, racism, schooling and education, sexual assaults on women and children, Ethiopia, South Africa, and party politics. In addition, the students made a substantial number of references to the coal dispute of 1984/1985, which had not ended in February 1985, when most of the discussions were held. The teachers' dispute was also commented upon, but more frequently in individual interviews.

In all, I organised twenty-six single-sex discussion groups with potential interviewees. They were all school students in their final year at school – that is, in the fifth form. Middington Education Authority has a system of sixth form colleges, as well as Colleges of Further Education to which those who wish to continue to remain in formal education can go.

The group discussions were not transcribed, as their main aims had been as described above. However, each was listened to carefully, a number of times, and notes taken on the topics raised, and the ways in which the topics were introduced into the discussions. It was necessary to do this so that if an individual interview became 'sticky' with too embarrassing a silence, I would have a means of introducing another topic into the interview in a way which resonated with at least one of the group discussions in which the interviewee had been.

4.3.3   Individual interviews

Individual interviews were conducted with seventy-six of the ninety school students who participated in the twenty-six group discussions. As described earlier, these interviews were voluntary. Of the interviewees, forty-seven came from the 'main' school in the study; of the remaining twenty-nine, five boys came from another comprehensive school and twenty-four girls from the girls' comprehensive school.

Every individual interview was conducted in a classroom or similar in the school and in school hours. Where classroom doors had glass panels through which others could see into a certain part of the room, the interview was conducted in that part of the room which could not be seen. All the interviews in the 'main' school were conducted at the end of February 1985 until the end of the school term, while the group discussions and interviews at the other two schools were held during April and May 1985.

Each school interview began with my writing down who else lived in the household of the interviewee and their employment status. In addition, I explained that I would probably want to re-interview them, and so needed an address and, if appropriate, a telephone number. Not one interviewee refused or even hesitated to provide their address. The tape recorder was then switched on and interviewees were first asked what examinations, if any, they may be taking in the summer, their birthdate and what they thought they would be doing when they left school. From this point, the interview was treated by me as a 'conversation with a purpose' (Burgess 1984). Thus, the topics in the informal agenda for the interview were presented in the order which seemed most appropriate, the only requirement I had placed on myself was that all these issues were raised with every interviewee at some point.

As stated earlier, the issues which comprised this agenda had been drawn from the group discussions. They were: employment, unemployment and the Youth Training Scheme, party politics, violence against women and marriage, racism, the 1984–85 coal dispute and the teachers' dispute, nuclear power and nuclear weapons, and the police. The interviews lasted between 30 and 45 minutes, using a semi-structured informal agenda with an open-ended interviewing technique.

Of the original seventy-six interviews, only two tape recordings were faulty. Thus, there were seventy-four usable interviews conducted between March and May 1985, amounting to approximately forty hours of recorded interview material.

Every evening, all the interviews which had been conducted during the day were listened to, with the aim of constantly trying to develop the next day's interviews. Details of the transcription process will be outlined in section 4.3.5.

4.3.4 Follow-up interviews

A letter was sent to each of the seventy-four interviewees whose interviews had been transcribed by the end of September 1985 asking how they were, reminding them of the study and asking if they were prepared to be re-interviewed. Given the well-known low response rate to letters requesting follow-up interviews, I then indicated that I would be contacting them in the coming two months to arrange a time to suit them. As the letters were photocopies, I also made a point of including a handwritten individual comment to each person to demonstrate that I did remember them. As the letters were going to their homes, I was careful never to refer to anything which had been said and which the interviewee may not have wanted others in the household to know about.

Methods of re-contact were telephone, calling round to their homes, and via contacts with friends whom I had also interviewed. In addition, I spent substantial amounts of time walking and driving around the streets in the locality as I often then met someone I had interviewed who wished to be interviewed again and whom I had not yet contacted. Sixty individuals were recontacted in this way, with a limit of seven attempts to re-contact my subjects.[4] Of the fourteen whom I was unable to reinterview, nine had moved away from the country, the town, or had not remained in contact with their friends.

These follow-up interviews, conducted from October to December 1985, were carried out in a variety of locations such as in my car, in a room at the local community centre and in the respondents' homes. Each interview was again recorded. Every interview began with the interviewee telling me their examination results if they knew them.[5]

---

[4] This is a commonly accepted criterion for follow-up contact, as for example, in Brown and Harris (1978).

[5] I later went into the schools, having explained to the interviewees I would do so, to note accurately the exact grades obtained as many of them were vague about the exact grades they had obtained.

Each interview then continued with my asking what the interviewee had been doing since leaving school. The technique used was the same as that described in the previous section – that is, conversations with a purpose – except that the number of topics I introduced was more limited. This was because the interviewees appeared pleased to see me, and eager to have the chance to discuss their lives since leaving school. Thus, the interviewees talked at greater length in these second interviews, limiting the number of topics which I could introduce. Whilst every follow-up interview covered employment, unemployment, the Youth Training Scheme, party politics, their futures, the recent events in Tottenham and Brixton, and leisure times, they were also much more open-ended than the first interviews. These interviews lasted between 45 and 60 minutes each, with the interviewees not demanding questions of me as frequently as they had in the first interviews.

4.3.5 Transcription of interview tapes

As stated earlier, all the interviews were transcribed. These transcriptions were done though a typing agency in Cambridge, so that there was very little chance that any of the transcribers would know any of the interviewees. The first interviews were transcribed during July and August 1985, and I checked each transcription for accuracy against the tape recording. Before every second interview, the interviewee's first interview was read carefully, and they were asked if they wished to either read or hear the first interview. They all declined that offer, but some asked that the cassette tapes be sent to them after the research had been written up.

The second interviews were transcribed in the first part of 1986, and again, transcriptions were checked against the tape. When there was a complete set of transcriptions, for both first and second interviews, I again checked all the transcriptions against the tape and noted pauses, laughter, hesitations and interruptions if this had not been done.

Following this, the interviews for each person were summarised into a maximum of ten-page narratives. This interview material will be considered in the following two chapters.

4.4 Sample characteristics

The area of Middington in which the interviews were conducted was mainly the constituency designated as Central Middington. In February 1985, unemployment was 17% in the Greater Middington travel-to-work area, and was at 31% in the locality in which the study was based (*Department of Employment Gazette*, October 1985). This level of unemployment was the second highest in Britain (February 1985). 80% of the sample lived in

Table 1. *Sample characteristics at time of first interview*

Afro-Caribbean	10 women	12 men	Total 22
'Asian'	18 women	10 men	Total 28
White	14 women	10 men	Total 24
Total	42 women	32 men	

All interviews were conducted between February and May 1985, with most of the sample being interviewed not more than three weeks before they were due to leave school. The age range at the time of the first interview was between 15 years 6 months and 16 years and 6 months.

council housing, with the remainder living in owner-occupied, predominantly Victorian terraced housing. Less than one-third of the sample had telephones, which compares with a national figure of approximately 60% of council tenants who have telephones (*Social trends*, 1986). Much of the housing is in high-rise flats, with the Shale estate in Middington having the reputation of being the largest council housing estate in Europe. This was built in the late 1960s, and much of the accommodation is now badly decayed. Many of the estates consist of 'deck access' flats, about which the local residents have, from time-to time, made representations to the Local Authority Housing Department regarding safety of access at night. Many of the sample were unhappy about the quality of the housing in which they or their friends lived:

> The whole country needs changing...like the buildings: they're not fit to live in the houses round here...
>
> PN74

However, this type of view, whilst echoed in many of the early conversations I had with the school students, was carefully delineated from any view which feeds into a 'culture of poverty' explanation (see Keddie 1973 for a critique). This can be seen in their comments on a newspaper article which appeared a few months before the interviews about the locality:

> She [a reference to a teacher in the school] wrote in the
> Evening News – Black people are immigrants. That all the
> pupils   at   [this   school]   are   tramps...they're
> undisciplined...that most of the children from round here
> come from broken homes. That's not right to say that.
>
> Tape IVa Discussion 381

This extract could be interpreted as a comment on the accuracy of the article. However, the context of the discussion suggested that the objection was to the implications which are often drawn from information and phrasing such as that in the quote. Thus, although the quality of the housing and the resources in the area is not high, and is acknowledged as such by the interviewees, there was a determination to not collude with the view that such indices of deprivation imply a lower quality human being.

Table 2. *Household composition of sample*

11	participants were living in households with one adult in a parent-relationship
29	participants were living in households with two adults in a parent-relationship
27	participants were living in households with >2 adults in the household, but two of these adults were in a parental relationship to the subject
7	participants were living in a household with >2 adults, but not necessarily with two adults in a parental relationship to the participant.

Thus, it can be seen that 38% of the sample was living in a pattern similar to the nuclear family of mother, father plus children, although the adults were not necessarily the biological parents of the interviewee.

An examination of the households' structure by employment status demonstrates that many of the subjects in the sample had experience of unemployment, in the sense that members of their households were unemployed. 25% of the sample (19) had no-one unemployed in their household, the remaining 75% (55) had at least one adult unemployed. Of this 75%, two-thirds (37) were living in households with two or more adults unemployed. Within these 37 households, 24 had two adults unemployed, 5 households had three adults unemployed, 6 households had four adults unemployed, and the remaining 2 households had five adults unemployed.[6]

Table 3. *Sample characteristics at time of second interviews*

	Girls	Boys	Totals
Afro-Caribbean	9	10	19
'Asian'	14	9	23
White	10	8	18
Totals	33	27	

85% (60) of the 74 individuals interviewed in the first half of 1985 were re-interviewed.

The sample was re-interviewed in October/November/December 1985. This was at least six months since they had left school, and the members of the sample had been either in a YTS scheme, in a college, obtained employment, or were unemployed.

The following table gives an idea of the post-school destinations of the sample:

Table 4. *Post-school destinations (4 weeks after leaving school)*

47 (78%) of the sample were unemployed
9 (15%) of the sample were on a YTS scheme
3 (5%) of the sample were employed on leaving school
(PN76, PN29, PN73)
1 (2%) member of the sample (a white boy) had a 4-yr apprenticeship

---

[6] 'Unemployed' here means either that the interviewee used that word, or said they 'didn't have a job'. In addition, if no comment was volunteered on the employment status of the adult, I asked; 'Do they have a job outside the house?' If the answer was negative, this was noted as unemployed. It seemed totally inappropriate to further discuss employment status in terms of registration, whether seeking employment etc. as this 'was not the point of the interviews'.

Table 5. *Occupation at the time of second interview*

---

14 (23%) of the sample were on YTS schemes
31 (52%) of the sample were at a FE college
10 (17%) of the sample were registered as unemployed
 5 (8%) of the sample had jobs/app.ships (incl PN59 now)

Table 6. *Examination results*[7]

On average, 3.3 CSE passes and 2 'O' level passes per person.
20% had over 5 'O' level passes,
14% had more than 7 'O' level or 'O' level equivalents.
Less than 50% with results available had any 'O' level or 'O' level equivalents.

4.5 Conventions for presenting interview material

There are two conventions for presenting interview material which retains the anonymity of the speaker. Firstly, individual interviews can be assigned a number, and this number is used to distinguish one speaker from another. However, this, it is argued, is dehumanising and is considered to be contrary to the spirit of particular research studies such as this one. The second convention is to assign new names for the interviewees. This assignation, however, is likely to imply a stereotype.

The pattern has been in much of the recent ethnographic work (e.g. Griffin 1985b) to provide names (albeit changed to ensure confidentiality of the speakers) whilst quoting from the interviews. However, in providing names for speakers who are white, of Afro-Caribbean origin or South Asian origin, is the researcher meant to provide a 'stereotypical' name to ensure that the reader realises both the sex and the 'racial' origin of the speaker? This appears to be an appealing strategy, and may be appropriate if the work has been done with only one sex, or one 'racial' group. But then these same stereotypical notions of groups can end up being reproduced in the research. In addition, continuities between the groups cannot be explored so easily if

---

[7]   Individual numbers of passes in public examinations have not been included in this book as this could possibly be a source of identification of individuals.

every participant within a psychological study is analysed as part of the group to which s/he is allocated by the researcher. Writers on 'sex differences' research in psychology (e.g. Griffiths and Saraga 1979; Fairweather 1976) have raised this point a number of times in their critiques of the discipline.

This is not simply a theoretical point. There are implications for the conduct of studies, and for the reporting of research. The point which is being made is that many of the interviewees in this study were born in Britain, and most of them had spent at least all their primary and secondary education in Middington. They are not, therefore, migrants or 'second-generation immigrants'[8] but are individuals who have spent their lives within Britain. The experience of racism is one distinction which may be teased out between the groups – white people are very unlikely to be able to experience directly the racism which is part of the daily lives of black people in Britain. In addition, the different ways in which young women and young men experience, and are experienced by their environments, both social and physical, is a potential point of analysis. A concentration on the differences, be it 'cultural' or 'gendered', leads to a static notion of the ways in which people relate to their social world. 'Race', class and gender simultaneously structure the lives of people – even when those people are white, men or middle-class. Ruth Frankenberg (1988), for example, has argued that what it means to be white can only be understood in relation to and with a separation of oneself from being black. Thus, by assigning the interviewees a name whilst discussing their arguments one can only fall into the trap of again setting up implicit notions of the static nature of cultural relationships – that, for example, it would not be possible for a white child to have a name like 'Winston' or 'Sushila'. There is another argument. Young black people and young white women are rarely present in studies exploring 'ordinary' youth, and when they are, they have to be made visible. On the other hand, the rarity of their inclusion can mean, if they are categorised into different groups, that the continuities across the experiences can get swamped in the search for discontinuities.[9]

For this report of the study, I have chosen to use the numbering system (see Appendix I).

---

8 See Bhavnani and Coulson (1986) for a critique of this term.

9 It is worth noting in passing that there have been a number of times when I have presented conference papers in which, although I have outlined the composition of the sample of the study, many people have offered comments which indicated that they thought the study was only with young men, or only with young black people.

Table 7. *Summary table of individual interviews*

A.	Qualitative method, i.e. open-ended interviews.
B.	Age between 15.6 months and 16.6 months
C.	Seventy-four subjects interviewed for between 30 and 45 minutes in first half of 1985. Sixty re-interviewed October–December 1985.
D.	Topics covered, generated by group discussions:

      - School

      - Post school

      - Employment/Unemployment/YTS

      - Teachers' strike

      - Coal miners' dispute 1984–1985

      - Voting and party politics

      - Racism

      - Police

      - Nuclear power and nuclear war

      - Sexual assault and marriage

      - Futures

4.6   Sample representativeness

Many criticisms have been put forward of the open-ended interview method as a means of allowing for accurate and insightful social analysis (see previous chapter). However, the question of the representativeness of the work seems to be an important one to tackle here. It is not enough to retort, as one is too often tempted to do, that statistical sampling techniques, along with statistical analysis, are also no guarantee of any representativeness. Often the theoretical framework which informs the choice of sampling technique or the analysis is not laid bare for non-statisticians to analyse. A productive way to discuss this point may be to outline the aim of this study which is to explore the themes within and around which young people discuss politics. As has been argued in the previous chapter, themes within discussions cannot be *measured* and a level of consistency across groups in relation to particular topics or issues presented; rather, these themes will emerge in the discussions. Taking this as the starting point, it can be seen that the discussions of politics will include a number of differing elements or themes within these discussions. Thus, studies such as this one can consider not only what is being represented, but, also, the relationship between this and the representer.

> Therefore, he [sic] always represents more than the process represented, and, at the same time, in certain respects, less. But the *tension between individual reality and general process is what must emerge in research* which aims to safeguard the integrity of the individual. For this reason, the psychological realm can never be completely deduced from social experience, but stands in a polar relation to it – both opposed and linked to it.
>
> Passerini 1987: 11 (my emphasis)

It is worth considering further this argument, so that the reader is not left feeling frustrated when reading the material in the next two chapters. The *range* of themes which are present in the interviews will be teased out. Whilst it may be of some interest to know whether a certain percentage of the group did raise a particular theme in a particular way, it should be remembered that when looking at the process of the development of these themes, one person's insight may be as valuable as the statements of the majority, by permitting an examination of the *process* of the development of the theme. That is, individuals will discuss and argue about topics in different ways; these differences are not merely idiosyncratic but reflect the differing social relationships which may lead to differing discourses of power. Thus, this study is not one in which it is necessary or desirable to utilise quantitative analyses in order to draw out the themes. Clearly, research strategies should, ideally, be able to combine both qualitative and quantitative analyses. However, for a project which is attempting to develop initial categories of analysis, the quantitative approach must take a back-seat for the moment.

5   The domain of the political. I.
Employment, unemployment, and youth training schemes

For my family, my strength
For my comrades, my light
For the sisters and brothers whose fighting spirit
   was my liberator
For those whose humanity is too rare to be destroyed
   by walls, bars, and death houses
And especially for those who are going to struggle until
   racism and class
Injustice are forever banished from our history.

Angela Y. Davis   *Angela Davis: an autobiography*

5.1   Introduction

The interviews will be analysed by an examination of some of the topics discussed in them. This chapter, following the arguments developed in chapters 1 and 2 will look at how young people discussed employment, unemployment and the training schemes. It has been argued earlier that 'politics' includes a discussion of modes of production; these are not abstract entities but are constructed through social relationships and so are both regulatory, as well as being possible sources of contestation of social relationships. Thus, discussions of employment opportunities are an aspect of the political, and the question examined in this chapter is 'What themes are present in young people's discussions of employment, unemployment and training schemes?'[1]

Some points need to be made here. Politics has been defined as the regulation and contestation of unequal power relationships. The young people, when interviewed before May 1985, talked very briefly in their first one-to-one interviews about employment and the related issues specified above. The reasons for this brevity require some thought, and the following considerations provide some insight. Firstly, it could be argued that employment, unemployment and training schemes were not ones which had been primary in the young people's lived experience, unlike, for example, schooling. Therefore, the interviewees were not confident in discussing these issues. However, it is clearly not accurate to assert that the respondents were only able to discuss issues which are part of their experience. Some of the topics, discussed in the next chapter such as marriage and voting are also issues with which the young people had no previous experience. That is, they had not voted, nor were they married; however, these latter issues appeared to have a greater resonance with their daily lives. Clearly, the nature of employment and the meaning of unemployment are differently conceptualised to marriage. As indicated in chapter 4, Table 2, 75% of the interviewees had at least one unemployed person in their household. So, like

---

[1]   This is sub-question 1 presented at the beginning of chapter 4.

marriage (or, more accurately, coupled heterosexual relationships), unemployment was present in the households of many of the interviewees. The difference, however, could be that marriage involves a set of social relationships which are extremely familiar from a very early age; the relationships are commonly rehearsed in the games children play in, for example, 'mothers and fathers'. Young children do not commonly, however, organise their play around games about working-class employment opportunities. Thus, it is possible that the social relationships of employment are 'abstract entities' in the lives of the young people until they leave school, and that this is a consequence of the social organisation of employment rather than of the 'limited imagination' of the interviewees.[2]

The first interviews, therefore, have little continuous explicit material about employment and unemployment. It is therefore difficult to analyse these with a view to specifying the themes present in the interviewees' discussions of employment-related issues. By contrast, these discussions in the second interviews are very striking for their richness; such a richness is mainly due to the ways in which the interviewees discussed the topics by using incidents and events to exemplify their arguments. This narrative structure of their accounts provides insights into the ways in which particular themes are central to their discussions of employment which the school-based discussions do not provide.

There is another means by which the contrast between first and second interviews can be explained. The latter interviews were *at least* the fourth time in which the interviewees met with me (twice in group discussions, and one individual interview), although many of them had talked with me in break times/free lessons at school, as well as chatting with me when seeing me on the street. Thus, it is likely that they were more relaxed with me; further, these second interviews were conducted in locations of their choice rather than in school class- or career-rooms. It is also likely that leaving school has connotations of the end of childhood, with its associated transition of status. Therefore, the interviewees at the time of the second interview probably had a greater self-confidence in themselves as non-children than when at school. A final point which is worth noting is that all the interviewees in both first and second interviews said they wanted a job. There is a related point. A number of the studies discussed in chapters 1 and 2 compared groups of employed and unemployed people with the aim of understanding the views of these groups as a consequence of their

---

[2] Castles and Wustenberg (1979) in *The Education of the Future* discuss some of the concrete consequences of the separation of employment from every other aspect of school children's lives.

employment status. There is considerable value in such studies, and the results from some of them have clearly informed the arguments and analysis of this one.

However, the present study is one which for theoretical reasons is not conducting its analyses within these more frequently encountered patterns. Firstly, the nature of youth unemployment in Britain means that an increasingly very small number of school leavers obtain jobs. Those interviewed for this study are not different to that overall pattern. Six months after leaving school, four of the sixty interviewees interviewed twice had jobs. One person had obtained an apprenticeship. Thus, over 90% of the group did not have employment. A substantial number of the remaining fifty-five were registered at Further Education Colleges. Many of them viewed this registration as a last resort, having searched for employment and tried out Youth Training Schemes during the summer. However, others who had registered for Further Education were seeing college education as a means of gaining qualifications for future employment. Of the remainder, all were on Youth Training Schemes or registered as unemployed. Chapter 2 has discussed the arguments that the YTS is not like employment because of its lack of a 'proper' job, its low wages, its rejection by many trade unions as exploitative and because it is specifically based on the notion that youth unemployment exists because school leavers do not have appropriate employment skills, and thus, need to be 'trained'. These characteristics suggest that YTS is more similar to unemployment, for example, in terms of the allowance it gives to trainees. Some analysts have also suggested that the quality of training is such that the schemes are a means of controlling the numbers of the registered young unemployed. Therefore, YTS may be treated as a training scheme by the participants, or it may be used as a means of bypassing the registration as unemployed, with the participants treating the scheme as somewhere to get their allowance but no training. The point of this argument is to suggest

(a) That the numbers of young working class people who obtained jobs in this study was very small.

(b) The groups of those at college and those on YTS were so very heterogeneous in terms of the way the young people related to them that, often, individuals within these groups had greater similarity in terms of income, and likelihood of employment, to those who were registered as unemployed than to others defined as being of that group.

(c) Therefore, it is not possible to compare the views of those associated with, for example, employment with those who were on a YTS with those who were registered unemployed. This is because such comparisons are only of some validity if they either have large numbers in the groups, or if the behaviours of assigned group members are homogeneous to the extent that some comparisons carry face validity. Neither is appropriate for this study.

(d) Finally, employment, unemployment, YTS, and being at colleges are not discrete and bounded categories. Not only are they one possible means of organising social relationships, rather than finite categorisations of human experience, but also, the fluidity in the ways in which those who are in those groups define themselves means that any type of comparison between groups becomes a nonsense.

To sum up, this chapter is concentrating on analysing the interviewees' second interview discussions about employment, unemployment, and training schemes. This is because it was in these interviews that a much greater interest was shown by the participants in employment-related issues. The possible reasons for this demonstration of greater interest have been touched on above. Further, it has been argued that to look at the interview material according to categorisations of the speakers as employed, or unemployed is not appropriate, given that these categories are not determinate states, and, for youth in contemporary Britain, are not easily demarcated.

5.2 Some general comments about the interviews

Employment, unemployment, and the Youth Training Scheme were mentioned in every interview, implicitly introduced at the beginning either for the first interview in terms of 'What will you do when you leave school?' or for the second, 'What's been happening since leaving school?' If the interviewee did not refer to any of them, the issues were picked up from any direct or indirect comment made by the participant during the course of the interview.[3]

In both chapters 3 and 4, as well as from observations made about other studies in the first two chapters, the reader will be aware of the limitations of using quantitative techniques of content-analysis to obtain meaning. For example, counting the number of times the word 'employment' was used by one interviewee cannot do justice to the length of time spent in discussing the issue (e.g. see PN51 in chapter 6), nor do justice to the ways in which the issues were or were not intimately integrated, both with each other, as well as with other issues. Counting the number of times a word is said is also not a guarantee of how importantly or unimportantly the issues were

---

[3] See chapter 4 for a detailed description of how the interviews were structured and conducted

viewed by the interviewees. In order therefore to present a hint of an overall picture, I have decided to use the word 'comment' when indicating how often particular topics were mentioned or discussed.

A 'comment' refers to the occurrence of the issue in the interview. However, in indicating the number of comments, there is no implication of for how long the issue was discussed by an interviewee. Neither, for example, is it possible to assume a consonance between a 'comment' and the length of time for which that issue was discussed. Therefore, one comment in one interview could still mean that the topic was discussed for a longer period of time than the time spent in another interview which contained three comments on that issue. Further, naming something as a 'comment' is not an implicit indication of how important the issue was for the interviewee. Despite these limitations, the counting of something as a comment does suggest the possible existence/occurrence of a discussion.

A second point relates to the specific issue of employment in relation to unemployment. Although the existence of unemployment is as 'natural' to capitalism as employment, the former is often publicly discussed as an 'unnatural' issue: hence it appears to make sense to ask questions about the reasons for its occurrence. This is not so for employment and was demonstrated in the pilot study. In that preliminary work there was a section of questions organised around 'why do you think people have jobs?', or 'why do you think people work?' Such questions were greeted in such a way as to suggest that the answer was self-evident – 'to get money, of course' – with further probes producing statements such as, 'well, it's obvious, isn't it?' Clearly, that something is seen as obvious or natural as marked by such short and non-discussion answers should be analysed: thus, the questions could have been retained for the Middington-based part of the study. However, the probes also tended to produce a 'clamming up' by the interviewees, who then behaved as if they had answered this question incorrectly, otherwise, why else would there be further probes on the same point? One-to-one interviews with young working-class people are a rare occurrence in their lives, and researchers need to be sensitive to the lack of self-confidence which may also be a consequence of the unequal power relationships with which many of the young people would enter an interview. If an interviewee considers that they have given the 'wrong' answer, then they are likely to look for other questions with right and wrong answers. Thus, probes on other questions such as trying to encourage an elaboration of a theme provided by the interviewee then resulted in 'I don't know; honest, miss, I don't know': a way of dealing with questions which is often present when an intelligence test or similar is being given. All the pilot interviews had been set up with my explaining there were no right or wrong answers; however, with the probes setting up an implication that there were right/wrong answers, it is likely that interviewees would not only have not trusted that initial statement, but also, ended up by not trusting me. This possible lack of trust is not conducive to interviewees developing either a self-confidence, or a confidence in myself as the interviewer. It is for these reasons that the interviewees were not directly requested to expand and elaborate upon reasons for the existence of employment while being expected to do so for unemployment.

5.3 Discussions about employment

This section will describe and analyse the three themes which emerged in the interviews when comments were made in relation to employment. These three themes were:

(a) income
(b) security
(c) jobs and careers.

5.3.1 Employment and income

Of the 143 comments about employment, 109 (76%) presented the theme of the income or wages from employment as an organising feature in their discussions. It is interesting to note, however, that this theme was used to denote either an acceptance of the current context of youth unemployment or to contest that context by stating the minimum wage they would like to receive.

> KKB: What sort of job would you like?
> PN59:   Anything as long as it's good money.
> KKB: What's good money?
> PN59:   £130 a week.
>
> I p.2

The above is from the first interview[4] of a boy who seemed very timid and uneasy at having to talk for any length of time, but who was, however, very keen to be interviewed by me. In his second interview, when he had got a job, he said:

> KKB: What did you do when you left school?

---

[4]   I and II indicate whether the comment occurred in the first or second interview, followed by the page numbers of the transcript.

PN59:	Sat down all day doing nothing for a bit then I got a telephone call to say that I've got a job interview.
KKB:	Where?
PN59:	Thomas Exhausts – you know, Chester Road. There.
KKB:	And you got the job, yeah?
PN59:	Yeah.
KKB:	Were you a bit scared when you got the job interview?
PN59:	A bit. But I've done work experience before.
KKB:	With them?
PN59:	Yeah. So I knew all of them.
KKB:	Is it a YTS?
PN59:	A proper job.
KKB:	Do you mind me asking how much you're getting?
PN59:	Forty...forty-eight a week. That's good money.

II p.2

In his first interview, this interviewee echoes the argument that wages are the single criterion by which a job may be defined as 'good' or 'bad'. By the second interview, however, the speaker has revised his notion of what constitutes 'good money', while retaining 'good money' as the defining criterion for a 'good job'. This downward revision of the amount of wage which is acceptable may be classified as a realistic revision, now the interviewee has had to look for, and, unusually, has been successful in finding a job as a 16-year-old. To categorise it as realistic, however, carries with it connotations of being 'sensible' and 'mature' (not merely 'accurate') and so implies a positive evaluation of his rethinking by the researcher. In order to get away from this implicit positive evaluation, it is more helpful to consider further why this rethinking has occurred. Jones (1983) has suggested that the rapid increase in unemployment, coupled with a dramatic decrease of resources for Welfare State Benefits have combined together to lower expectations especially on the part of young people – expectations in relation to employment, working conditions, future security and a general quality of life. Jones suggests that the existence of the Manpower Services Commission with the variety of schemes which exist to tackle youth unemployment have led to a strategy aimed at lowering expectations of both wages and the types of job which may be available. The speaker quoted above, PN59, appears to be an exemplar of Jones's argument about wages.

KKB:	What sort of job do you want?
PN47:	One that pays good money – I'll enjoy.
KKB:	What's good money?
PN47:	A certain amount what's tax free like say £200 a week – I might be exaggerating a bit but...something like that. And you don't have to work too hard for it. Physical that

	is. I mean doing it with your mind and everything.
KKB:	So that would be good money to take home – £200...
PN47:	Well, no less than a hundred. I'd take up to a hundred pounds tax free. But below that, I mean you can't really survive with £100 can you – a week? Gotta buy your clothes and food, pay the house or things like that. I mean I'm still living at home now but like say when I move out I really want more money to set myself up – set up my own environment.
KKB:	What's good about having a job? What are the good things?
PN47:	I don't think there's anything good about having a job actually, apart from the money. I mean you might get around a little bit, yeah. The money and getting around...'cos you've got to be sociable to be a secretary.
KKB:	Would you like to be a secretary?
PN47:	Yeah – it's indoors isn't it – you keep warm and everything. I wouldn't mind working outdoors and everything but abroad – I'd like to do something abroad as well. Might go abroad sometime anyway...

II pp. 6–8

The speaker above is also insistent that the wage is the ultimate determinant of working out what job he would like.

His acknowledgement of the very low possibility of a 16-year-old receiving £200 a week, despite the average male wage in Britain being close to that, is reflected in his assumption that my echo of his figure was not simply an echo but an evaluation of his definition of 'good money'. Hence his response – 'well, no less than a hundred', suggests that it had been implied he should reconsider this figure. That he is a little defensive about the wage level can also be noted from his detailed explanation of why £100 would be the minimum. At a time when the allowance from the Youth Training scheme, overwhelmingly the only possible source of income, was under £30 a week, his determination not to lower his expectations can be understood as a means of his not simply accepting the 'realities' of youth unemployment – of not simply accepting the argument young people are 'pricing themselves out of jobs' – by uncritically being grateful for any job, but a means of demonstrating, that, as wages are the reason many people have to work ('I don't think there's anything good about having a job'), the wage must do what it is supposed to do – namely, allow people to eat, house, and clothe themselves.

Further, the hopes of PN47 about the wages he would like to receive, with no direct reference to the actual wage levels of 16-year-olds, indicate that it may be more accurate to suggest that Jones's argument is only partially sustained. That is, expectations have not been lowered 'wholesale'; this speaker is attempting to ignore the current context of the wages young people actually receive. This ignoring can be analysed as a strategy of contesting one aspect of the hegemonic project of Thatcherism. However, precisely because it is partial, it is not able to be *clearly* oppositional to that project. Thus, the theme of income and its occurrence with employment expectations is one theme which organised the discussions of employment.

Other aspects of employment were introduced when discussing the theme of wages. Interwoven into their views of the wages they might receive for a job, the young people included other conditions of employment, such as PN47 wanting to be a secretary because the job requires being indoors.

KKB: What do you think is good about having a job?
PN05:   You're enjoying life 'cos you're earning, plus you feel good – feel quite good doing something, not just sitting about.
KKB: How do you mean when you say that what's good about having a job is enjoying life? What's involved for you in enjoying life?
PN05:   I'm not really sure.
KKB: Try and tell me. [Pause] Like, what would you be like? [Longer pause] OK, say you could have a job, what would be the things you'd ask about it?
PN05:   The wage, what people are like up there, how long do I have to work there for, how many days a week, and if I have a day off what do I do - when I come back do I have to sign something saying what are my reasons for having that day off.

II pp. 8–9

The above speaker, in using the theme of income, is interweaving it with his argument that obtaining employment income can be a source of self-respect ('plus you feel good'). In other words, he is expressing the theme of income as a means of signalling his strategy to develop his self-confidence by gaining self-respect.

KKB: Are you fed up?
PN72:   Am I fed up? No, not really, because I might be getting a job as an apprentice double-glazer and it starts off at £60 a week and it goes up, and when you're 17, you get the car to go round in. They're sending me a letter...
KKB: Do you think you've got a good chance?
PN72:   As good a chance as any.
KKB: Uh huh. Do you like being on the dole?

PN72:   I'm not on the dole, I'm on supplementary benefit.
KKB: Are you? What's that like?
PN72:   I don't mind really. I can just go out the same as me
          mates because they only get £26 on a YTS. Anthony and
          all of them are at college – they get a grant and it seems
          big but they...it only works out about eleven a week so
          I'm just the same as them really. I can go out where they
          go out, so I'm not missing out on anything really.
                                                              II p. 1

This speaker is also organising his arguments about employment around
the theme of income. In suggesting that he is in no different position to his
peers who are on a YTS or at college ('I can go out where they go out, so
I'm not missing out on anything really') he is using the criterion of
disposable income to suggest that the quality of his life when receiving
supplementary benefit is the same as that of his contemporaries. That he has
aspirations to obtain a job with a car in the near future implicitly indicates
that he may also be wanting a job in order to have greater freedom of
movement than is often possible, at present, for 16-year-old school leavers.

The final way in which the theme of income from employment was
expressed may be seen below:

KKB: What wouldn't you like about a factory job?
PN06:   So much boring, you don't get a lot of money for it do
          you? I mean you do quite a bit, it's a boring job, you do
          exactly the same every single day, same thing all day
          long, over and over again. Like yours is exciting 'cos
          you're meeting all different people every day aren't you?
          If you enjoy what you do it doesn't matter, sometimes it
          doesn't even matter how much you earn, I mean just as
          long as you enjoy it. I mean you don't have to earn a lot
          of money, as long as you like it, it's exciting to you, but
          I do think in a factory it'd be boring. You couldn't do
          that if you had a job in a factory – like you can go
          outside like, you know, I mean meet new people, seeing
          new things, I mean not just being stuck in a place all day.
                                                              II p. 12

The above speaker in articulating the theme of income from employment
suggests that income, for her, may not compensate for boredom and routine
as epitomised in factory work. She discusses the theme of income in relation
to enjoyment and excitement and foregrounds her fear of boredom in relation
to wages. Thus, in her discussion of employment and income, this speaker
interweaves the issues of her dislike of repetitious and unstimulating
occupation into her narrative and implies that the use of income as a

criterion for evaluating employment is not satisfactory for her.

There were four distinct ways in which the theme of income from employment was discussed – in relation to expectations, self-confidence and self-respect, freedom of movement and fear of boredom. In the differing expression of the relationships between the above few issues and the theme of employment income, it can be seen that the theme can be considered to be part of the domain of 'politics'. This is because it was discussed not only as regulatory, but also as a point of entry to begin to contest current wages for 16-year-olds, as well as to contest routinised and dull employment.

In saying the above, I am not wishing to suggest that the interviewees had no career aspirations. Rather, it is being argued that if jobs are considered not to be part of careers (with 'career' being seen as a guarantee of regular adequate income combined with higher status), then *any* assessment of a job is centred upon the size of the wage. This suggests that merely being employed is not considered to be the criterion by which the young people marked their entry into adulthood. A job it appeared could only mark entry into adulthood if it provided the possibility of this financial independence. This, I am suggesting, is the subtext of wages being the main criterion for a job for the 16–17-year-olds interviewed in this study – that wages represent their entry into adulthood and, therefore, independence. Thus, wages/income are a theme around which the regulation and contestation of the social relationships of employment can occur.

5.3.2   Employment, jobs, and careers

Of the 143 comments about employment, 89 (62%) organised their arguments around careers as well as income. Of those who stated in their second interview that the main reason for getting a job was income, twenty-five were men (out of a total of twenty-seven who were interviewed twice) and nineteen (out of a total of thirty-three who were interviewed twice) were women. It was thus that the young men argued that job or employment satisfaction would be determined by the wages received. When the young women discussed this issue of satisfaction, twenty-seven out of the thirty-three women interviewees organised their arguments around career prospects, which were sometimes explicitly related to income but not necessarily so. That is, interwoven into the theme of income was a notion of wanting 'proper' jobs, which were defined as not only distinct from the opportunities available on the Youth Training Schemes but also as distinct from routinised employment. The passage in the previous section which quotes from the interview transcript of PN06 is one demonstration of these two themes, income (discussed in the previous section) and careers-as-distinct-from-jobs being interwoven.

> KKB: And what do you think, you said, oh, you know, you said 'I think I'd like to get some "A" levels and get a proper job'. What does that mean? What's a not proper job?
>
> PN25: A not proper job is something like me mum used to do like working in a biscuit factory, packing biscuits. I want a proper career you know.
>
> KKB: And what's a proper career – what's good about having a career.
>
> PN25: A proper career is like what I've told you I want – say like a career in banking. I want that cause it gives you a steady income, and hopes of the job being interesting, if you sort of stick to it, working among nice people.
>
> II p. 3

While she is referring to the theme of 'income', the above speaker also suggests that the steadiness or regularity of an income from factory work is overlaid with a lack of security. A 'steady income' (like a 'steady' boy/girlfriend) implies security, reliability and regularity, aspects which she implies are not present in factory jobs, but are present in careers. The use of the theme of career in her hopes and aspirations is not taken to mean that a career is a necessary guarantee of an interesting job, but that it is possible that the interest will develop – 'and hopes of the job being interesting' – if an individual displays a determination to remain in it.

PN06 who was mentioned in section 5.2.1 had earlier worked with the theme of 'career' to suggest that following a career could be of specific benefits for women.

> KKB: You said you wanted a career. Why? What's good about a career?
>
> PN06: Well, I'd like nice clothes and nice house, nice car, I don't think you have to depend on somebody. I think it's nice to know that you're somebody in life, you know, and I'd just like something in life, and not just a family. I would like a family too.
>
> KKB: Would you?
>
> PN06: Yes, but I'd rather earn some money, you know what I mean, it's something to do, isn't it? Can't just sit down all day, do nothing.
>
> KKB: 'Cos some people say a woman shouldn't have a job, a woman shouldn't have a career [pause]
>
> PN06: No, I don't believe in that. I think it's nice, you know, just to go to work. No, if you [pause] but everyone's different now aren't they, but to me you need a career, especially now.

KKB: How do you mean?

PN06:   Well, there's not a lot of jobs, you've got to have a career, you can't just, I don't – I wouldn't like a job in a factory, you know getting me chance and getting a job in a factory like some people think they're lucky. I've got nothing against it, but, I'd rather have a, you know, a job somewhere above that.

II p. 11

Thus she uses the theme of career versus jobs to argue that the former not only implies reliability, security and variety, but also a lack of financial dependence on one other person. For women, who are often financially and emotionally dependent, she is suggesting that a career may allow an identity separately defined to the identities usually available to women – that of wives and mothers. In chapter 2 it was noted that levels of unemployment were almost identical for 16–17-year-old young women and men (unlike post-20 or post-25 unemployment levels) which would suggest that employment levels are similar, too, at that age. That young women are less likely to be concerned with careers because of their own and others' expectations that they will marry and have children is an argument put forward by, for example, McRobbie (1978) and Griffin (1985b), but is not borne out in these interviews. Why there should be this difference between the present study and the other two needs more thought. It will simply be noted here, as well as noting that every time a woman interviewee discussed employment, in relation to the theme of careers versus jobs, she always discussed these issues in relation to future marriage, or possible wishes of her husband, or future child care and family responsibilities. Not one of the young men when discussing the theme of careers in their discussions of employment referred to wives, marriage or child care. Thus, although young women were more likely to discuss future employment prospects in terms of careers than has been indicated in earlier empirical work, this was also interwoven with the consideration that they would get married and have children.

Some researchers (e.g. Bowlby 1963; Kellmer-Pringle 1975; Riley 1983) have suggested that the tasks of mothering need to be reconceptualised so that 'mothering' is seen as a career in itself. The young women interviewed in this study did not appear to be sympathetic to this argument when they discussed employment in relation to the theme of careers as distinct from jobs.

KKB: What's important about having a career?

PN18:   You've got to have something behind you – it's better
           than having ten kids behind you.
KKB: What's better about having a career than having ten kids?
PN18:   A lot! [laughs] 'Cos then you've got to fork out for them
           and everything as well, haven't you?

II p. 11

Many of the young women concretised employment by reference to the
theme of careers and argued that careers implied possibilities of interesting
tasks, reliable income, security as well as independence. At the beginning of
this section, it was noted that the men who were interviewed assigned a
certain primacy to income from jobs. The women, however, systematically
interwove the theme of income with the theme of careers, into their
discussions of employment. If having a job is an important symbol of
adulthood and independence for 16-year-olds then it would seem that for the
young men, it was the income which could provide the means of entry into
adulthood. For the young women, however, it was both careers and income.
Some writers (Campbell 1984; Wallace 1986) have implied that present
youth unemployment levels mean that the only entry for young women into
adulthood is through marriage or bearing children; further, they have
suggested that young women are themselves having children at earlier ages
for this very reason. Not one women interviewed for this study presented
that argument.

KKB: What are the good things about having a career?
PN24:   Independence I think – and if you've got your
           independence you've got a lot and you can do what you
           want – you can sort of branch out on your own – be like
           an adult. I wouldn't like to be staying at home for another
           three or four years – I hope I'll get a flat in a couple of
           years when I've hopefully got a job. But you sort of
           branch out a bit more on your own and you've got to
           learn to stand on your own two feet – and that's what I'd
           like to do – get a job and be able to move out.

II p. 18

The ways in which the theme of careers-as-distinct-from-jobs was
interwoven with the themes of income, and the desired consequences of
independence can be seen in the final quote, which begins from the
interviewee discussing her employment around the theme of career in her
school interview and then continues with what she is doing at the time of
her second interview.

KKB: What sort of job do you think you want?
PN76:   I ain't really bothered. I want a career. I'm doing catering [when I leave school] and I'll go to college first and see what happens from there. Work in a hotel or something, make up me own shop.

I p. 6

When the above interviewee did not obtain a place at a college in Middington she decided that she would get employment:

PN76:   When I found I couldn't get into college I was going to the Job Centre every day.

II p. 3

However, her comments on her employment as a machinist at the place where her mother worked, with a take-home pay of approximately £65 suggest that the theme of careers was still implicitly present in her discussion and description.

PN76:   I'm getting a bit sick of it now, but you've got to stick it out, haven't you?
KKB: And what do you think about the job? 'Cause I haven't seen it – tell me a bit about the job, tell me what you think about it, whether you like it, what you like and what you don't like about it.
PN76:   Well, it's a job, that's what I like about it. [laughs] It's a job and you get the money and everything.

She is here signalling that the theme of income from employment is only a partial source of satisfaction from this particular employment. Placing it in the context of her disappointment at not obtaining entry into a college to follow a career of nursery nursing makes this last statement all the more revealing.

In her description of the workplace and the tasks she had to do, that she got up at 6.30 every morning, and returned home at 6/6.30 every evening, she described the tasks as being the same every day, plus the fact that the workers there were not allowed to talk to each other. She did point to potentially interesting aspects of the job such as working on pillowcases as distinct from mattress covers, whilst simultaneously noting that the task was the same for both.

KKB: What are the good things about having a job?
PN76:   None! [embarrassed laughter]. It gets you out of the house and gets you off roaming the streets – some money in

your pocket [pause]

KKB: And what are the bad things about having a job?

PN76: Getting up in the morning! No, for some people it's alright – I'm alright [pause]

KKB: What are the other bad things about having a job?

PN76: Just depends what sort of job you're in. If you don't like it and people are being nasty with you and everything – you've just gotta know people. That's another thing – if you get to talk to people, right, and they've got a great career ahead of them and everything and they've got a job, you talk polite - they might then get you a job. They might find you somewhere.

II p. 6 and p. 11

She then went on to describe how her sister had got a 'proper job' in this way, through happening to be talking to an officer from the Education Department, who then found the sister a job. The account she presented of her sister's career suggested that she, PN76, was hoping that some such event would allow her in the future to be able to leave her current job as a machinist and be able to have a career.

The above section has demonstrated that second organising theme in the interviewees' discussions of employment was that of careers. The themes of income/wages and careers are intimately interwoven, and from a close examination of the interviewees' discussion, a crude categorical separation between the two themes is not justified. However, it has been noted that, on the whole, the young men appeared to specify the theme of income as an important organising feature of their employment discussions, while the young women presented the theme of careers as a central organising feature of their discussions of employment.

There are two ways in which to approach such empirical evidence. Firstly, it could be argued that young women and young men, as an indirect consequence of gender stratification, considered that identities which may be developed from employment were a result of either the income obtained, or the 'career prospects' (remembering that 'careers' were defined in distinction to routinised, repetitious and unstimulating jobs). That is, that the young men considered control over their lives and the consequent independence to be possible as long as there was an adequate income, while the young women viewed the possibility of controlling their employment tasks as a means of being independent. In other words, the men considered that control could be a consequence of income and independence, while the young women considered that independence itself was a consequence of control over their employment. This can be further understood if it is argued that a consequence of patriarchal structuring is that men's employment opportunities are less circumscribed than those of women. Therefore, for working-class men to be able to assert control over their lives necessitates an income which may permit them to exercise this control. In contrast, the greater circumscription of employment opportunities for women means that the working-class women interviewed had to negotiate and attempted to contest this circumscription by being desirous of greater control within their employment. This greater control, it is implied in their interviews, is more likely to lead to independence for them.

It should be noted that both these themes were not racialised. There is a prevailing view that young women of Indian sub-continental origin may be less likely to be interested in employment and careers than their white or other black contemporaries. This was not present in these interviews, although the 'Asian' young women did discuss the ways in which they would hope to integrate career and marriage; this, too, was not different from the other young women, except that the 'Asian' women were looking forward to arranged, as distinct from love, marriages (see chapter 6 for a more detailed discussion about this). There is, however, another complementary way to approach this. The young women I interviewed are likely to have defined me as a woman with a career (e.g. PN06 quoted in previous section). The themes which are being discussed in this chapter and the next one are not merely reflections of the 'true' selves of the people interviewed. The interviews are social events in that dialogues of the interviews are precisely that: they are communications between two people, one of whom was always myself, the researcher – a black woman in her mid-30s of Indian sub-continental origin, also likely to have been perceived as a woman with a career. Clearly the process of the production of these themes is part of the theme itself and also an aspect of the power relationships within the interviews. This issue of power relationships in the present research is discussed in the final chapter.

5.3.3 Employment and security

Of the 143 comments about employment, 117 of them (82%) referred explicitly to the theme of security.

> KKB: What's good about having a job?
>
> PN41:   Well, you can think about the future if you've got a job, you've got more security if you've got a job. If you haven't, well, you've got to think where your next penny's coming from, or where your next meal's coming from. If you've got a job then you can look forward to

	the future otherwise you've just got to struggle on.
KKB:	Is there anything else that's good about a job?
PN41:	If you've got a job, first things first, you've got to like it. I don't think it's right that anyone should have a job that you don't like, if you do that, you're going to be unhappy. I couldn't see myself... if I had a job I'd prefer it to be the one I'm happy at. If I got offered a job and I didn't really think I'd be happy in it, I'd...I wouldn't take it. Even if that meant being unemployed still, I wouldn't take it, 'cos I'd like to get satisfaction out of what I do, not disappointment.

II pp. 17–18

The way in which the above speaker relates the theme of security to a job by outlining the possible processes and linkages between them is clear. However, whilst presenting the theme of security in his discussion of employment, he is also integrating this theme with that of contentment with the employment. Thus, while he acknowledges that security is a possibility as a result of having a job, he is not advocating an uncritical acceptance of any job, for he implies that 'looking forward to the future' also necessitates 'satisfaction out of what I do, not disappointment'. In this way, he may be considered to be detailing his contestation of a public discourse which suggests that job security will be threatened if those who are employed attempt to improve the conditions of their employment. Also, by implication, this type of satisfaction, or contentment when associated with the theme of future security in relation to employment implies a satisfaction which can produce self-respect. Thus, the theme of security, like the theme of income is linked to self-respect when the topic being discussed is employment.

PN20:	The good thing about having a job is you've got something to do, you've got somewhere to go, your system keeps going every day, you know the next day and every day you're going to work and then you get your pay and go home and think, 'oh well, I've done something, I've made something. I've got money we're doing alright', you know. But if you've not got a job you've got to rely on other people and you just can't rely on yourself.

II p. 11

In describing the regularity of going to work, and the regularity of receiving pay she implies that employment allows for security. She suggests that without employment the necessity of having to rely financially on other people implies a lack of security, because of its consequent lack of independence. The explicit notion of predictability is thus related to the theme of future security, this latter being integral for the attaining of self respect by not relying on others; in addition, this security is intimately bound up with its essence being financial.

Thus, predictability, satisfaction, self-respect, and independence are all seen as linked to the theme of security in the discussion of employment. It is the linkages between these which form part of the reasons why an attitude that employment was desirable was always discussed as a central feature of the interviewees' lives. There is a lack of the theme of the Protestant Work Ethic *per se* in the discussions. Further, it may be noted that the themes of income, career and security were presented not simply as regulatory in terms of the social relationships of employment but also as potential sources for contesting these unequal power relationships.

5.3.4   Employment and the domain of the private

Sections 5.2.1, 5.2.2 and 5.2.3 have traced the ways in which the themes of income, careers and security were expressed and discussed in the interviews. These themes, which appeared with outstanding regularity within the interviews, appear to have little in common with Jahoda's argument about the five latent functions of employment.[5] Jahoda (1979) has suggested there are five latent functions of employment. These are discussed in chapter 1, but briefly, they are that employment imposes a time structure, it compels social contact, it links an individual to goals which transcend individual goals, it imposes status and social identity and it enforces activity. Whilst such a functional approach to employment is unsatisfactory, Jahoda's theory may be suggestive. Employment is defined as lying within the domain of the public. These latent functions suggested by Jahoda, however, are defined, in general, as part of the domain of the private for individuals.

The section began with an outline of how it was not possible to ask reasons for employment, because employment was defined as being 'natural'. Although arguments were present in the interviews which discussed employment in relation to income, security, and career, these themes were discussed as if such issues are private concerns and aspirations. These themes which are present in the discussions of employment were set in a

---

5   It could be argued that to expect a concordance between a theory which suggests *latent* functions of employment and how the people themselves talk about employment is unreasonable, precisely because the functions are latent, or implicit. However, the strength of qualitative analysis is that it can permit analyses which look at latent or implicit themes in interviews, and if, when using this analysis the interviewees have not organised their arguments with these latent functions as central, it can suggest that a more critical look at that theory is necessary.

context, by all the interviewees, of personal responsibility, personal hopes and personal aspirations. Ortner (1976) has argued that 'female is to male as nature is to culture'. Combining these two complementary arguments, it could be suggested that employment, in being seen as 'natural', is reconceptualised and discussed by the interviewees as within the realm of the private. Therefore, these interviews, when discussing employment, are an example of how the distinctions between the private and public realms are not as clear cut as suggested by Elshtain (1981). One final point: women are considered to be closer to the realm of the private, and men to the public; this argument has implications for the reproduction of gendered differences in behaviour. If, however, the interviewees are redefining the private and the public in their discussions of employment, then it may be speculated that this redefinition permits an entry into the contestation of gender roles and behaviours (see Siltanen and Stanworth 1984).

5.4 Unemployment

All the interviewees stated that unemployment was high in contemporary Britain, and that this was undesirable.

There were three main themes which informed the interviewees' comments in relation to unemployment. These were:
(a) welfare benefits,
(b) qualifications and the advents of new technology and
(c) the government.
In describing these, it should not be assumed that the views about how each of these three related to unemployment were consistent across the group. However, following from section 5.2.4. above, it is being argued that these three themes suggest that unemployment was mainly discussed within the realm of the public. However, it was not discussed in opposition to employment. Rather, it was discussed as something totally different, and was not consistently compared and contrasted with employment.

5.4.1 Unemployment and welfare benefit
Of the 159 comments about unemployment, 129 (81%) were organised around the theme of welfare benefits.

> KKB: What do you think about unemployment?
> PN65: If the money was higher it'd be good! [Laughter] But I don't like signing on, I hate it.
> KKB: Why?
> PN65: It's like lowering yourself, I don't like it. Me Mum goes you might as well, cause she's paid all tax for us so we

might as well use it. But I feel dead low. You know, when you go in and you see those people – all you're doing the same day is going in, signing your name, and walking out and waiting for your Giro. It's a horrible feeling. But when you get the Giro it's nice! [Laughs] 'Cause you've got no money. But it's just going to sign on – it's horrible. Feel ashamed – hiding my face when you're walking in.

KKB: How much do you get?

PN65:   £36 a fortnight. But half of that goes to me Mum for family keeping sort of like, and the rest of it goes on dog food, so I don't get anything out of that. So that's why I need a job...So, I get money off me Mum and then when me Giro comes I owe it her back and everything. So you have to have a job as well, or you never survive.

II pp. 11–12

This speaker has related unemployment immediately to welfare benefits. In his first sentence, with the accompanying laughter, he is making a comment about his criterion for employment; there is an echo, therefore, of the theme that income is an organising feature of discussions of employment. The speaker's description of his discomfort at receiving welfare money, parried by him using his mother's argument as a justification for taking it, is a clear statement about his shame, his embarrassment and the tension on the day of signing on – his personal reactions. But his immediate linking of unemployment to welfare benefit is analogous to the ways in which the interviewees related employment to personal income. It was noted that the theme of income in the discussions of employment was often presented as a possible means of obtaining self-respect and independence. However, the theme of welfare benefits is not discussed as a means of the retention of self-respect and independence by those who sign on. Rather, it is used to exemplify the removal of self respect ('feel ashamed'; 'hiding my face when you're walking in'). It could, therefore, be speculated that it is not unemployment *per se* which necessarily produces a loss of dignity, but that it is the ways in which the receipt of welfare benefits are viewed which does so.

The theme of welfare benefits in the discussions of unemployment did not always lead to the same attitude towards social security.

KKB: What would you say unemployment was?

PN28:   Well, like you're looking for a job and you go looking every day and you just can't get one I'm moving about aren't I [referring to the tape recording].

KKB: It's alright [pause] Why do you think they can't get
           them? Why can't people get jobs?
PN28:   One reason is that they can't be bothered 'cos they can
           stay in bed till what time they want, and get money off
           the dole for doing nothing.

                                                              II pp. 11–12

This speaker again uses the theme of the 'dole' or welfare benefits in
organising her discussion of unemployment. However, not only does she
introduce this theme into the interview, but she also links it to a cause of
individual unemployment. The previous speaker discussed the theme in
relation to *consequences* of unemployment for him, while this speaker uses it
to suggest a *cause* of unemployment. It may, therefore, be argued that the
first speaker is marking a possible point of entry into contesting the
ideologies surrounding unemployment, while the second speaker is using it
as a means of reproduction or regulation.

KKB: Do you think jobs are easy to get?
PN09:   Well, with the unemployment these days – you know you
           have all these figures on TV – means nothing to us
           children but if you look for a job, I think you can get
           hold of it if you're really willing to go out and look,
           whereas if you're willing just to stay at home and get
           your...and you're on the dole money, it's different isn't it?
           'Cause you'd rather stay at home where you can be paid
           for nothing – don't want to go out to work.
KKB: Would you...
PN09:   Stay at home and go on the dole? No, I don't think that's
           right to stay at home.
KKB: What's wrong with it?
PN09:   Well, first of all it's people like our parents paying for
           this dole – our parents that have worked hard all their
           lives – you know they pay through their taxes and so
           forth. I don't know all these political bits and that, but I
           just know the point of view of a 16-year-old now. And I
           wouldn't, no. But if I had to, then I think it's a different
           matter. If I had to. But I wouldn't – not me, no. It
           doesn't fit in. I'm a person who'd go out and do
           something. I'd be bored anyway wouldn't you?

                                                              II pp. 2–3

   In this interview, the interviewee demonstrates how unemployment is
discussed through the theme of welfare benefits, in this case, via the issue of

taxation.[6] A comment which may be noted here is her lack of confidence ('but I just know the point of view of a 16-year-old') and her reluctance to discuss 'all these political bits' – issues mentioned in chapter 4 when discussing the design and conduct of the interviews. It may also be noted that she discusses 'our parents paying taxes' as if none were unemployed, although her two closest friends both had unemployed parents in their household.

Thus, the theme of welfare benefits was present in discussions of unemployment. The ways in which the theme was presented, whether as a cause or a consequence of unemployment, was different within the interviews. However, it was used to organise the interviewees' arguments in relation to unemployment.

5.4.2 *Unemployment, qualifications, and new technologies*
The need to obtain qualifications often as a consequence of the changing technologies being developed in employment is a second theme to be introduced by the interviewees when discussing unemployment. There were 97 out of the 159 comments about unemployment (61%) which considered the theme of qualifications in their discussions of unemployment. Similar to the ways in which the theme of welfare benefits was introduced, this theme when related specifically to changing technologies was used as both a cause and consequence of unemployment.

> KKB: So what do you think are the reasons that people don't have jobs?
>
> PN12: It's either qualifications actually at school or [pause] umm - qualifications.
>
> KKB: How do you mean? How are qualifications good to help you get a job?
>
> PN12: If you were to get – alright if you had 'O' levels, there's plenty of jobs going for 'O' levels, most jobs they say if you've got an 'O' level grade in a subject or if you've got higher grade at this subject, you've got to have a little typing and all that lot, there's plenty of jobs like that. And if you've done a computer course like some people have just come out recently, the courses have. If I'd have

---

6   The way in which the theme itself is discussed is of interest, and reflects some of Gallagher's (1987) comments on categorisation and particularisation. That is, this speaker categorises those who receive welfare benefits as preferring to stay at home and receive money ('be paid for nothing'). However, she also particularises herself in her discussion. That is, that while she acknowledges that part of being unemployed is outside the control of an individual ('But if I had to – then I think it's a different matter'), she also argues that her approach to life is different from that of those who she categorises as 'unemployed' ('But I'm a person who'd go out and do something').

been sort of like a more, if I'd have been a first year
now, and the computers have come out, I would have
taken that straight away and said right, I'm sticking to
computers 'cos computers are first you know, it's going to
come in the future now, everything's working as
computerised. So I said to me brother if you go back to
college, you're not old yet, and do a computer course,
that'd get him somewhere, like I know this teacher in
Meadow Plain, he's a teacher but he's going off to
college, and he's going to University and he's going to do
two years' computer course, and he said because in the
future, computer teaching's needed.

II pp. 13–14

This interviewee is developing the theme of qualifications in general and
exemplifying the argument by introducing specific types of qualifications as
related to 'computers'. The interwoven way in which the theme of
qualifications was considered as central in discussions of unemployment was
reflected in many of the interviews when the speaker was discussing
unemployment.

KKB: D'you think high unemployment is a good thing or a bad
          thing?
PN53:   I think it's a bad thing.
KKB: What's bad about it?
PN53:   Well, there's no money so people can't really make a
          living and there's a lot of work is done by machinery but
          I reckon man could do some of the work that machinery
          does as well. The money that the government are
          supplying they're just making more machinery and it's
          not necessary when they've got a man there to do the
          work – so they could save a lot of money there as well,
          by employing people to do the work.

II pp. 12–13

The above interviewee is presenting a very straightforward and direct
explanation for why unemployment exists in Britain. Rarely, however, did
interviewees present a 'single-issue' argument such as this when discussing
unemployment, but it serves to demonstrate how 'new technology' was used
to explain the reasons for levels of unemployment. His implicit suggestion
that Britain should use labour-intensive rather than capital-intensive means
for dealing with high unemployment is based on his philosophy that
unemployment is 'a bad thing' for people ('man') and that it ought to be
alleviated over and above things like efficiency, higher productivity, and
better control of the producer (e.g. 'computers don't go on strike' said

PN63).

A similar argument based on the same theme of new technology was also presented.

> KKB: So why d'you think there aren't many jobs around?
>
> PN58:   If the person who created all these robots and machines and everything – if they took all them back there'd be a lot of jobs 'cause that's what's made most people retired. If they took them away again there'd be more work.
>
> KKB: D'you think they will?
>
> PN58:   No, they're trying to make more, not demolish them. It's stupid. They should take them all out.
>
> II p. 5

However, although the theme is the same as the ones above, and echoed within many of the second interviews, the responsibility is not presented as resting upon the government but on a more generalised 'them'.

5.4.3   Unemployment and the government

Eighty-five (53%) of the 159 comments presented 'the government' as a theme in their discussions of unemployment with most of these comments (78 out of 85) occurring in the second interviews. This is not to suggest that the speakers organised their arguments as being either in favour of or opposed to the present government's policies about unemployment, but rather, that unemployment was discussed as an issue for which either the government had responsibility, should take responsibility, or could take responsibility.[7]

> KKB: What d'you think are the reasons that there aren't a lot of jobs around?
>
> PN51:   No market for manufacture. All these stupid spending cuts and that – the country's in a bad shape. But it's worse now. The country was in a bad shape before she [Margaret Thatcher] got in, but it's worse now.
>
> KKB: How d'you mean?
>
> PN51:   The rich are getting richer and the poor are getting poorer – that's all there is to it. I mean she wants her head testing.

---

[7]   That 'the government' has the potential power to deal with unemployment was revealed in the 60-second interviews when thirty-two respondents, in discussions about 'if you were in charge of the country, what would be the three things you would want to change', stated they would do something about unemployment, or create more jobs as their first priority, with nineteen of the remaining twenty-eight interviewees including this theme as one within their three priorities.

KKB: Why?

PN51:   How can you make the rich richer and the poor poorer? You should bring it till everybody's equal, or even everybody's comfortable – just even that. She wants to be put away. Or shot – one or the other.

II p. 5

The above speaker introduces his theme of 'the government' via a specific reference to the Prime Minister. This theme is introduced in the context of his argument that there is a decrease in the demand for manufactured goods which, by implication, suggests that there is less need for the production of such goods. However, despite his articulation of an 'economic' description, it is clear that he sees the theme of 'the government' as integral to his discussion of unemployment. What is also of interest, however, is that the theme of 'the government' is also related to his arguments about economic inequalities. That his reference to the Prime Minister is not intended to imply that it is the present government, specifically, which is being considered can be realised through his suggestion that 'the country was in a bad shape *before*'. It is this use of 'before' which indicates that he is presenting a theme of 'the government' in general, rather than a specific reference to the present administration of Britain.

Although the present Prime Minister of Britain was often referred to in terms of her personal characteristics, these references did consider her to be representing 'the government' as a whole. In other words, a distinction was not made that she, as an individual, is in distinction of opposition to 'the government'. Jenkins (1983a) for example has suggested that the young people he spoke with tended to hold individuals responsible for aspects of structural inequality. This was not so in the present study. This point can be further explicated through considering statements which refer only apparently to the Prime Minister.

KKB: What do you think about jobs? Do you reckon they're easy to get?

PN40:   Are they heck easy to get – Jesus man, no way are they easy to get! It's Margaret Thatcher up there – she's wicked. As I was saying before, the other day, she's bad – she's not letting us have no jobs. Look at all these riots what are happening now – oh God! Bad news, man, the world's a mess.

II p. 6

While this speaker does argue that the Prime Minister is the cause of unemployment, his reference to 'the world's a mess' also provides an inkling that he is referring to an individual as an *exemplar* rather than as being the one and only cause. This can also be seen when looking at his whole interview.

The linking of unemployment to 'riots' through the theme of the government was present in interviews, and was also linked to both racism and police activity. Rarely were these events, however, seen as the consequence of 'mindless rioters' by the interviewees. The discussions tended to focus on whether 'rioting' was a means of achieving any change; while some interviewees did argue that 'the government' should be harsh in its dealing with those who were arrested during the 1985 events in Tottenham and Brixton, there was no interviewee in the second interview who suggested that 'outside agitators' had sparked off the riots.

The ways in which the themes of welfare benefit and the government were linked together in the discussions of unemployment was not always conducive to a categorisation along the right or left of the political spectrum.

> PN63:   And also, if she [Margaret Thatcher] does put them out of work, all they're doing is going on the social (welfare benefits) – and they're having to be paid to be kept you know. Other people who are working have got to pay to keep these people. I mean I know the unemployed should have financial help, but if the government keeps putting people on the dole it's just draining the resources of the people that are working and it becomes more economic to lose your job.
>
> I p. 14

This interviewee was an active and committed member of the Labour Party at the time of this first interview, who attended Labour Party meetings regularly and who agreed with the miners in the coal dispute of 1984–1985. The way in which he organises his argument through the topic of unemployment, and using the themes of welfare benefits and 'the government' is not one which would be expected of an individual with his public political commitment.

Thus, it is clear that any exploration of the themes used to organise discussions of un/employment and politics cannot begin with an assumption that some speakers will be clearly identifiable as being of the left and others of the right. That type of exploration is closer to an attitude study or a study of belief systems rather than one which attempts to examine how relations of domination and subordination are both regulated and contested through the ways in which particular topics within the domain of the political are discussed and dealt with. However, to trace the themes – which for unemployment were welfare benefits, qualifications (new technology) and the government – allows for an examination of the themes around which the ideologies related to un/employment are organised. In this way, it is possible to 'home in' on the continuities which are present in the accounts of un/employment across those who claim to be opposed to each other.

5.4.4 Unemployment and racial structuring

The main themes which organised the interviewees' discussions of unemployment were welfare benefits, qualifications and the role of the government. In section 5.2.4 it was noted that the discussions of employment were often gendered by the interviewees. The discussions of unemployment were however racially structured.

KKB: Why d'you think there aren't many jobs around?

PN69: I reckon it's due to Margaret Thatcher. On telly she says she wants employment but she doesn't really.

KKB: What makes you say that she doesn't really – what makes you think that?

PN69: When you watch telly and the way she goes on [pause] there was this programme we was watching on Sunday and they were talking about how the West Indians should go back to, you know their thingy, 'cause they don't want to work and I was watching that. She's like saying that and if they pass a law all the West Indians will have to go back to their own country. 'Cause we don't want to work we just want to laze about – that's what the telly said. Me Mum was watching – she went mad.

II pp. 3–4

This young woman has used the theme of the government (more specifically, the Prime Minister) to discuss unemployment. However, integral to her argument is that the issue of repatriation is closely linked to public and government discussions on unemployment, and that a racist stereotype of 'West Indians' is used to justify the linkage presented between unemployment and repatriation. Clearly, she uses the theme of 'the government' in her comment, but the way in which it is embedded in a discussion of racism and repatriation demonstrates what I mean by 'racial structuring'. Of the 42 black interviewees who were interviewed for a second time, all of them discussed unemployment, with 29 (71%) racially structuring their comments. The racial structuring did not only occur in relation to the government, but in relation to all the themes which arose in the discussions of unemployment.

KKB: Why d'you think it's hard to get jobs?
PN53:   I think because a lot of people haven't got the
          qualifications they need really and I know that there's a
          lot of black people that have got good qualifications but I
          reckon it's because of their colour that they can't get the
          job they want. I think the room is there but I think people
          just don't want them because of their colour. I reckon if a
          white person came along with less qualifications but still
          had a good chance of getting it, I think they'd give it to
          him.

                                                          II p. 12

It is worth noting that only two of the white interviewees explicitly
racially structured any part of their interview with me. Explicitly racist views
in relation to unemployment were also not put forward by any of the white
interviewees. This is contrary to much research done with young people (e.g.
Cochrane and Billig 1984; Coffield et al. 1986; the Economic and Social
Research Council 1987). Why this should be so is explored in the final
chapter in the section on the methodological implications of this study.

Thus, the three themes which dominated the interview discussions of
unemployment were welfare benefits, qualifications, and the government. In
the previous section on employment it was suggested that the themes of
incomes, careers and security were all ones which can be thought of as
being part of the sphere of the private. It is now being suggested that the
three themes of welfare benefits, qualifications, and the government are
similar to the employment themes, but could be categorised as being located
in the realm of the public. Thus, employment was gendered and discussed as
part of the private, while unemployment, with similar themes, was racially
structured and part of the public arena. We can view the three themes,
whether in the realm of the private or the public, as being components in the
ideologies of employment and unemployment. It is these elements or themes
which seem to persist in such discussions: they may also be considered to be
the assumptions upon which ideas of un/employment rest and are informed
by.

5.5   The Youth Training Scheme

At the time of the second interview, in the autumn of 1985, the Youth
Training Scheme (YTS) was almost the only form of 'employment' available
for school leavers. Its structure was outlined in chapter 2. Although the
scheme has been changed in the past two years, it will be discussed and the
interviewees' comments presented as if that scheme still existed; that is a

12-month experience for which an allowance of between £27 and £28 was paid, and although it was difficult to obtain welfare benefit if you refused to go on the scheme, its compulsory nature was just beginning to be made more explicit at the time of the second interviews. Thus, in October–December 1985, the YTS could still be discussed as if there was a choice available for school leavers not to go on it. When reading this section, therefore, it is important to bear in mind these points. The three themes surrounding YTS were

(a)   the allowance,

(b)   the training aspect, and

(c)   future security.

The YTS was discussed in both the first and second interviews. In common with employment and unemployment, it was considered from a more intimate perspective in the second interviews when the young people had either tried one out, were still on one, or had definitely rejected going on to it. Thus, most of the interview comments presented below, as with employment and unemployment, are from the second interviews. The YTS was discussed in terms of three main themes: the allowance or income from the scheme, the type of training and whether it constitutes a 'proper' job, that is one with security and a regularity of income. There were 130 comments about the YTS. Out of these 130 comments, 115 (88%) were ones which elaborated their views (that is they were more than merely a statement such as 'It's a waste of time').

An overall picture of the attitudes towards YTS shows that every single second interview incorporated criticisms of the YTS, even when suggesting the scheme was a good idea, or did provide some training.

KKB: Do you think everyone should have to go on a YTS?

PN68:   Everyone should? No. They should be able to go to college or supposedly everyone should be able to get a job as soon as they leave school.

KKB: 'Cos they might make YTS two years. What do you think of that? Do you think, umm, just when you hear that YTS is going to go from one year to two years, what do you think?

PN68:   In between. Trust me! I don't know because, oh gosh, YTS for two years. I suppose in a way it's a good idea because if people don't get a job in the first year it gives them another year to have a chance because they won't be just getting money off the dole, sat around, they'll still be earning money and learning things at the same time. A good idea in a way, yeah... So I went for the interview and got that YTS at Elm Street, and I like it there, it's

good. You know, people are friendly and kind, they're
alright.

KKB: Are they? How many other people are working with you?

PN68:   Well, at the Centre, about eighty but we're split up into
          different groups, 'cos like, some started in July and some
          started in August. I'm in the last group 'cos we started
          the latest. I've been learning office work, doing typing,
          office equipment, well, just used the computers, haven't
          really learned much about them but just using them. It's
          been alright, I'm enjoying it.

KKB: Do you like the YTS?

PN68:   Well, I like the YTS but the money, that's what lets you
          down, it's not really good. I mean after you take in your
          housekeeping, your bus fare, dinner money out of it,
          you've got nothing left, nothing to buy clothes.
          Sometimes you're walking down the street and you see
          something you like and you haven't got the money to buy
          it. 'Cos things are so expensive now, you know like
          you're guilty going to Chelsea Girl paying £13 for a
          jumper. I mean, on the YTS you can't afford it at all. Just
          get fed up sometimes.

                                                            II p. 12

However, in looking at discussions of paid work, this study is less
concerned with the attitudes towards YTS and more interested in the themes
which organise the interviewees' arguments about paid work, and the lack of
it. It is for these reasons that comments about the YTS are explored below.

5.5.1   The YTS and the allowance

Of the 130 comments (as distinct from statement comments) about the YTS,
91 of them (71%) talked about the allowance. The following speaker
presented her argument in her school interview, about six weeks before
leaving.

KKB: What do you think about YTS and getting jobs and stuff
          like that?

PN28:   I think the YTS is stupid, it's just slave labour because
          you get £26.50 for doing the same amount of work. 'Cos
          say like if I got that job at MacDonalds I'd be coming
          out with say £50/60 a week, but take tax away from that
          so it'll be less. I am getting that money for so many
          hours and if some boy or some girl working there on the
          YTS they're getting £26.50 for doing the same amount of
          work as I'm doing, it isn't fair, it just isn't fair [pause]
          £26.50 a week for doing exactly the same amount of
          work as somebody coming out with £70 a week is stupid.

                                                           I pp. 5–6

It is worth noting that this speaker, in her first interview, is critical of the allowance when compared to other wages for older people doing identical work. She has not explicitly stated that the allowance is not enough to live on, as PN68 above did, but this absence may be understood in the context that she has not as yet had to experience paying for her food, her travel or her housing.

In all the second interview comments about the YTS allowance, every speaker argued the money was not enough to permit independent living, with some also including the 'comparative argument' as well.

KKB: You're not on a YTS?
PN73: Yeah. I wouldn't go on a YTS.
KKB: Tell us why. Tell us what you don't like...
PN73: I just don't like them – it's slave labour. It's £26.50 now – pittance money and you're doing the same hours as everyone else except you get paid less than the others. I wouldn't go on one anyway. If I wouldn't have got the job I would've gone to college.

II p. 4

The use of MacDonalds as an example of where YTS trainees may work provides an echo for Finn's (1986) analysis of the main employers who are using the YTS: fast-food chains such as MacDonalds as well as the leisure park industries. His analysis of these being the main employers suggests that the training benefit is low (not much skill needed to serve hamburgers or organise people into queues at Alton Towers), while the payment of very low wages increases the amount of profit for the employer. Thus, it is private employers who benefit from the YTS, he argues, not the trainees.

The principle of not entering a YTS because the allowance paid is lower than the wage someone may receive who is working next to you was extended as a justification for going to college for training or qualification, receiving less money, but at least not being 'cheated':

KKB: Are your mum and dad pleased that you're at college?
PN25: Yes.
KKB: They wouldn't want you to go on a YTS or get a job –
PN25: No, me mum definitely didn't want me to go on a YTS. I don't think she minded whether I tried to find a job or go to college. I think me dad preferred me to go to college, to try and get some more qualifications. And I wanted to go to college, so we were both happy.

KKB: Why didn't your mum want you to go on a YTS?
PN25:   Because of the fact you're working next to someone who's getting say two, three, four times the wage you're getting for the same job. She wouldn't want me to be a mug like that.

II p. 4

5.5.2   The YTS and training

A major public argument presented by the Manpower Services Commission (MSC) about the Youth Training Schemes is that young people are not employable, on leaving school, for they have no skills. Therefore, the YTS was necessary to provide this training; the training with its implied potential to allow someone to get a 'proper' job is the justification for paying a very low allowance – the implication being that because a 16-year-old is being trained, s/he will do less work, will require time from other workers in order to be trained, and so hamper a higher level of productivity. The interviewees in this study, although discussing the YTS in terms of its training aspect, appeared to agree with the logic of the MSC position, but did not consider the YTS to be providing training.

KKB: You didn't go on a YTS?
PN72:   No I wouldn't go on a YTS.
KKB: Why not?
PN72:   It's a waste of time, just slave labour I think.
KKB: How d'you mean?
PN72:   They're supposed to be learning you a trade but I've got mates who go on and they have them making cups of tea and all that, and I don't think that's learning anything. If I knew for a fact you could go on one and learn a specific trade in about two years and you're guaranteed a job at the end of it then I would go on, but you ain't guaranteed a job. They know that, because they don't really have to accept anyone for a job because they know if they take anyone on for a job they'll be paying them a full wage, so at the end of the year, or two years, they can lay everyone off on the YTS and just take fresh ones and they're getting the job done but cheaper. So, I don't see the point in it really.

II p. 6

The integrated way in which the allowance, training, and future security were discussed in the interviews may also be noted in the above quotation.

Seventy-nine (60%) of the 130 comments discussed the training aspect of the YTS and suggested that in general further training was desirable and necessary for 16-year-old school leavers – an argument similar to that to the

MSC mentioned above. Thirty-nine of these comments were made in the first interviews, before any of the interviewees had had any close experience of being on the scheme; of these, two speakers suggested that the YTS itself may not provide this training, with the remaining thirty-seven arguing that the undesirable aspects of the YTS could be compensated for by good training. It was in the second interviews however, when interviewees had either tried out a YTS or had close friends who had, that the 40-second interview comments about the YTS and its training appeared to be overwhelmingly critical of the type of training available on YTS schemes. Of these forty, two speakers did feel that the training on their scheme was appropriate, and the extract cited from PN68 at the beginning of this section is one. However, the remaining thirty-eight comments were critical of the training on YTS.

> KKB: What do you think of YTS?
> PN60:   They're a waste of time. 'Cos it's taken away all the apprenticeships and that, ain't it? They're a waste of time. All they do here, all they want to do, is dock your money.
>
> II p. 7

This interviewee, at the time of his second interview, was on a local authority run YTS scheme for electronics and computing – a scheme which he did not consider to provide the type of training and skills he had hoped for.

That the issue of training is not one which is separate from other aspects of the YTS is indicated in all the quotations for this section. The following interviewee had decided that he would obtain more qualifications by attending a Further Education College from September 1985.

> PN46:   So before that [going to college] we all decided to go on a YTS and make some money, you know, 'cos you don't get a lot of money at college, so we went on a YTS and everything...
> KKB: What YTS were you on?
> PN46:   I was doing painting and decorating at [Name of Place]
> KKB: What was it like?
> PN46:   It was only inside the base itself 'cos they give you so many weeks training, it's like a centre, and it's just got artificial rooms and that and you put wallpaper up and then you strip it down and you've got to do that day in day out, stripping off what you've put up and it gets boring.

KKB: What does? Stripping down what you've put up?
PN46:   Yes. And it depends, the attitude of the section in there, you know painting, decorating and plumbing and joinery, and on decorating, the tutor I had was called Dan and he was horrible, and I was swearing and calling him all sorts – and he used to say 'oh I'm not prejudiced I've worked with black lads in my life' and I used to hate him. And once I got out of there – you know you can – qualified and what have you, they put you out in a team, and I got put with this guy called Tom Beerstone and he was alright...There was about 15 doing painting and decorating, about 15 doing joinery and 15 doing plumbing. There was a girls' section as well. They had to wash the clothes and make tea and all that, and they go to old people's homes as well, and help out there [pause].
KKB: And how many black people, black kids, black youth were on it?
PN46:   There was quite a lot really, it was in Old Trafford, so there's a lot of blacks up there, but when I first went in the Manager said to me we don't want any trouble on racist grounds, and he just laid down the rules saying, you know, 'we don't want to see blacks fighting whites and we don't want to see whites fighting with blacks or Indians fighting with blacks or Indians fighting with whites, we all like to be treated as equals'. That was how he went on and things. There was four of us that started and I was the only black one [interruption into the room]
KKB: Yeah, there were four of you when you started and you were the only black one –
PN46:   Yes and he asked us when we went in there if we'd been in trouble with the police and that and when I went out and asked the other lads he'd never asked them that, he only asked me, so he must have thought that more black lads than white lads get in trouble with the police. That surprised me.
KKB: Did you say anything?
PN46:   No, 'cos he seemed alright...

The interview continued:

KKB: And when did you quit it?
PN46:   About two weeks before I started college so I'd have a bit of time for, you know, just a bit of spare time.
KKB: And did you want to quit it?
PN46:   For the money, no, but for the actual YTS, yes. I don't like YTSs. It's boring. It's slave labour, you have a work card and you work just as hard as a man on any job – it's just the money is worse. You do the same work. 'Cos it

	is hard work.
KKB:	What hours did you work?
PN46:	We worked from half eight to four. Sometimes when you

PN46: We worked from half eight to four. Sometimes when you were on a team they'd let you off half an hour earlier, it depended on the supervisor, if you had a bad one he'd let you off straight on time, but another would let you off earlier. Inside the base it's worse though, 'cos you'd start half eight, you'd work through to ten, then a 15-minute-break, you work through till twelve, have a half an hour break for your dinner, work through till half two, then a 15 minute break and work through till four. So you only get one hour a day, you know. It's rubbish.

KKB: What do you think of YTS's then?

PN46: Well, when I was there, the supervisors, people in there used to swear and I used to think if that's the way you're teaching, I mean, people are gonna be dead bad. And when I was there I was there for just over three months, and in the time I was there about five people got sacked. And since I've left there, I heard about twelve more got sacked. They sack people like grease up there, 'cos when we first went there, the first three days we were there, all we did was sit down and watch, and that was driving me round the bend, that was very boring. And when we actually started this guy used to say 'Get that fucking wallpaper up' and he used to go on like that – that was Dan – and people used to say, 'who you talking to?' and he'd go 'Right, if you don't like it get your coat on and go home' and you just got your coat on and walked out. He used to say it to me but I never used to walk out – some of the guys, you know what I mean, just used to put their coats on and then they'd get sacked. And I just used to stand there and not go home – and he couldn't do nothing about that. There was a lot of people got the sack there, there was a lot of people got suspended as well.

KKB: For what – for doing what?

PN46: For answering back really, or not doing what they were told. Like there used to be a time when, you know, you have to put paint in a kettle, and you used to leave your kettles on the side, and he used to pick on one person – even if it was a woman – and say 'Wash out them kettles' and if they didn't used to wash them out, then he used to sack them. Or send them home, or suspend them, or whatever, he was really bad.

KKB: Would you tell other people to go on a YTS?

PN46: No. We used to have arguments about that in school, whether they were any good or not. What's the point in taking on someone, if at the end of the year, they can just get rid of him and at the end of the year just bring in another person on cheaper pay.

II pp. 5–9

This whole comment has been presented for a number of reasons. Firstly, in relation to the present discussion of training, to demonstrate that this interviewee did learn some skills on his YTS (stripping off and putting up wallpaper), although the pedagogic techniques used, that of constant repetition, were not ideal for him – he states he became bored. Secondly, to demonstrate not only how racist practices were embedded in that particular scheme, but also to demonstrate his insight into some of the unequal power relationships present, for example the young women doing different jobs to the young men and trainees being treated as workers who could be, and were, suspended or sacked 'like grease'; this clearly led to the development of a fear of unemployment so that trainees felt they could not 'answer back' if they wished to continue. The third reason for including this quote was to provide a description of the hours worked and the work done – a description which demonstrates that many interviewees based their arguments that the YTS schemes used the trainees as 'full' workers by describing their particular scheme in detail.

5.5.3   The YTS and social stability
The third theme which informed the discussions of the YTS was that of social stability. Of the 130 comments about the YTS, there were fifty-eight in the second interviews. Of these fifty-eight second interview comments, forty-seven (81%) made some reference to the 1981 or 1985 uprisings in their comments. In the earlier discussion of unemployment (section 5.3), the subsection which examined the theme of the government included a quote about how unemployment levels are related to the uprisings of 1981 and 1985. Chapter 2 has looked at the 'common senses' in relation to youth unemployment and conscious political activism, as well as 'riots'. The theme of social instability as a consequence of high unemployment levels was not a dominant one in the interviewees' discussions of unemployment. However, it was dominant in the discussions of the Youth Training Schemes and arose spontaneously – that is in the sense that I did not link the 1981 uprisings to the introduction of the YTS in the interviews.

KKB: Do you think YTS is a good idea in general?
PN47:   Yeah, gets people off the streets, doesn't it? I mean, something to do, get a bit of money, keep yourselves going.
KKB: Tell us, what's good about getting people off the streets.

PN47:   Well, less harassment and that. They don't cause so much
             trouble when they're doing something and they'll
             probably stay in the house and sleep all night, something
             like that.

                                                            II pp. 4–5

This comment emerged fairly early in the interview, and later in the
interview, when I tried to encourage the interviewee to expand on these
ideas, he claimed to have nothing more to say. It is worth noting that this
purpose of the YTS is rarely, if ever, explicitly present in official
representations of the schemes; the interviewees have clearly noted the
public discussions surrounding the schemes and suggested a theme which
may be dominant, but implicit, in these discussions and represented the
theme explicitly. In this sense, the theme, it is being argued, becomes part of
the discussions of YTS, even if it is not present in official discussions.

Another interviewee:

KKB: ...but you still didn't like your YTSs?
PN67:   No, that's a big con. You might just as well say it's to
             keep people, to keep school leavers from when they leave
             school, put them on a YTS, 'cos you know, they're gonna
             be clamped down, that means everybody, school leavers,
             have to go onto YTS straight away, and that's just
             keeping unemployment down for a year, and then after
             that year, school leavers for that year can go on YTS and
             the others have to go on the dole...

                                                              II p. 7

The above speaker has developed the idea further – namely, that the
curbing of social unrest may not be the only consequence of the YTS – that
unemployment itself can be temporarily presented as lower than it really is.

And a final example of ideas about the YTS:

KKB: What do you think of YTS, like in general?
PN45:   It's OK if you haven't got any money and you're not
             going to college. You should get more dole.
KKB: Why do you think people are making YTSs, why are they
             providing YTSs?
PN45:   'Cos the riots before, when they had the riots, people had
             no money so they started making them.
KKB: What d'you mean by that? When?
PN45:   The riots, when was the riots? [Pause] 1981. There
             weren't no YTSs then, but soon as the riots had finished,
             they started making them 'cos they knew a lot of people
             needed the money, so they gave them a bit more so they

could stay on the dole or go on the YTS.

II p. 3

Linking issues of youth unemployment, youth training, and social unrest, this interviewee has much in common with the authors of the 1981/2 Scarman and Hytner reports, and so reflects young people's experiences, and media coverage. In chapter 3 it was argued that views and ideas do not simply appear from either 'out/inside', but rather, are re-presentations of an amalgam of prevailing ideas. The strength of interview material is that it reflects this while also showing the complexity of the ways different co-existing representations are related to each other.

The previous 3 subsections have argued that the young people's social representations of the YTS are those of the allowance, the training, and social stability.

5.6 Summary and conclusions

From the arguments and descriptions of the first four chapters, this chapter has discussed the themes present in the young people's discussions of employment, unemployment and the Youth Training Schemes. The themes for each topic were used to organise interviewees' arguments and to provide a starting point for the discussions of their attitudes. Further it was shown that the themes were not only regulatory in the maintenance and reproduction of relations of domination and subordination, but were also used to contest such relationships.

The themes specified for employment in section 5.2 were income, careers-as-distinct-from-jobs and future security. For unemployment, specified in section 5.3, they were welfare benefits, qualifications and 'the government'. In section 5.4 the themes which emerged in discussions of the Youth Training Schemes were the allowance, the training and social stability. From these specified themes, it may be argued that one conclusion to be drawn is that the young people's discussions in the arena of modes and relations of production clustered around three overall themes: of

(a) disposable income,

(b) differing needs as a consequence of the changing nature of employment and

(c) control implications – social and individual – of these changes.

These three overall themes are aspects of the ways in which the domain of the political, i.e. regulation and contestation of social life, is lived and experienced by the interviewees.

A second conclusion concerns the relationships between the public and private spheres. Employment etc. is most frequently considered to be within the domain of the public in contrast to the domestic and personal domain which is considered to lie in the private sphere. However, these spheres themselves are not discrete from each other (e.g. Siltanen and Stanworth 1983), and the interviewees' discussions have demonstrated that within discussions of paid work, employment was defined as 'natural' and expressive of private hopes and aspirations, while unemployment was discussed as 'unnatural' and expressive of public issues. That is, a second conclusion which may be drawn is that whilst employment is defined as being located within the domain of the public, with its concomitant implications for the definitions of some actions as legitimate, and some not, this is not a monolithic location but one which is discussed differently according to whether employment or unemployment is being considered.

A third conclusion to be drawn from the issues discussed in this chapter concerns the ways in which such interviews are produced. It was suggested in chapter 3 that a discussion of discourses requires an understanding of how power and knowledge are integral to such a discussion. When considering empirical social research, this point can be reconceptualised as one which points to the need for an analysis of the power relationships within which the 'data' are produced.[8] There are areas of the interview material in which young women discussed aspects of their potential employment lives differently to the way in which the young men did. Further, the black interviewees discussed unemployment differently to the ways in which the white interviewees did. Clearly, the continuities in the interviews so far discussed are of considerable interest and carry certain implications for psychological analyses. But the discontinuities as specified above also warrant analysis. Such analyses must, however, begin from the position that the interviews are forms of communication and hence are discourses. Therefore a third conclusion which may be drawn from the interviews is the need to analyse the ways in which the 'data' are produced. This point is discussed in more detail in the final chapter.

---

[8] 'Data' is placed within quotation marks for the etymological origin of the word lies in the Latin verb 'to give'. A strand of argument in the design and analysis of this study has been that interviewees do not simply transmit their arguments. Rather, the process of communication involves transmission, reception, and response. Therefore the interview material is not information which is given, but information which is communicated.

What is life?
A friend tells me, 'Life means finding happiness in hardships.'
'No!' I say. 'Life is an endless battle with fate'

                                        Zhang Jie   *Leaden Wings*

6.1 Introduction

This study is examining the domain of the political. It has been argued in
chapter 2 that politics refers to relations of power and domination and,
therefore, the ways in which waged work is discussed require systematic
analysis and are one means of understanding the reproduction of these
relations. However, politics also incorporates the idea that these unequal
relations may also be reproduced through relationships centred around public
power as well as within the private domain. Thus, in this chapter I will look
in detail at three specific issues which were discussed in the interviews and
which are examples of public power (democracy and voting), the operation
of public power directly on the individual (racism and racialism) and power
in the private domain (marriage).

The first example is the topic of parliamentary democracy. In the first two
chapters it was suggested that while the processes of parliamentary
democracy are too limited to, by themselves, encompass all that is political,
they are, however, a necessary part of what constitutes politics. This is
because the notion of universal suffrage is one which is held to be the
lynchpin and an important criterion by which it is possible for citizens to
exercise their rights and therefore have some say in the type of society
within which they live. Thus, it is necessary to examine how the concept of
democracy is discussed by the young people and what the prevailing themes
are which together enmesh themselves to constitute the democratic process.
The second issue is that of racism. Sivanandan (1985) has recently repeated
his distinction between racism and racialism: racism refers to institutional
practices by which black people are maintained in unequal and subordinate
positions: examples of racism would be the British immigration and
nationality legislation, and the way in which the legal institutions operate
(e.g. de Muth 1978). Racialism may be taken to refer to individual acts of
domination such as racialist attacks on the street, refusal to serve black
people in shops, that is, conscious decisions on the part of a white person to
treat a black person unfairly. Clearly, racism fuels and legitimates racialism
with the consequence that both are not only reproduced within the economic

sphere, but also via the ideological. Thus, discussions of 'race'[1] lie with the realm of the political. The third topic is that of marriage. The hopes expectations and aspirations expressed by the young people permit an examination of their everyday lives and, therefore, the possibilities they may consider to be available to them. These possibilities are shaped by and shape the political terrain:

> Treating everyday cultural phenomena as important does not mean isolating them from politics; on the contrary, the[se] reveal the temporary and shifting nature of the boundaries between politics and everyday life.
>
> Passerini 1987: 75

Thus, although marriage is defined within the private domain, a clear-cut distinction between the public and the private is not possible.[2]

6.2   Social representations of democracy and voting

There were three ways in which discussions of democracy and party politics were introduced in the interviews by the interviewees. These were:

(a)   that politics is boring,

(b)   that politics is difficult to understand,

(c)   that there was no point in voting.

There were 115 comments in all centring on voting and its relationship to democracy. Of these 115, 98 comments (85%) were organised around the point that 'politics is boring'. Of the 115 comments, 103 (89%) integrated the argument that 'politics is difficult to understand', while 71 of the 115 comments (61%) argued there was no point in voting. Two points need to be made here. As these aspects of arguments about voting were interwoven with each other by interviewees, like the comments in the previous chapter, more than one of these aspects were present in the interviews of each individual. The second point is that 27 speakers argued they would not vote in both the first and second interviews. Of the 71 comments, 56 on 'no point in voting' were made by the 27 interviewees just mentioned. The remaining

---

[1]   Quotation marks are used around 'race' in order to signal that while the word is rooted in social realities, it is not based on a biological reality.

[2]   It is necessary to explain here that while the previous chapter used mostly second interview material, this chapter in looking at democracy, racism, and marriage will utilise material from both sets of interviews. This is because the two interviews differ in the extent to which the interviewees felt able to discuss employment and unemployment (see chapter 5). Although the interviewees clearly felt more relaxed with me in the second interviews, they did discuss the issues in this chapter at length both while still at school and six months later.

15 comments were made by 15 different individuals in either the first or second interviews, who, nevertheless, argued that they would vote in future general elections.

6.2.1 'Politics is boring'

As was described in chapter 4, the experiences of the pilot work suggested that to use the word 'politics' in the interviews was taken to refer to British party politics, which the interviewees claimed to find boring. However, a discussion of party politics was present in every group discussion, and so raised, if necessary by me, as an issue in every individual interview. In addition, I had decided that if an interviewee introduced the word 'politics' or 'democracy', I would follow this up with an encouragement to expand.

> KKB: Do you feel more of an adult? Now you've left school?
> PN05:   Sometimes...
> KKB: In what ways...
> PN05:   I still like watching the odd things like cartoons – it's something I can't get over. I do try and avoid it as well, but I just like watching them. Hearing politics is hard, though.
> KKB: How do you mean?
> PN05:   Yeah, too boring.
> KKB: What's boring about it?
> PN05:   Well, I can't understand it – don't know what it's about. I suppose I'm just not clever enough to think about it.
>
> II p. 2

It is clear that a separation between politics as 'boring' and politics as 'something I don't understand' is not totally satisfactory. The above speaker, for example has elided his theme of politics is boring into an apparent explanation of why it is boring – namely that he cannot understand it. However, because the two aspects are so closely interwoven, it is not possible to suggest how they shape each other unless they are considered separately, and the specific aspects of each are teased out.

Politics was usually taken to refer to 'boring' pronouncements from spokespersons such as leaders of parliamentary parties – the party political broadcast was seen by a large number of interviewees to be the epitome of politics. This implies that no change is possible unless those who want change are also prepared to be 'boring'. Billig (1986b) has shown that the Young Conservatives defined their meetings as 'fun' and did their best to get the 'boring, political parts' over with as soon as possible, whereas the Young Socialists talked earnestly and at length about Labour Party policy and how to influence the Parliamentary Labour Party. With two exceptions

(PN63 and PN41), none of the young people interviewed claimed to have an explicit desire to develop an interest in party politics.

> KKB: So, what do you think of Margaret Thatcher?
>
> PN60: What do I think of her?...I don't know. I don't really think about politics and that. Don't understand it really, can't really be bothered with it. No matter what I think, it ain't gonna change the way everything is, is it? It isn't really, so I just leave it and go on living me own life.
>
> II p. 10

Not only is the above speaker saying he has no interest in politics, but he is also suggesting that there is no purpose in attempting to understand 'politics' because social change will not happen. That is, that politics is boring because it appears to him to change nothing. This lack of change is what is found 'boring'. The interview continues:

> KKB: But what don't you like about her?
>
> PN60: I just don't like her. I don't know what I don't like about her, I just don't like her, full stop. I don't like the way she speaks, I don't like her hair, don't like anything about her, don't like anything at all. She don't know what she's going on about. She sees things, right, from her point of view, she doesn't see it like from our point of view.
>
> KKB: Who's our?
>
> PN60: People like me – she thinks we're daft, dumb cos we don't understand everything, but she don't see it from our point of view at all. Well, I suppose it's because she's got power and that...It'd probably change anyone. Labour, SDP, Liberals – it'd probably change them all. Once they get in there, once they're sitting in the seat and that, probably change them as well. They forget all what they said...I don't really think about it.
>
> II p. 12

Thus, if politics is boring, there is no reason to want to understand it. Not only will nothing change, he argues, but also, because he does not see there being accountability among Members of Parliament, he is implying that there appears to be no point in trying. In this way, democracy comes to be seen as synonymous with the parliamentary process, which is defined as boring, partly due to the lack of accountability of elected representatives. Thus, 'politics is boring' is one thread in these interview discussions of democracy. 'Boring' has very strong negative connotations, and it is these negative connotations which then become key mediators in the reproduction of these relationships.

6.2.2   'Politics is hard to understand'
In equating 'democracy' with 'politics', the latter being defined as
synonymous with parliamentary and party politics, the interviewees also
claimed they did not understand 'politics'. As was suggested above, whether
politics is boring and therefore difficult to understand, or whether politics is
difficult to understand and therefore boring cannot be totally separated from
these interviews. This is because the interviewees often used the two themes
interchangeably – although it is clear that to argue 'politics is boring' places
the responsibility upon professional politicians not to be like that, whereas to
argue 'politics is something I don't understand' places the responsibility
upon the speaker. This seemed to be implicitly recognised by the
interviewees.

KKB:	Do you like her?
PN70:	No.
KKB:	What don't you like about her?
PN70:	I don't know – I just don't like her. I can't just sit down and listen to her anyway 'cos her voice goes right through me...
KKB:	What do you think of the Labour Party?
PN70:	I don't know nothing about them.
KKB:	Do you like Neil Kinnock – do you know who he is?
PN70:	Oh, I think he's great, him. Is that the one with the bald hair – it is isn't it – yeah – I think he's good...I was watching him a couple of weeks ago on the TV. I don't understand it all – [I] don't think I'm a brain box about things like that – I was just watching him and I think he's good.

II p. 10

This recognition may be seen by her asserting that she is not a 'brain box
about things like that'. The use of the notion of intelligence and necessity to
have it implies that without it, views such as liking Neil Kinnock, the
present leader of the British Labour Party, are not legitimate. In this way,
the concept of intelligence comes to be seen as a necessary criterion for
being able to comment on the parliamentary process. However, 'intelligence'
as a concept has been widely criticised (e.g. Richardson, Spears and
Richards 1972; Simon 1971; Coard 1971; Rose and Rose 1979). In general,
the arguments have pointed out that there is little evidence for its genetic
determination (e.g. Kamin 1976) and, further, it has been suggested that the
concept merely serves to perpetuate divisions, especially along class and
'race' lines (Rose and Rose 1979). Despite these scholarly and detailed
critiques, there are widespread and received notions of intelligence based on

the idea that it is genetically controlled: also, because the concept is defined implicitly as measurable (thanks to IQ tests and the assumption that intelligence is normally distributed), it is then taken as given that some people have a lot of intelligence, some have very little, with most in-between. This accepted and common-sense notion of intelligence, with its associated baggage, has tended to sustain and justify economic, social and racial inequalities. Thus, the concept has sustained political inequality and is used in this way to regulate relationships and action in the area of voting. This means that working-class young people define themselves as being knowledgeable or not being knowledgeable, and equate this with intelligence. This equation then implies that those who are not intelligent are unable to understand 'politics', and, therefore, do not have valid views. The logic of this is also based on what is defined as knowledgeable:

> KKB: What do you think politics is [name]? If you had to
>   explain them to someone – what is politics?
> PN29:   Well, dunno, I'm not really sure what it is actually. Like I
>   said before I'm ignorant towards politics, so maybe I
>   shouldn't say.
> KKB: Go on, have a go
> PN29:   Like I think politics is like people trying to sort out this
>   country and money matters and you know, and
>   unemployment and everything like that, but I don't really
>   know a lot about politics, so if somebody asked me I'd
>   say, well, I'm not, I can't explain it proper but I take it
>   that it's people trying to sort everything out for
>   everybody, but they're all arguing about it, aren't they?
>   'Cos they've all got different ideas, I know as much as
>   that.
>
>   I p. 4

In her argument which is based on a claimed ignorance she suggests that her views may not be accepted as valid. Her diffidence and uncertainty as to whether she is 'correct' in her description of politics – that politics is about national and economic organisation, and that it involves debates and discussion – is clear in this passage. However, she warmed to this theme in the next part of the interview, when I asked her 'How would you sort out everything, if you were in charge of England say, what are the first three things you'd try and sort'? She itemised housing, reducing income differentials, and 'make like everybody have an equal chance'. She also suggested that personal experience of hardship was important amongst politicians. However, this type of life experience is defined as distinct from knowledge and intelligence and she implies that such experiences are likely to produce compassion in political leaders. The actual passage from her interview which is discussed in this paragraph is presented below:

KKB: How would you sort out everything, if you were in charge of England, say, what are the first three things you'd try and sort?

PN29: I'd try and sort out people's housing, because I mean there's a lot of bad housing and that. I don't know where I'd get all the money to do it from but I'd you know, try and sort out the housing and that. I'd try and give people who can't afford things more chances to afford things, but I don't know how I'd do it, but try and make like everybody have an equal chance, you know, and everybody sort of not have loads of money but have enough, to get them all what they need, sort of thing. I'm probably saying that because I know like it's hard enough for mum and dad and that, 'cos if I was from a very rich family I wouldn't be bothered at all about the people who were unemployed and all, I'm only bothered 'cos I've got a lot of people in my family who are, and I know what it's like. But I'd try and sort something out for them 'cos Margaret Thatcher's got no idea. If she – I bet if she had a family like so many people who've got a lot of kids and they've got tiny houses, I bet she wouldn't be able to cope, 'cos she has never probably known – well I don't know what sort of childhood she had but I should imagine that she never had to struggle for things and save up for things for weeks and stuff like that. You know what I mean? If I was in charge I'd know what it was like, sort of thing. Probably sounds as if I feel dead sorry for myself, I don't feel sorry for me, I feel sorry for people who haven't got things they want because I've had most things – well not everything that I've wanted, but I've had, they've given me as much as they can of what I wanted, and now I'm getting it back, buying a lot of stuff meself, I'm always buying clothes and that. But I want to get mum and dad a really good Christmas present this year.

II p. 5

Not every interviewee who began tentatively developed a self-confidence in their views:

KKB: What do you think politics is?

PN66: Something I don't understand! [laughs] I don't really understand politics at all, no.

KKB: What's it about then?

PN66:   That's got me stuck, 'cos I don't know. I still don't
          understand politics at all – you've got one side and
          you've got another side – what have you got, you've got
          the Conservatives, you've got the Labour and you've got
          the Liberal thingsy alliance – I don't even know the
          names you know.

KKB: That's alright.

PN66:   That's how bad I am. [Pause]

KKB: Will you vote when you're eighteen?

PN66:   I don't think so. I can't be bothered.

KKB: Tell us why.

PN66:   It's not worth it – I mean I don't understand about that
          kind of thing. I know that sounds a bit funny, but I
          actually don't – couldn't be bothered either way...

                                                          I p. 8

The notion of 'couldn't be bothered' cannot be accurately described as
political apathy. This is because the speaker has related it to her lack of
knowledge and understanding of politics.

This subsection has suggested that the theme of intelligence, which is
linked into the theme of boredom, becomes an organising feature of
arguments about democracy. The theme is used to imply that the opinions of
some individuals – mainly those who are defined as not intelligent – do, and
should, carry less weight in discussions of democracy than the views of
those who are intelligent. Thus, intelligence (often combined with boredom)
is an element within discussions of democracy which operates to undermine
and negate the received common wisdom that one adult/one vote is a
safeguard to ensure the existence of government by the people, rather than
government by any one section, interest or class.

6.2.3 *'There is no point in voting'*

The arguments and empirical work about apathy, cynicism, realism and
pragmatism in relationship to the democratic process were outlined and
discussed in chapter 1. Reservations were expressed about all these terms
because, it was suggested, they are descriptive rather than explanatory.
Further, the words 'apathy', 'cynicism', 'realism', and 'pragmatism' are not
terms which are specific to parliamentary processes – they are used with
reference to a wide variety of issues, although within the political science
literature they are often used in relation to voting behaviour. It was further
noted that the use of 'apathy' and 'cynicism' were often present in
descriptions of potential voters who had not voted, and that this description
was not always accurate in implying that those so described did not vote

because they had no interest in politics.[3]

Twenty-seven of the interviewees in this study (in both the first and second interviews) had claimed they would not vote when they became eligible to do so. This percentage (38%) of potential no-voters is similar to levels of non-voting in British general elections. Of these, five demonstrated no interest in elaborating or presenting their reasons. The remaining twenty-two presented arguments. This subsection will initially give three examples from the interview material of such arguments, with brief comments on each. The arguments will then be considered in relation to each other and the themes identified and specified.

> KKB: What do you think about politics?
> PN31:   There's nowt I can think about it. Just got to take what they give you – that's it. If they're gonna make the inflation rise what can you do – go on a march – what are the marches doing? Nothing. So take it – they can do what they want, you can't stop them. It's supposed to be a free country – it's free to a point and that's all – to that point.
> KKB: To what point?
> PN31:   To the point you're not under orders, you are free to go where you want – some places you might be getting chucked out of – you're free to leave the country if you want to – that's all the freedom you've got. When it comes to having a say in the country the only thing you can do is put your little X in the box – that's your vote – that's it.
> KKB: So...[pause]
> PN31:   Well, it's not enough, but nowt you can do. I mean the government that are in, they're running it their way – she wants the country her way and no-one else's – gotta accept it.

> I p. 9

This interviewee had earlier indicated that he would not vote and is elaborating on his reasons in the above. For him, 'freedom' becomes a meaningless concept because he is not happy that voting in elections is synonymous with 'having a say in the country'. That he says 'gotta accept it' suggests that he does not consider non-parliamentary methods ('what are the marches doing?') to be of any value in challenging government policies and practices with which he does not agree. He may be described as apathetic ('gotta accept it') or pragmatic, 'What are the marches doing?'

---

[3]   This point was also related to the methodologies used to obtain such groups of people.

may suggest that his views should be categorised as cynical or realistic. 'That's your vote – that's it' would suggest realistic or apathetic and 'so take it – they can do what they want, you can't stop them' may be seen as pragmatic, cynical or fatalistic. It is clear, therefore, that no *one* categorisation of his views, e.g. as in 'pathetic', 'cynical', 'realistic' or 'pragmatic', would be adequate.

> PN47: Then again it ['rioting'] won't really get you anywhere will it?
> KKB: Why do you think people riot?
> PN47: Trying to get something across – to the government, you see, 'cos like a single person can't really go up to the government and start talking – they won't listen to them. I mean they'd probably think 'he's mad' and throw him back in the crowd. So they've gotta put themselves over in a crowd themselves. Gotta cause disturbance. To get heard and get seen. Let them know what's going on.
> KKB: What is going on?
> PN47: All sorts – things aren't going right, full stop.
>
> II p. 13

This speaker has also indicated the likelihood of not voting, but differs from PN31 in that, in this passage, it is indicated that non-parliamentary means may be one method of 'get[ting] heard and get seen'. In addition, the implication present is that organising with others is necessary ('So they've gotta put themselves over in a crowd themselves') in order to effect change. As with the previous speaker, it would be difficult to categorise this set of views in any simplistic one-dimensional manner.

> KKB: Will you vote when you're 18?
> PN41: [pause] It depends really...[pause]
> KKB: Go on
> PN41: I'm definitely not voting for the Tories – there's no doubt about that. I don't think I'll vote in the next election, even though I will be 18 by then. But I'll have to see if Labour win it...if they get in the next election I'll have to see you know, their policies for minorities and all that. If that's alright, then I suppose I'll vote Labour by the next election – after the next one – which is 1992 or something like that.
> KKB: How d'you mean – policies for minorities?
> PN41: Well, some people want to kick us out, they say we're stupid and all that – and sometimes the police and the government do provoke us, but I think it's true, if you're going to riot you're just going to prove what people say about you that you're stupid and all that...but if you don't,

some people might think that a riot's the only way out of it, but it ain't, you've gotta talk, you've gotta talk things out. If you don't talk then you've got problems, 'cos violence it's not really that nice, it's not nice at all it's better to talk than to fight.

KKB: What about South Africa?

PN41: That's just the biggest joke I've ever seen in my life. That Botha – he goes on like he's trying to abolish apartheid but he ain't, he's doing nothing at all about it, even Britain, they're just avoiding the issue. They're just putting sanctions around it, they're not going to the central issue. The country – there's 22 million black people live there, the majority, there's not even 5 million white people in the country and they've got the rule. I'm not saying no to them [the white people] but it should be equal rights for one and all. It's not right at all. I don't believe in that. Apartheid should be stopped altogether. I think it's, I think they're thinking it's time they had to riot, the government are doing nothing for them, but really, they should – well, riots the only way they can do it now 'cos with their political party ANC being abolished there's nothing they can do. They can't talk 'cos they won't listen to them so they've got no choice but to riot. That's all they can do.

II p. 3

This speaker is not someone who is anxious to vote the minute he becomes eligible to do so, although he does not see 'rioting' as an alternative. In fact, his argument implies that rioting will only serve to reinforce stereotypes about black people ('if you're going to riot you're just going to prove what people say about you that you're stupid and all that').[4]

His approach to the issues of 'rioting' and 'violence' is worth noting because, although the first part of his argument may have suggested he had a general principle about violence, it becomes clear that he is arguing about violence in relation to specific circumstances and contexts.

6.2.4 *Democracy and disenfranchisement*

'Apathy', 'cynicism', 'realism', and 'pragmatism' are not adequate to cover the range of arguments presented by the above three speakers. Some writers (e.g. Ullah 1987; Coffield et al. 1986) use the term 'disaffected' to describe those who, like the above speakers, as a consequence of unemployment are

---

[4] I asked him about South Africa because in a group discussion, he had argued that the visit of Edward Kennedy (an American politician) to Southern Africa in early 1985 was for opportunistic political reasons, not for principle, and that the black groups challenging apartheid there should not have legitimated this opportunism.

defined as 'politically militant' and 'anti-authority' as well as those who are 'resigned' and 'dejected'. The term thus includes categories of views which are more accurately defined as mutually exclusive. The Oxford English Dictionary states that 'disaffected' can mean: 'evilly affected; estranged in affection; usually, unfriendly to the government; disloyal'.

When considering these aspects in relation to the arguments presented by the above three speakers, questions immediately arise such as 'disloyal to whom?' or 'unfriendly towards which government?' Further, the term appears to be based on 'affect' which is most commonly seen as an individual emotional state rather than being rooted within the political arena of regulation and contestation of social life. Thus, although the term 'disaffection' is initially rather attractive, it can be seen, on reflection, that it is a ragbag term which can incorrectly imply a homogeneity amongst those so described. Rather, the common themes amongst those who have presented reasons for not voting are those of social/political change and rights. The speakers are discussing how power may be exercised in relation to democratic rights, using 'power' as Flacks (1983) does – that is, the capacity to make history and to influence the lives of a community or society.

It has been argued above that the young people interviewed presented three points in their discussions of democracy. These points – of boredom, lack of intelligence implying lack of political efficacy and the exercise of power to safeguard rights – may be more usefully considered as different aspects of disenfranchisement, which, in, turn may be seen as an overall theme in their discussions of democracy. 'Disenfranchisement' has connotations, by definition, of political rights for it means the removal of political privileges, or, more specifically, the removal of voting rights. The interview material has demonstrated that the young people did have views and arguments to present about issues considered to be in the realm of the political, but that certain aspects prevented them from participating. It is the theme of disenfranchisement which appears to capture the different configurations of these points.

6.3 Racism and the interviews: an introduction

Racist ideology in contemporary Britain has shifted and changed from the direct 'we [whites] hate blacks' variety to the racism of the new right, so clearly analysed by Hall et al. (1978) and then developed further by Lawrence (1982) and Gilroy (1987). This racism is associated with rightwing newspapers such as *The Times* as well as with far-right journals such as the Cambridge-based *Salisbury Review*. Many of the writers in these publications have not discussed racism explicitly within the frameworks of 'aliens swamping this tolerant and peace-loving nation' but, rather, have directed their vitriol towards anti-racist initiatives, discussing multiculturalism as an undesirable principle.[5] This style of argument is epitomised in the discussions surrounding Honeyford, the Bradford headteacher who claimed in 1983 that the victims of racism are white children who were being taught 'to denigrate [sic] the British Empire' and 'classes were constantly being interrupted when Asian parents took their children to India' – 'wildly and implacably' resenting 'simple British requirements of keeping attendance during the term' (from Murray 1986: 13). Murray then comments:

> White victims endured all of this in silence – until, that is,
> Ray Honeyford, the man on the spot, the former Labour
> supporter who at last saw the light, dared to say enough is
> enough.
>
> Murray 1986: 13

In the same period, Murray points out that the 'top people's' paper (*The Times*) said that '"Nig Nog" was a term we [who?] all say'. If top white people do use such terms regularly, the implication is that the similarly explicit racism expressed in tabloid newspapers such as *The Daily Mail* and *The Sun* expresses the racism of their readers as well.[6]

Phoenix (1988) has argued that psychologists have often worked with 'narrow definitions of culture' (the title of her paper) and take little account of the fact that a large number of young people under 20 have shared experiences of institutions such as schools, as well as non-shared experiences of aspects of power such as racism. It is this argument which is here being outlined, albeit with a different emphasis to that of Phoenix. Thus, although the white interviewees could not have experienced racism in the ways in which the black interviewees did, a similar social network for some of the interviewees meant that some of the white interviewees had experienced being disliked because they were friendly with black people.

The young white people, on the whole, in this study (most of whom read *The Sun*) did not express such racism in their interviews. Whilst some of their comments were situated within British racist discourses (e.g. PN75 defining her school friends as 'half-caste' whilst saying 'I don't care what

---

5   Murray (1986) quotes Sherman as writing that the Conservative controlled Swann Committee on Education would recommend 'a procrustean, pidgin culture to be imposed on majority and minorities alike' which would, therefore, be 'cultural genocide' (Murray 1986: 12).

6   Who may or may not be 'top people'.

colour they are – they're just my friends' and asserting that her parents 'wouldn't like me to marry a black lad') of colour-blindness until heterosexual relationships became a possibility, by no means all colluded with such views. The following speaker claimed that 'equal rights' (which he had not specified) was desirable, which led to:

KKB:	Do you think people have equal rights?
PN74:	Not the black people I don't think.
KKB:	You don't?
PN74:	No.
KKB:	What makes you say that?
PN74:	They can go anywhere they want, can't they, black people, but when I go out with them I get people looking at me saying 'what are you doing with a nigger' and all that, just 'cos they've got a different colour. I don't agree with that.
KKB:	Would you ever get into a fight?
PN74:	I have been into a fight.
KKB:	Yeah – what happened?
PN74:	I was in a club and they called [this means insulted] all me mates and they called me a 'nigger lover' so I just steamed in into them. Just because he's a different colour don't mean that he's different inside. 'Cos I was brought up with black people.

I p. 11–12

It is worth noting that the above speaker does use the theme of a common humanity *despite* different experiences (i.e. no equal rights) and oppressions.[7]

The following white speaker also introduced the issue of racism before I did in the interview, after a discussion of whether he would consider going

---

[7]   The young black interviewees also asserted this common humanity while discussing differences:

KKB: Do you think there's racial prejudice or racism or whatever around? In Britain?
PN55:   Yeah...National Front – that's getting bigger and bigger.
KKB: Is it? What round here?
PN55:   Yeah...I've got white friends. I've got nothing against white people. I'm not racist – no way - whether they're Chinese, black, white or you know what. They could still become my best friend. White people that are racist they think it's a white country – let's only have white people in it – and they want to send us back. If they only want English people here why not send the Americans back then? I don't see them as English...
KKB: Have you ever been called on the streets?
PN55:   You mean 'paki' and all that? Yeah I've been called loads of times. More people don't realise me as a Pakistani...people at my church wouldn't believe I was an Indian...just took a bit of convincing. Now everyone knows that I'm Indian.
KKB: Do you like being Indian?
PN55:   I like being human.

I p. 12

on a march or a demonstration:[8]

> PN33:   I don't like the [police]. They're the same as Margaret Thatcher, they're all for theirself. I mean I was at a football match, I mean a couple of weeks ago and there was one coloured lad stood with me, doing nothing, and everyone was throwing coins at the other supporters. And this coloured lad was just stood with me talking and the copper just goes like that [hand action to demonstrate] and takes him away for no reason at all. I mean if he'd have made a formal complaint about that I mean, yeah, maybe he'd have got somewhere but you can't do that against the police. Even if you take 'em to court you never win. It's the same with the council.
>
> I p. 9

As explained in chapter 4, issues surrounding racism were included in every interview and were introduced at an appropriate time by me if the interviewee had not raised it her/himself. The following speaker had been discussing private education and had suggested that while she would send her children to private school if she could, because they 'teach you manners, don't they?', she was also concerned 'they might go into snobs - bit snobby'. She had then continued with 'If my child had prejudices [pause] there's no need to be prejudiced'.

> PN49:   I think prejudice is stupid. There's no need for racial discrimination – we're all the same inside, just different colours. When people say [pause] 'all black people are horrible' – you can't just judge them by their colour – it don't matter what colour they are – you get some real horrible white people as well. Like they say most of the Rastas do the muggings round here, but you get some white lads what do it as well. I mean it is them what do it, but it's not 'cos they're black – it's 'cos they're a horrible person, not 'cos they're black [pause]. These days, most white families are being brought up with disrespect aren't they?
>
> I p. 15

Again, 'race' becomes the means through which she discusses her everyday life, and her use of categorisation and particularisation simultaneously, in her discussion of the myth of black criminality, echoes an argument raised by Billig (1987).

---

[8]   In this interview, 'race' became the means through which he discussed his relationship to the police (echoing Hall et al. 1978).

This introduction to the section on racism and social representations has demonstrated that a claimed panic from liberal social scientists that all white working class young people are explicitly and virulently racist (e.g. E.S.R.C. Report 1987) is not necessarily the case. Racism is endemic in British institutions and social relationships – of that there is no question. However, it is epistemologically impossible given the arguments raised earlier in this book about the production of views in the context of the interviewer and interviewee to imply, suggest, or assert that racism is more prevalent amongst those who are defined as disadvantaged (young, working-class, poor, unemployed) than amongst the dominating groups. Rather, the shared experience of powerlessness (for example in relation to education, to the police) may also become the basis of a shared set of experiences and arguments between young black and young white people - and *some* of this continuity across their socially categorised differences is demonstrated above.

The rest of this section will consider the themes which organise arguments about the experience and existence of racism.

6.3.1 Racialism and strategies

The introduction suggested that issues centred on 'race' were either individually or institutionally based. However, the theme of strategy, or ways to change racialist or racist behaviours were present in the discussions of every black interviewee.

PN53: ...you know like a lot of white people live down there you get a lot of young guys in cars driving past, they wind down the windows shouting 'black bastards' and this and that...I don't think there's any need for it.

KKB: Why do you think people are like that?

PN53: I don't know – because if we were white they wouldn't do stuff like that – it's our colour. And then they criticise us and everything and then they want to be like us. I mean they criticise us like our colour - and they want to go on holiday and get our colour - they criticise everything on us – even criticise you know – hair like that and then they go and try and get it done like that – you know like girls when they got beads in their hair – you see them all white girls in the town with beads in their hair – that's what I don't understand – they try to be like us but they don't like us – it's funny that.

I p. 12

This speaker begins with a description of incidents and then moves into a questioning of the value attached by many white people to acquiring a tan –

'that's what I don't understand – they try to be like us but they don't like us – it's funny that'. It is clear that he does understand this, that he is pointing to a contradiction in expressed values of explicit racialists, but in commenting upon it as 'funny' is implying that in pointing to such a contradiction, there is a possibility for developing a strategy to undermine racism.

Other strategies for dealing with incidents were indicated:

> KKB: What would be the first three things you think you'd change if you were in charge of England? What are the things that you think would make it a better place?
>
> PN57:   Well, I would change people going around killing old ladies and grabbing their handbags – innocent people. Change racism. Can't think of another one.
>
> KKB: OK, so let's take them one by one.
>
> PN57:   Racism – well, only once was I called a name. I felt terrible – wanted to grab and choke them.
>
> II p. 8

This interviewee, who was very shy with me and anxious to explain that social ills were a consequence of the lack of a widespread acceptance of the beliefs of the Jehovah's Witnesses, appeared surprised at herself for the vehemence with which she would have liked to have dealt with the abuse.

Such incidents did not only occur on the streets, where strategies of fighting or belittling were put forward as possible means of dealing with them.

> PN23:   ...You do, usually get [racism] in schools and colleges. At the school I was at they always used to pick on me every single time you know, third, fourth and fifth year. Used to hate them...They're quite nice round here, they're friendly. The ladies say 'hello' when they go past and that...
>
> KKB: What used to happen at school?
>
> PN23:   They used to be jealous, say that you've got more money than us and you've got all, you know the Asians have got more jobs than our lot...
>
> KKB: What did you say?
>
> PN23:   Me? Nothing at all, it's not my fault is it? That we're more richer than you are...we used to fight always.
>
> KKB: Who used to win?
>
> PN23:   It used to be them, 'cos there used to be more of a bunch of girls than us, they used to stab cigarettes in your faces as well. They got us in the toilet, they got me in the toilet – and say, 'did I want a ciggy?' and I kept saying 'no, I didn't want any' and I was saying 'I don't want to'. You

> know, I used to act tough on them and the others used to
> be scared, so they used to pick on me the most. But you
> have to be a bit tough you know. You can get away with
> it, but they pick on you the most. Once I gave them some
> lip and they'd stab a cigarette on your face. Told the
> teacher and the teacher never did nothing, never bothered.
>
> II p. 11–12

Here, in providing information on the strategy she used to deal with the
attack – that of informing those in charge of the institution – she is also
pointing to the particular consequence of her strategy.

Thus, for the young black people interviewed, the development of
strategies for dealing with racism and racialism in their daily lives was
embedded within their discussions of racism. The interweaving of a theme of
strategy suggests that these speakers considered that racism could be altered
by being challenged. In suggesting that patterns of racist behaviour can be
altered, there is a consequent implication that, therefore, racism is not natural
and, therefore, strategies for change are integral to the discussions. These
strategies involved the pointing out of contradictions, and sometimes using
laughter which can be a way of acknowledging the contradictions without
labouring the point.[9]

> KKB: Do you think racial prejudice, or whatever, exists in
> England?
>
> PN51: Yeah. It doesn't bother me. The only time racial attacks
> bother me is when they're on me family or if they're
> stopping me from doing something – like if I want to get
> a job and they wouldn't give it to me 'cos I'm black. I
> mean if someone was to call me a 'nigger' or something
> like that, I mean I'd be mad - probably laugh at them –

---

[9] The following brief comments are examples of that.
KKB: Do you think you can do anything about it [racism]?
PN64: No, not really.
KKB: Do you think anyone can?
PN64: No.
KKB: So, do you accept it?
PN64: No.
KKB: So, what do you think can be done?
PN64: Just laugh it off.

The use of humour was often suggested as a means of not only deflecting the barb of racialist
insults but also as a means of belittling the aggressor. In general within the interviews, laughter
was often present when an interviewee had recognised a tension between something they had said
earlier and what they said at the point of laughter. Thus, it was not only in discussions of
racialism that humour or laughter was used to signal a contradiction, although this signalling can
be noted most clearly in such discussions.

> they've probably got more colour than what I've got –
> they've got more colour than what I have.
>
> I p. 8

The strategies suggested include fighting back ('wanting to grab and choke
them') as well as reporting the incident to someone in authority (PN23).
Rarely were institutional changes suggested, although the interviewee below,
who has been very critical of her school, is clearly considering whether such
a change would be appropriate.

> KKB: How do you think you could make the school better?
> PN70:   Don't know – get more teachers in you know to make
>   this school better – I think you should get some coloured
>   teachers you know that are always in, not just doing
>   teaching some kids. That all the kids have a turn of them,
>   getting taught by this coloured man or woman to see what
>   they're like, see the differences or anything. I think they'd
>   be different. I don't really know why – don't know – it's
>   just like you – you going to teach someone, now I think
>   you'd be different from those daft teachers in this school.
>
> I p. 11

Racialist attacks had been experienced by many of the young people,
although it was so much a part of their lives that it was not always given an
especially distinct salience by them within the interview. It was interwoven
with, and embedded within, their comments.

> KKB: What do you think about racial discrimination?
> PN68:   It exists, but I don't really hear much about it [pause]...
> KKB: Has it ever happened to you?
> PN68:   ...only in South Africa, you hear a lot about it. It's
>   happened to me in Moss Side, yeah.
> KKB: What happened?
> PN68:   People, you know, we'd just moved there and people
>   were calling us 'black bastards' and all that, and 'go back
>   home, get back to the jungle' and try to burn us out of
>   our home by catching the drainpipe on fire. They broke
>   our windows, plastering and on the windows and all that.
> KKB: Is that why you moved?
> PN68:   Yeah.

After discussing the details of where her household had moved to:

> KKB: Why do you think people do that?
> PN68:   I don't know, honestly.

KKB: Do you think there's anything you can do about it?

PN68:   Anything I can do about it? – no. If I set up a campaign they'd kill me off or something. Like Martin Luther King, the rights of blacks.

KKB: Do you think if black people got together –

PN68:   No, the police would get in the way.

KKB: How do you mean – get in the way?

PN68:   They'd try to stop us, you know, wherever we were grouping up they'd split us up and all that, keeping us all alone, I don't know.

I pp. 12–13

She later suggested that 'the government' could do something about racism 'if they wanted to, but I don't think they want to. I don't think they want to at all'.

The final type of strategy was a personal as well as a public one, that of how an interviewee would choose to describe themselves. This issue was only raised by me if I was confident that the interviewee would not take offence at my interest – that I was confident that they had an accurate sense of me and would know that I was not prying into their personal lives, but was interested in them.

KKB: Like, how would you describe yourself?

PN41:   Well, I'm English, whether or not anyone likes it, I was born here, so that's the end of it, I mean there's nothing else I could say about it.

KKB: Would you say you were black?

PN41:   Yes, I am black.

KKB: Would you say you were black English?

PN41:   No, I'd say I'm English.

KKB: What's the difference?

PN41:   I don't see why colour should come into it, there's no need for colour to come into your nationality, some racist people would say, you're black, so you're not English, if you're born here, you've got a British passport and you are British. That's the end of that, I'm not – colour doesn't come into it with me – colour's one thing I ain't too bothered about.

II p. 17

Although he finishes with his claim that colour is one thing which does not bother him, it is not as someone who is denying being black, but as someone who is asserting his right to live in England and not be continuously defined as an outsider.

Self-definition is not, however, a necessarily 'touchy' subject. The following speaker, who had in her first interview suggested that her school could be improved through a strategy of employing more black teachers, in her second interview, six months later, discussed her self-identity almost as an aside.

KKB: What if you were in charge of England – and you could change three things – make three things better...

PN70:   Housing – I'd make the housings better – these houses are falling to bits. All you've gotta do is look up there. And jobs. I'd try and change this prejudice against people 'cos there's a lot going around. What do you call it?

KKB: You mean racialism?

PN70:   Yeah, can't say that, so I'll say prejudice...I don't think there's a lot of prejudice round Moss Side though. 'Cos Moss Side you're either white or you're either black – not half-breed – I don't believe in that word – you're either black or you're white and I'm black, know what I mean? If anyone calls me a half-breed, that's it – war. No, I don't think there's a lot around here. You get one or two posh people who don't like coloured people but you don't really cause trouble over that do you – it's when you can't walk in the precinct because you're white or you can't walk in because you're black – you know, things like that. I think it's stupid anyway, 'cos in the end you're all normal people aren't you – you're all human.

II p. 10–12

These last two speakers are also rejecting static and rigid notions of culture – that is, British culture for them is heterogeneous by definition – and both of them can therefore be seen to be contesting discourses such as those in the recent Dewsbury schools issue.[10]

This subsection has shown that for the black interviewees, any discussion of racism or racialism is based on the assumption that racism is not *natural*. This can be seen by noting that their discussions of racism had embedded

---

[10] This refers to a situation in Dewsbury, West Yorkshire, where a group of parents of twenty-six children (mostly white) did not want to send their children to a local school which had 85% black children in it – children of South Asian origin. The parents said that they wanted to send their children to schools where they would receive a 'traditional English education' (*Sunday Telegraph*). These Dewsbury parents claimed that they 'are not racially, only culturally prejudiced' (*New Statesman*, September 1987 p. 3). The parents were also apparently concerned about language problems (*New Society*, 2 October 1987). However, they also favoured another school because they claimed that educational standards were higher (*New Society*, 11 September 1987). Apart from *Marxism Today* (October 1987), most of the weekly periodicals were clear that the issues were about racism on the part of this parent group.

within them a notion of a strategy for change – a notion of dealing with racism. Therefore, the theme of strategy is an organising feature for their discussions about racism.

6.3.2   Racism and strategies

In the previous subsection it was suggested that discussions of racialism almost always had strategies embedded within them. At the beginning of this chapter it was argued that racism referred to systematic institutional practices. The British police force is one institution which all the interviewees discussed, either through telling me about their own contact with the police, through others in their households or friends' contacts with the police. There were nine interviewees (all young women) who did not refer spontaneously to the police and who were then asked by me for their comments. When considering the police as an institution, in anticipation of the argument that my asking about the police may have conveyed an image to the speaker that I was critical of the police, I have decided to analyse for this subsection only the interview material in which the topic of the police was initiated by the interviewee.

The following speaker had described to me an incident with the police to which I asked him if he liked the police:

> PN60:   You haven't seen the way the police act though, have you? Like you walk down the street and some of them start calling you names for nothing. 'Cos me and me friend – me and me two friends were walking down the street in Shale and this police comes up to us and goes 'What are you doing you black bastards? – Where are you going?' And I went 'What!' and he came over to us and started harassing us for nothing. For no good reason he just started on us and then they go 'Go on – you'd best get on your way now'. And on Wednesday when we [a group from the school] went to see the play we were late and we were all at the bus stop – and me and X (a white boy) said we'd run to the Royal Exchange to tell them to keep the tickets. So we were running up and X was tired so I gave him my coat and I carried on running – and this policeman stopped me and said to me what had I nicked – just because I was running. For no such reason the guy comes up to me and says what have I nicked? I said 'I've not nicked nothing'. he says 'Where are you going?' I says 'The Royal Exchange'. he says 'Why, are you going to rob it?' No such reason they're going on like that.

KKB: What did you say?

PN60:   Nothing – I just ignored him and went on. 'Cos I learnt my lesson – 'cos once I gave them cheek and they took me in...

His assumption that I would be in disagreement with his criticisms of the police at the beginning of this extract can be noted. He does not feel he has a strategy, however, for dealing with the racism of the police force, and implies that once, when he had attempted a strategy of pointing out contradictions and using laughter, the power inequality between the police officer and himself was used to block the interviewee's challenge. Attempting to use violence as a strategy for challenging police racism was a strategy which the interviewees argued would be unlikely to be effective in achieving the aim of the strategy – that of trying to eliminate racism. The use of laughter does not appear to have empowered the above speaker in his dealings with the racism of police.

The third main strategy suggested in the previous section was that of answering back:

PN72:   There was me, right, I was the only coloured guy there – there was me, A, B and C and we was all sat outside a shop window and they came past and because the women had, had comp... you know because it's shops and it's got old people's flats upstairs, and they kept complaining saying that there's youths down there, and it was the first time I'd been there. And I was sat there – everyone was sat there and they [police officers] came straight up to me and said 'stand up'. I said 'why me?' and he just said 'shut up and stand up'. He took me name and everything and they were still sat there outside the shop, shouting and everything. I said what about these? He said 'shut up – give me your name, give me your address' – and he took me name and address and he radioed and said 'how old are you?'. He checked up with somewhere and then he said 'alright, go on, get home, back where you belong' – he was just cheeky.

II p. 11

I later asked him if he considered that the employment of more black police officers (a strategy for institutional change analogous to the suggestion by PN70 for more black teachers in schools) may ameliorate the racism of the police force.

KKB: What about having more black police – is that a good idea?

PN72:   I think it's all crap when they say they should recruit more black policemen – that's just – it's using them to help – it's using them to help – it's using black people to help the police against black people. I don't think that's right. At all.

II p. 13

However, despite their criticisms of the police force and their reservations as to whether the racism in the police force could be challenged, very few of the black interviewees claimed to be in total agreement with those who had participated in the events which occurred in Tottenham in London in October 1985.

PN72 who, above, is clearly suspicious of the police force and unhappy about racist policing argued:

KKB: What do you think of what's been happening down in London?

PN72:   I think it's the police that's causing a lot of it. But I don't agree with that Bernie Grant, you know, that black – Haringey. I think it is – I don't agree with him, don't think he's right. Don't think he's right at all.

KKB: Where don't you think he's right?

PN72:   The way he said – I agree with that policeman by the sound of it – you know, that PC Blakelock who got killed well he's got a family and all that, you know, what he's left behind and the police wanted to – I'm not sticking up for the police but the police wanted to erect a memorial on the spot and I – but Bernie Grant said 'no, if there's one for her there's got to be one for that Mrs Jarrett' or something. And I don't agree with that. I can't put it into words but I know what I mean inside me. Like [pause] the copper was killed but I think the memorial should be erected 'cos by the sounds of it he was helping one of his mates, one of his colleagues. And I think that makes him a sort of hero there and then. So I think they should erect a memorial for him. But Mrs Jarrett – but the thing that I don't agree with is that once she collapsed the police were just stepping over her – they wasn't sort of trying to help her or anything.

KKB: Why do you think people rioted?

PN72:   It's just to show how you feel. There's a point where all the aggression, all the hassle and stick you've got through the years – once you come to an age – it was mostly 17, 18-year-olds weren't it – that's the age when it all sort of bubbles up and you start to realise what's happening around you and you feel, 'well, this ain't right, the way I'm being treated' and it all bubbles up and you want to let it out.

[The next part is omitted for it could identify him.]

KKB: Do you think unemployment's got anything to do with it?

PN72:   No. [pause] *No*. [pause] Because if a lot of the blacks was employed more the police would still push them about. A lot of it is police harassment I think.

II pp. 14–16

Rather than produce a number of extracts from different speakers in relation to my argument that the black interviewees did not feel happy with any of the strategies for challenging the racism of a state-controlled institution, it was more appropriate to follow and trace through the arguments presented by one speaker. (The next two pages of this interview are presented as Appendix II.)

From the above it can be seen that whilst there are criticisms of the police and reservations about being able to challenge the racist policing which was discussed by the interviewees, they also did not necessarily agree with using uprisings as a means of challenge. This is not to say that they were totally hostile and had extremely punitive attitudes towards the uprisers, for they did not. Rather, while having an insight into the reasons for the events, the black interviewees did not have a position of unconditional support. Thus, it can be seen that 'rioting' was not argued to be a useful specific strategy with which to challenge racist police practices in contemporary Britain.

6.4   Social representations and 'marriage'

At the beginning of this chapter it was argued that an analysis of future hopes and aspirations permits an insight into the changes which the interviewees may desire in their present daily life. In addition, 'futures' can indicate the possibilities which young people may feel are available for them, what they consider to be prescribed, and whether they discuss such social prescriptions in an eager and enthusiastic way or not.

Passerini has argued that

> [it] is impossible to deduce the presence of consent from the absence of political opposition.
>
> Passerini 1987: 65

The previous two subsections of this chapter have demonstrated the accuracy of her argument. The themes of disenfranchisement and the development of strategies in relation to racialism suggest that the interviewees may not be consenting to the ways in which the state, parliamentary democracy and social relations are structured, but that this is not necessarily an organised political opposition. However, neither is it, necessarily, an indication of consent to the present organisation of social relationships. Rather, it is that the dominant themes which were used to organise their discussions of racism and racialism – i.e. disenfranchisement and strategies for dealing with racialism – may be constituted such that these themes are re-presented not only as regulatory of social relationships, but also as possible points of contestation.

Passerini continues her argument:

> Equally, it shows that political dissent is not to be confused with cultural opposition.
>
> Passerini 1987: 65

Neither, therefore, is cultural consent to be confused with political consent. Further, it is also appropriate to consider whether cultural opposition may be a necessary, but not sufficient, aspect of political dissent. For example, if an individual argues that they do not want employment because it is a human right to develop one's own creativity, and the alienating nature of employment within capitalism will not permit the development of such creativity, this is not necessarily a clear form of political dissent, but may be considered to be part of a cultural opposition. Similarly, having a 'different' hairstyle (such as, in the mid 1980s, of green and blue hair) is a suggestion of cultural opposition but may not be considered to be political dissent. However, a man who considers himself to be a Marxist and struggles untiringly outside his household for the revolution, but does not challenge the domestic division of labour and is serviced by a woman or employs a black cleaner could not be considered to be challenging a racially structured capitalist patriarchy. It is in this sense that I am arguing that the cultural and political spheres are shaped by each other - Passerini's 'temporary and shifting nature of the boundaries between politics and everyday [or, I would suggest, 'cultural'] life'.

From the above it follows that social and interpersonal relations are separate from but also part of the sphere of the political. Thus, the comments of the interviewees about their possible future relationships and the themes which inform these comments, will provide an insight into social and cultural regulation and contestation. Marriage and the nuclear family are institutions legitimated by the state which are about coupledom and heterosexuality, and power inequality between adults and children as well as women and men. Writers such as Mitchell (1971) have argued that through these institutions the unequal power relationships between women and men, and the relations of subordination and domination between children and adults are reproduced. Further, the notions of the nuclear family and love marriage, as distinct from extended families and arranged marriage, are used by the state to legitimate and perpetuate racism (Bhavnani and Coulson 1986).

Thus, future hopes about marriage and family are analysed in this section as examples of an issue about private manifestations of power.

The speaker below had just said that she imagined being married in ten year's time (in response to 'what do you think you'll be doing in ten years' time?') and I had asked her how she imagined her future husband to be.

PN08:   Someone, like, say if I marry a rich fella and that, I don't think I'd like to marry someone like that 'cos the people I know like that are snobby and a bit stuck up like. I like people to be down to earth, to understand me and me ways sort of thing. Someone who'll dig the garden on Sundays. Someone who'll be me friend and help in the house and everything so it won't be 'mother cleans the house and dad washes the car' sort of thing, it'll all be mixed in together.

KKB: What's good about that?

PN08:   'Cos it's a team sort of thing, it's not right 'you do that, and I've got to do this'. It's working together, getting on with someone while you're working as a team.

KKB: Would you expect him to change nappies?

PN08:   Yes.

KKB: If your husband didn't want you to have a job, would you have one?

PN08:   Just for spite?

KKB: No [laughs] if you wanted a job, and your husband said 'I don't want you to get one', what do you think you'd do?

PN08:   I'd be quite happy. I think I'd like to be a housewife, even with one kid, if we was alright for money and everything, I'd like to be a housewife 'cos that's a big job in itself really. If you get on with that and your husband's bringing the money in, I think it's quite a hard job being a housewife.

KKB: You'd like to have a go?

PN08:   Yeah. I think if we needed the money I'd like to go out to work, but if we didn't, I'd stay in. Like me Mum goes out to work as well as comes home and she's shattered half the time. She like does two jobs really, she's got a lot to contend with. I think if when I was married and we both did go out to work it would have to be both of us doing the cleaning and the ironing and the washing 'cos then you're both doing the same amount of work sort of thing and no-one's sat down doing nothing.

I p. 13

This speaker certainly expects to be married, but it should be noted that twice within this passage she argues that she wants a relationship which is not based on the most frequent division of domestic labour ('it would have to be both of us doing the cleaning and the ironing and the washing'). Thus, her cultural consent is tempered by a questioning of power inequalities within marriage. She implies that mutual respect for each other is an important part of marriage (''cos it's a team sort of thing...'). However, she also accepts that her future husband could decide whether she be permitted to take employment. Thus, the theme underlying her argument is that of marriage being based on equality in daily life with the man being the overarching authority – an unequal partnership. However, in her arguments it can be seen that she also contests particular aspects of that inequality, such as the most frequently encountered division of domestic labour.

KKB:	What do you think you'll be doing in ten years' time?
PN69:	Housewife...I don't know if I'll be married by then 'cos in ten years' time – yeah, could be, 26, hmmm.
KKB:	Yeah?
PN69:	I'll have kids but I don't know if I'll be married yet. I want to have kids when I'm married though, don't want to have them without being married.
KKB:	What's wrong with it?
PN69:	Nothing's wrong with it but I'd just prefer to be married.
KKB:	How do you mean?
PN69:	It's just like really you've been waiting to get married from since you were come to sense sort of thing. Say, like, from the age of 15 onwards or maybe lower than that you've been saying I want to get married and I do want to get married...I'd prefer to get married. Invite all me good friends to me party and have some of me sisters and some of me friends as bridesmaids – things like that. I'd be looking forward to that. And I'd be inviting people from school. A white dress.
KKB:	What's good about wearing white?
PN69:	Just makes you know that you're pure. You can't go to church with a red wedding dress – or blue! [Laughs] Or people will know.
KKB:	What will they know?
PN69:	It just shows that you've had a – done something before – you're not a Mary Virgin.
KKB:	And you think that's important?
PN69:	Yes, I do.

KKB: Do you think it's important for men as well as women?

PN69:   I think it's importanter for women...'cos like boys who've left our school, they say that they can go out with one girl and then go with all the others – now if girls were to do that, they'd be called. They get ratings if you get what I mean. [Laughs]

KKB: Why do you think that is?

PN69:   I don't know – I don't see why they should be able to go with girls and get called good and the girls do it and get called bad. That's like unequality, ain't it?

II p. 19

The above speaker has firm ideas about how her marriage ceremony will be, all of which comprises an idealised notion of the bride. However, although she does not question these symbolic forms around the Christian marriage ceremony, she is clearly aware that a double standard in relation to sexual experience is dominant. In pointing to this double standard, the speaker is describing the lack of respect accorded to 'bad girls'. Thus, again, the issue of inequality between women and men, particularly in reference to marriage informs her discussion. This theme of inequality between women and men may also be seen in the comments of the following interviewee. She had said that she, too, thought she would be married in ten years' time, and then volunteered that she was engaged. So I asked her what he was like.

PN58:   He treats me right and everything [a reference to her 'boyfriend']

KKB: What does that mean?

PN58:   Well, when I was at me sister's he used to come up and stay in the spare room and everything and he could be just sitting down and he'll have his arm round me, just watching telly, and then I go 'Oh, will you make me a cup of tea, do you want one?' and he'll just get up and make it. No, 'Oh, bloody hell, make it yourself' – no hassle and things – he's not like that. And if you go to the shop he'll ask you what you want and everything - you know, he'll buy it you. Or like if you say 'Can you pass me a cigarette?', he'll get a cigarette out of the box, give it yer, give you a light and everything, pass the ash tray. He's really nice. He looks after me niece – he changes the nappy, he dresses her, he feeds her and everything – he's really good.

I p. 11

Her description of her relationship with her present boyfriend is suggestive of her ideal relationship. Thus, not only does she desire equality on a daily basis (changing nappies, feeding children) but also, enjoys being treated with respect. This issue of inequality appears to be intimately influencing of and influenced by the theme of 'respect for the woman'. This can be seen in the earlier extracts.

The theme of self-respect, sometimes expressed as independence for women, underlies the argument of the following speaker, and it also provides the rationale for her present desire not to be married in ten years' time.

KKB: What do you think you'll be doing in ten years' time?
PN68:   Don't know.
KKB: Imagine I'm holding a gun to your head [laughter], so you have to say something. What do you think you'll be like?
PN68:   Hopefully, I'll not be married. Hopefully, and I won't have any children...
KKB: And when you say hopefully I won't be married and won't have children, what do you mean?
PN68:   I don't want to get married yet and be tied down, you get tied down quick when you're married.
KKB: What do you think marriage involves?
PN68:   Looking after children, cooking for the husband, cleaning, washing, ironing and doing it day after day after day after day. [pause] Oh gosh!
KKB: Do you think you will ever want to get married?
PN68:   I might one day, but not now, I want a job first, I want my own money you know, so I can do what I like with it. Be independent, be my own self.

II p. 16

Thus, being one's own self for women may be seen both as wanting respect from others as well as retaining one's own self-respect within marriage. At the beginning of this subsection it was argued that 'love' marriage and 'arranged' marriage are presented overwhelmingly in public discussions in Britain as being opposite to each other, with the former claiming that it allows women to experience their true fulfilment through an ideology of romantic love, this ideology masking the maintenance and reproduction of unequal power relationships within marriage. In Britain, 'arranged' marriage is seen to be associated with South Asia and is discussed as implicitly barbaric for it is asserted that it forces women into a heterosexual relationship which has no claims to being based on romantic love. Clearly, the mythologies about 'love' marriage are varied, and 'love' marriage can take a number of forms within it. So it is for 'arranged' marriage. The underlying philosophy of the latter approach to marriage is that the institution involves a life-long commitment between a woman and a man and that such a commitment is likely to be fulfilling if the partners have interests, histories and aspirations in common. Thus, potential partners are considered with the aim being that a contract may then be possible. The way in which the heir to the throne of England had his choices of future wife proscribed demonstrate that the aspects of lifelong commitment and compatibility (as well as an 'unsullied' woman) are identical to those of arranged marriage. Thus, public noises of 'how wonderful' for Royalty and 'how barbaric' for South Asians would suggest that the hypocritical outcries over the latter are informed by racism. All of the young women of sub-continental origin who were interviewed for this study stated that they would be married in ten years' time and did expect to have arranged marriages.

PN11:   I think they're both [arranged and love] alright. I mean arranged marriages have got a high success rate - most probably because they don't want to get divorced anyway, you know, but love marriages at least you know you're gonna like the person you're marrying.

KKB: What are the good things about marriage? What do you think are the nice things about marriage?

PN11:   Well, you get to know somebody else and you know that you've got a husband who's gonna be there, you've got security and you know you're gonna be well provided for and that. And you know when you have children you know they'll have a father – at least he'll still be there, whereas sometimes they run off you know – the love marriage ones. And he'll eventually – you know you're gonna get married anyway if you know you're getting an arranged marriage. 'Cos you don't have to go out looking for someone – I couldn't.

KKB: You couldn't?

PN11:   No. Must be like a hunter with a spear and net, hunting for a husband.

II p. 17

Her unease at the idea of 'going out and looking for someone' rests on the theme of self-respect and an argument that marriage ought not to be about capturing and imprisonment. In addition claimed public anxieties that 'arranged' marriages restrict the freedom of the woman serve to remove the gaze from the ways in which relations of domination and subordination are reproduced within 'love' marriage: violence against wives, child physical and sexual abuse, lack of financial independence for women, the non-recognition as a criminal offence that a wife may be raped by her husband are all part of the sphere of marriage whether 'arranged' or 'love'. Thus, when the young women discuss their hopes for their future marriages and use the theme of respect around which to organise their arguments, this theme is used not only to regulate and mask the prevailing unequalities within the institution of marriage, but also used to contest such inequalities. However, just as clearly, this is not dissent as such, from the institution of marriage, for most of them definitely wanted to be married by their mid 20s.

The following speaker however *is* dissenting from marriage, but not necessarily as rejecting the motherhood aspect often associated with marriage:

KKB: What do you think you'll be doing in ten years' time?

PN70:   Gosh – 26 then – I'll be a mum, yeah. Not yet though. First of all I want to go through college, get a flat or a little house, set that up and then when the time comes for me to be a mum the baby will have a home to go to. You know the baby won't have to doss with me or anything. All these little 16-year-old girls having babies – I think it's disgusting – they've got to live with their mum – that means the baby's gonna crack up, gonna make the mum and the daughter argue and she's homeless again, know what I mean? No, I'm gonna go through college, get my flat – set up my flat before I start having my own family. I've always said that though.

KKB: Do you want to get married?

PN70:   No. Don't.

KKB: Why? What's awful about marriage?

PN70:   I don't know really. I think it's just the word marriage. But these people say they'll never get married and most of them end up getting married. I don't think I will though.

KKB: Why not?

PN70:   'Cos you have to be in, have the dinner on the table when your husband comes from work – do this, do that. You can only go out when he says you can go out – no-one can tell me I can't go out else there's trouble - I'd have him. That's why you don't really want to have kids now 'cos when you've got a kid you can't just go out and leave the kid – you've gotta have someone there to look after it. Some people can't afford to pay these babysitters, then they end up staying in by themselves. I want to spend some of my life doing what I want to do before I have a family.

KKB: You say you don't want to get married yet – do you go out with boys now?

PN70:   Yeah. I do. They crack me up now, see, so if I get married they'll just do me head in and I'll go mad.

KKB: How do you mean?

PN70:   They're too fussy and they moan too much – yeah that's it, they moan too much and they're too fussy. And they think they can rule you, you see. I think that's the top and bottom of it. Men think they can rule women and they can't – not me, anyway, not me. If they hit me, I'd just slap them back in the face – I don't care. What is true though is that these men think they can rule the women and they can't you know. Some can, some can't. No-one can rule me – except me mum – well, she can't really, no more, I'm 16, but – she still tells me what to do, you know, she still gives me a time to come in and if I'm late I've gotta explain to her.

II p. 21

The young men who were interviewed often argued that marriage tied them down and restricted their independence.

KKB: Do you want to get married?
PN47:   No.
KKB: Why not?
PN47:   Getting tied down to somebody for all the time – not for ever! I'd live with her, you know what I mean, but I wouldn't get married to her. Too much hassle.
KKB: Tell us why – like tell us how it's a hassle.
PN47:   Like getting tied down to one person you can't move around, associate, she might start getting jealous and all that and giving you a lot of trouble. I don't want a divorce – go through a lot of trouble to divorce her, then go through another lot of trouble to get married again.

I p. 18

It can be seen from the above that despite saying he did not want to get married, once the young man began to talk about divorce, he also assumed that he would get married again. Hence his reason to avoid marriage in the first place. While many of the young men claimed they did not want to get married, a little probing into their reasons led to their 'confessing' (for that was how many of them saw it) that they did want a close relationship with another person – usually a woman.[11]

---

[11] It should be made clear that the issue of sexual orientation, and the possibilities of a future partner being of the same sex were not raised in the interviews. I had decided that the subject was an extremely sensitive one, and, as I had conducted the interviews in schools to begin with, did not want to set up a situation where the schools felt uneasy that I was raising the issue of same-sex sexual relationships. I had, however, decided that if any interviewee raised the issue with me, I would follow it through. Not one of the interviewees did so.

Willis (1977) amongst other men researchers who have worked with young men has suggested that young working-class men epitomise ultra-masculinity when they discuss women.[12]

KKB:	What do you think you'll be doing in ten years' time? Ten years from now?
PN74:	Ten years? Be married – a married man. Well, I hope to be. Have a happy family – children and that.
KKB:	What's good about marriage – what are the good things?
PN74:	Don't know – don't really believe in marriage but – it has to happen. I don't believe – 'cos all it is is a slip and if you love each other, why have a ring and that – it's wasting money and money's precious.
KKB:	But say you were like living with someone, or married, right, whatever – what's nice about that do you reckon?
PN74:	It's love, ain't it? If you love someone you want to be with them, respect them and look after them – that's what I want to do anyway.
KKB:	How do you know if you love someone?
PN74:	Don't know – don't think I've been in love.
KKB:	You don't?
PN74:	In me own way, but not the way people feel. I've liked someone a lot – like I like my girlfriend a lot and I've only been with her seven months – things like that.
KKB:	Would you say you love her?
PN74:	In me own way.
KKB:	What does that mean?
PN74:	Don't know. Like if I care for someone and like them a lot, I must love them, sort of. So, I most probably do love her. But I don't know.
KKB:	But what is it? You don't have to talk about yourself, you just have to say – describe – what you think love is.
PN74:	Love is caring about someone and respect and living with each other – things like that – getting on with each other and really being nice and proper. That's what I think it is anyway – caring about each other.

II p. 14

Thus arguments about marriage in the interviewees' discussions of their futures were organised around a theme of respect.

---

[12] In this study, with a woman researcher, for many of the young men (although most had to be asked about marriage rather than that they raised it spontaneously), this was not necessarily the case. For example, Spike in Willis's study is quoted as saying. 'I've got a right bird. I've been going with her for eighteen months now. Her's is good as gold. She's fucking done well, she's clean. She loves doing fucking housework... she's as good as gold, and I wanna get married as soon as I can' (Willis 1977).

6.5 Summary and overview

Chapters 5 and 6 have, in looking at specific topics, suggested that discussions of 'politics' include some or all of the themes of income, changing conditions of employment, control, disenfranchisement, strategies for change and respect. These themes are not discrete and finite elements. Rather they are interwoven and intermeshed in different configurations in discussions of different topics. Thus, these themes are located within the domain of the 'political' for they have been presented by the young people in the context of discussions of particular issues and have been used to suggest how the regulation and contestation of the processes of subordination and domination in social relationships can be considered. The following passage is one example of such an intermeshing and interweaving by means of which political arguments are advanced.

KKB: What else has been happening?

PN51:   Oh, there's been a lot of talk about these riots and things like that.

KKB: What do you think about that?

PN51:   The policeman deserved everything he got. [This is a reference to the death of PC Blakelock at the time of the October 1985 events in Tottenham, London.] I'm not saying all policemen, right, but I mean my Mum's saying to me the policeman didn't deserve it and all that. I mean I want to... the woman who got shot cannot walk again, right, that's her life finished, she can't walk again, right. The policeman who shot her, he was suspended. This policeman [Blakelock] got stabbed out of anger. The fact that it happened right – I mean you take the Brixton riots, Brixton was a mess – there was buildings broken down, the lot, and they had councils and all that having meetings and things like that – because I mean I was there at the time – they was having meetings and nothing was being done. So if we've got to wait, the only way we can respond is through violence – so they mashed up everything and had to rebuild it back, right, and now the GLC is being kicked out, right, everything is going to go back to normal. We're gonna have more riots. Because the GLC – when we mashed up Brixton, the GLC thought we'll wait, you know what I mean, we'll listen to them now so the GLC wants to give us a whole new sports place and that, whole new shopping precinct, the lot, right, and we said fair enough, but now Maggie Thatcher's now saying that the GLC is spending too much money on us, right, so they're kicking GLC out. The same thing as they're going to do here one day –

kick out the GMC [Greater Middington Council] – and there's gonna be trouble. There's gonna be a lot of trouble. You know I was saying about this woman who got shot, right, people burst in the house and shot at her – they're too trigger happy. This man, the policeman has got suspended, right, because the black people got back to show how angry they was, and a policeman got stabbed – that is a sin, that is a sin – 'cos he got stabbed and lived. Right, he can get up and walk again now. Or – I think one of the policemen died, but that is his fault. I'm not blaming him, but I mean why should a person who's stabbed a policeman get charged for it when the policeman has shot the woman for not doing nothing at all and get away with it – just get suspended. So there's been a lot of arguments in our house about that, but I mean – the only way we get heard and the only way the miners got heard is through picketing and rioting. The only way we black people get heard is through rioting. And they call us – what is it? What do you call them people who hijack planes a lot – terrorists. Margaret Thatcher calls it terrorism. She wants a kick in the head for that. She can't even govern the country properly. I mean I'm not saying that Labour can do it any better but I mean she's so rich she doesn't think about the poor people. I mean how can the poor people go to these posh schools, they don't get any reduction. They don't get in courts – it's people like us who get in courts and the crime rate goes up. Well, I mean you don't get recreation centres and all things like that so they go out and look for excitement by breaking the law. I mean everybody – it's a known fact right, but when you break the law the adrenalin starts pumping. And when you do something, like you go for a battle for instance, your adrenalin starts pumping and you enjoy it... I mean if there was recreation centres and all things like that around here you wouldn't get that type of thing – and she calls it terrorism – she doesn't understand nothing – she wants to come down to the ghetto. You can't call this Moss Side a place, you've got to call it a ghetto because it is – it is a ghetto. She's not giving it enough money. She can spend money on a £25,000 picture portrait of herself, a £125 hairstyle and all things like that, but that £25,000 could buy a lot for this school. [The interview was being conducted in my car parked in the car park of his old school.]

KKB:　　Do you think Labour would be better?

PN51:　　No. I'll tell you what would make this country better, if it was communist. If the country was communist this country would be alright – everybody equal, no rich no

poor – if everybody was equal, like China. Look how far
China is in the field of electronics, things like that, and
Japan as well – they're all communist, that's the way to
be – everybody equal. I don't mean communist where you
wear the same clothes and all that rubbish, everybody
exactly the same, rated exactly the same. If this country
was communist then I think it would be alright – if there
was no rich and no poor – everyone just, well managed –
be alright. SDP, Labour, they're all the same. There's
nothing you can do about it, you've just got to live
through it. People like me have got to live – I would
never, ever rob somebody or mug somebody who I feel is
poor. I mean there's this guy in the precinct, he's just like
a tramp, right, and he's got wads of money in his pocket.
Someone like that, I would rob because he doesn't need
the money, right, 'cos he's rich. I know this man is rich,
we've heard everybody say he's rich. A man in a Rolls-
Royce I would rob somebody like him because he's rich
– he's got the money – but some of these old ladies here,
no I wouldn't do it. I'd rob the rich to give to myself –
you know what I mean – give to the poor. But I'd never
rob somebody...

II p. 12–16

In this piece of narrative, the speaker has used the theme of income to
organise his arguments ('no rich, no poor', 'people like me have got to live',
'I'd rob the rich to give to myself... give to the poor'). He has also used the
theme of both government and personal control – the former by his
organising topic of the police and its relationship to local authorities, and the
latter by reference to possibilities of street violence in Britain and the
comparison with the actions of the miners in the 1984–85 coal dispute. The
theme of disenfranchisement is expressed through his assertion that the
Prime Minister was abolishing metropolitan authorities, which are implied in
his reference to the provision of sports centres to be more accountable than
central government; the themes of changing conditions of employment (his
reference to 'field of electronics'), a set of possible strategies for change and
respect for all human beings are also integral to his arguments. For example,
his claim about the Prime Minister's reference to terrorists, and in his
discussions of the assumed personal expenditure of the Prime Minister, he
implies that she has little respect for people like himself for otherwise she
would reconsider her definitions and her policies. This interweaving of most
of the themes identified in these two chapters forms the basis for the
argument that he is discussing politics – that is, that the themes are used as
organising features to discuss relations of domination and subordination, and

the ways of contestation and regulation of these relationships in the discussion of specific topics.

7 Summary and issues for the future

You see, I have survived so long,
my habit of observation grown so strong
that sometimes I think I almost belong.
I know exactly how a tiger drinks
how a tiger walks, smiles and thinks,
but find somehow that I cannot ape
that unthinking pride or its manifest shape.
I fully understand the Tigrish Cause
and keep my distance from those massive jaws.

Suniti Namjoshi   'Among Tigers'

7.1 Summary

The central focus of this book is the empirical study designed to analyse and understand the ways in which young people discuss issues within the domain of politics. The present political context in Britain, that of rapidly increasing unemployment, and the ways in which young people are situated in this context is an important aspect of their lives, and hence, is part of the background for any contemporary arguments about politics. For this reason, chapter 1 considered shifting definitions of employment and unemployment in Britain. Following that, an examination of the 'psychology of unemployment' literature demonstrated that a substantial part of the studies are based either on an assumption of determinism and passivity (e.g. Jahoda 1979) or on voluntarism (e.g. Fryer 1986a). This critical evaluation suggests that there is a need to look at how individuals arrive at political understandings within structural constraints. In an examination of empirical evidence on the relationship and assumed distinction between unemployment and political attitudes, it was noted that the studies had defined politics very narrowly, had confused terms such as 'alienation', 'apathy' and 'cynicism', had not looked closely enough at the relationship between personal and public issues, and had not always acknowledged that the group defined as unemployed is heterogeneous, for example in respect of age, gender and 'race'. Chapter 2 moved on from there to look closely at young people and unemployment. From an examination of youth unemployment, the argument developed into a commentary on theories of youth cultures. It was suggested that some of the empirical work, in focussing on regulation and cultural reproduction, often rules out the possibility of contestation of social relationships by young people. This consequence of the sociological approaches is due partly to their predominant concentration on young white working-class men, although the specificity of the analysis is often unacknowledged. However, the use of quasi-ethnographic methods in these studies has considerable potential value in beginning to develop the means by which individuals arrive at political understandings – in this instance, young people in the context of unemployment.

Chapter 2 continued by noting that psychological studies of young people are often conducted within the framework of adolescence, which can assume a biological basis for the social behaviours and cultures associated with young people. It was argued that youth is a social category not a biological given. Psychological studies have tended to examine the impact of unemployment upon young people, and this formulation, often combined with the use of one method, the survey method, has again made invisible the possible means by which youth may be contesting social relationships in the context of their current levels of unemployment. The work of Billig and Cochrane was examined closely in chapter 2, to demonstrate that studies within psychology can approach the issue of political views in a sympathetic way, although that work was conducted in a period of substantially lower levels of youth unemployment.

Chapter 3 focussed upon potential theoretical and methodological frameworks for examining the ways in which youth discuss issues within the political domain. It was suggested that social representations theory could provide a starting point for such an analysis. A critical examination of this approach suggested that while some of the reservations expressed by those preferring concepts of linguistic and interpretive repertoires were helpful, both means of analysis lacked an *explicit* conceptualisation of the ways in which systems of meanings and understandings regulate and contest the unequal power present in social relationships. Thus it was argued that an analysis of the themes around which attitudes and views were organised could be the starting point for gaining insights into the regulations and contestations referred to above. The methodological implications from this assessment of possible analyses were considered in the second half of chapter 3, and it was argued that qualitative analyses were necessary in order to specify the above-mentioned themes.

Chapter 4 described the design and conduct of the empirical research. The manner of interviewing and transcription plus the characteristics of the sample were presented.

Chapters 5 and 6 focussed upon the interview material. Chapter 5 examined the themes around which the issues of employment, unemployment, and YTS were discussed. Three themes emerged from the interviews: the availability of the disposable income, the consequences of the changing nature of employment, and control. These themes were the organising strands around which the interviewees stated the views and presented their arguments. It was also noted that although the labour market and political life are frequently defined as being in the public sphere, the interviewees discussed employment in relation to personal hopes, aspirations and expectations of wages, careers, and future security, that is, the private sphere. In contrast, discussions on the issue of unemployment were located within the public sphere – by focussing upon welfare benefits, the need for computer-type qualifications and government policy. Further, it was noted that in contrast to the young men, the young women interviewed organised their discussions of careers in relation to future marital relationships and child-care responsibilities. It was also noted that the black interviewees integrated comments about racism and racialism into their discussions of unemployment.

Chapter 6 examined the interview material on democracy and voting, racism, and marriage. It was argued that the themes around which the interviewees' views and arguments were organised were those of disenfranchisement, a strategic approach to racism and the theme of 'respect'. It was noted that black interviewees' discussions of racism had embedded within their discussions arguments and practices for challenging racialism. In contrast, the white non-racialist interviewees, tended to exclude such strategies for change in their arguments. When the issue of marriage was discussed, it was evident that both the young women and the young men organised their views and arguments around the theme of 'respect'. The contrast between these discussions, and those reported by Willis (1977) on how young men discuss present and future sexual partners, was commented upon. Thus, chapters 5 and 6, in specifying the themes around which issues in the political domain were discussed, point to ideas for further analyses of how the unequal power present in all social relationships may be both regulated and contested by the organising themes which are used to discuss specific political issues.

From the above, it can be seen that there are a number of ways in which issues present in the research may be considered in the future. Three aspects will be focussed upon here: methodological issues, theoretical issues and substantive issues. Each will be considered as subsections of the next section.

7.2   Issues for the future

7.2.1   *Issues for the future. I: Power and methodological considerations*
In the past few years, the issue of power within social research has re-entered some of the discussions of contemporary social psychology.

> It is necessary to insert into social psychology a concern
> with problems of power, or, more precisely, with

> relationships of power. If this is not done... [there is a] risk
> of skirting around a number of phenomena the study of
> which is indispensible for our understanding of certain
> forms of social behaviour.
>
> Deschamps 1982: 97

There are a number of ways in which it is possible to analyse power
relationships within the research context, two of which will be considered in
this section in relation to the present study. On the one hand there is the set
of power relationships between researchers and those who are defined as the
interviewees in the present study. Another set of power relationships flow
from the socially ascribed characteristics of myself as the researcher, as well
as the interviewees; these socially ascribed characteristics carry hierarchical
loadings of their own.

7.2.1.1 Power relationships between researcher and researched

The power of the researcher, in relation to the researched, to define the
parameters of the theoretical framework, the design, the conduct and the
write-up of a research study are rarely explicitly noted or analysed. This is
not meant to imply that there is a conscious decision on the part of
researchers to ignore this aspect of their research. Rather, it is to suggest that
the transparency of these power relationships does not provide an easy entry
for analysis. However, if these power relationships are shifted away from
their clean, see-through framework, it may be possible to see some aspect of
these relationships; in being seen, these relationships can then be examined
and analysed. Some writers who are attempting to develop a feminist
analysis are beginning to do this (e.g. Griffin 1986c). Further, Oakley's
(1981) arguments that 'subjects' of research are not merely informants and
so should be attended to and treated with respect when they pose questions
of the researcher, again point to a means of analysing the unequal power
relationships within social research. The insights provided by such questions
– in this study they revolved around issues of my marital status, my
relationships with my parents, my contacts with the police force plus
comments from the black interviewees which indicated that they defined me
as having a personal insight into the experiences of racism – all provided
ways for me to carefully consider my interviewing content and style. This is
one means of focussing upon the power inequalities during the conduct of
the research.

The examples specific to this study, such as the ways in which the black
interviewees discussed racism and unemployment, how the women discussed
careers-as-distinct-from-jobs, and the ways in which the men and the women

discussed marriage are all testament to the above argument – namely that the interviewees were discussing these issues with *me*, that is, they were communicating with a black woman researcher in her mid thirties. That these issues were discussed in these ways indicates that the research interview itself was a site of power relationships. It is this point which provides a direction of analysis in future social research.

7.2.1.2   Socially ascribed characteristics and power

While it is accurate to suggest that social psychological research has tended to ignore the power inequalities which result from the hierarchical loadings assigned to socially ascribed characteristics, it is also necessary to state that the unevenness in these characteristics is sometimes 'controlled for' by women interviewing women, black researchers interviewing black people and so on. Reference is usually made to the 'experimenter effect' (Rosenthal 1966) to explain this matching. However, if it is accepted that such a synchrony between researcher and researched is desirable in order to minimise the impact of power inequalities, the argument may be taken one step further. That is, that rather than side-step the question of power, more may be learnt about its functioning in research if the usual balance of power which flows from socially ascribed characteristics is both inverted and subverted. The present study through an inversion of the more frequent balance of power had such subversion as part of its structure. A black woman researcher (therefore defined as socially middle class) in her mid thirties interviewing black and white working-class 16-year-olds, both women and men, means that I, and the interviewees in the study were inscribed within multi-faceted power relationships which had structural domination and structural subordination in play on both sides. It is this less frequently encountered power asynchrony, or this 'messiness' which could allow for the analysis of power relationships within social research. In addition, as conscious attention and interaction with the dynamics of power in research is focussed upon, so, a more complex view of how research subjects view themselves and their worlds may become available.[1]

7.2.2   Issues for the future. II: Theoretical considerations

It has been demonstrated that an analysis of the themes around which the interviewees discussed and presented their views and arguments of specific issues provides an insight into how relationships of power within social interactions may be regulated or contested. It was argued in chapter 3 that

---

[1]   These ideas are expanded upon in Bhavnani (1988).

Moscovici's writings and arguments on social representations could be developed further than at present. The empirical work reported in this study has, however, suggested that the notion of 'representations', associated as it is with visual images, implies too static and concrete a formulation when considering the organisation of views and arguments of political issues. The themes which emerged from the analyses in chapters 5 and 6 were flexible and mobile. The boundaries of these themes as well as the ways in which the themes were articulated with each other pointed to flexibility and mobility. The ideas of 'figuration' and 'configuration' seem to be more appropriate than that of 'representation'.[2] Not only do the first two words suggest a plasticity and mobility which is not present in 'representation' but also, they do not have connotations that they may be 'held' by an individual, or situated only *within* an individual. Rather, they contain connotations of giving shape to ideas and arguments. As Moscovici has argued, the aim of social representations theory is to reconsider and divert the current project of social psychology. This current project relies not only on positivistic frameworks for the analysis of human behaviour (although, for example, Billig 1982 and 1987 are significant exceptions to this), but also, is unable to analyse the cognitive structurings of social reality as being embedded in the social relationships of structured domination and subordination. The word 'figuration', whilst implying that individuals may give shape to ideas by communicating arguments and views, also has built in the notion that such ideas do not originate nor reside only within individuals. Rather, they are shaped by individuals, as well as shaping social relationships. The empirical work of this study has indicated that the interviewees discussed issues within the domain of politics by organising their arguments around certain themes. But 'theme' is, in itself, too static and too 'neutral' a notion, and to discuss the ways in which the themes combine together again implies a distinct loss of plasticity – a desirable hallmark (although not unambiguous) of social representation theory. However, 'figurations' can combine together, or be articulated with each other into configurations. Again, this notion of configurations requires an analysis of who is bringing together certain arguments and what the context of the communication is. The weakness of these words, however, is that they are not, as such, associated with unequal power relationships. The term 'discourse' is (see chapter 3). An issue for consideration in future research, therefore, is that 'social representations' be recast as 'discursive configurations'.

---

[2] The verb 'figurate' means 'to give shape to'. Thus 'figuration' means both the process of giving shape, as well as meaning the resulting form. 'Configuraton' means both the arrangement of figurations, as well as the contour or outline of a given form.

7.2.3   Issues for the future. III: Substantive considerations

The two previous subsections which discuss theoretical and methodological issues for the future are not, of course, free standing. While their implications for the conceptualisation, design and conduct of research studies has been outlined, it would also be accurate to state that theory and method are starting points for suggesting why this study, unlike many others, found young working-class people to be interested in discussing issues in the domain of the political. But, also embedded within the theory and methodology are the implications for the substantive aspects of this work. For example, the interviewees' discussions of unemployment and employment suggest that the young people did not conceptualise the spheres of private and public life as separate and distinct; this then provides further substantiation for the arguments put forward by Siltanen and Stanworth (1984) on this issue. In addition, the study has also been able to tackle claims put forward by, for example, the Economic and Social Research Council that young people in Britain are 'political[ly] innocent, naive... and ignorant' (ESRC 1987, p.6). The reason it is important to provide both empirical and theoretical arguments for such claims is that otherwise, a statement such as the above-quoted one from the ESRC leads to a position in which it is argued that it is political innocence which is the reason for the 'overt racism which the research projects [contained in the report] commonly reveal to be endemic among white youth in Britain' (ibid.). What needs close examination is whether such political innocence is the norm for young working-class people, and whether it is political ignorance which is the cause of the endemic racism, and, indeed, whether racism is a necessary consequence in the lives of young working-class white people. The study reported in this book, in refusing to locate itself in an implicit 'blame-the-victim' framework, avoided starting with the assumption that expressions of racism are always central in the lives of young working-class white people. The study has also indicated that the ways in which young black people discuss political issues have considerable continuity with the discussions of their white peers. However, that the black interviewees discussed racism in a strategic way may suggest a different point of entry for further explorations of how endemic racism can be contested and challenged. Further, the study has demonstrated that issues of private and public power are intimately related to each other in the arguments of the interviewees. It is these substantive considerations which flow from, as well as provide a source of rethinking for the theoretical and methodological aspects of the work.

Thus, the turning of the project of social psychology away from its positivist history and towards an understanding of how relationships of power and subordination are reproduced is exciting, although challenging. The final words of this book must be the words of one interviewee:

KKB: What's your ideal job?
PN60:   I'd like the job of the Queen.
KKB: Why? What does she do?
PN60:   Well – she gets paid a lot of money for doing nothing...
           Put it like this, she gets paid for breaking bottles against ships and we get arrested for breaking bottles on the street.

Appendix I

Number allocated to interview	Sample characteristics	No. times interviewed
PN01	Asian boy	2
PN02	Asian boy	2
PN03	Asian boy	2
PN04	Asian boy	1
PN05	Asian boy	2
PN06	White girl	2
PN07	Asian girl	1
PN08	White girl	1
PN09	Asian girl	2
PN10	Asian girl	2
PN11	Asian girl	2
PN12	Asian girl	2
PN13	Asian girl	1
PN14	Asian girl	1
PN15	Asian girl	1
PN16	Asian girl	2
PN17	Asian girl	2
PN18	White girl	2
PN19	White girl	2
PN20	Asian girl	2
PN21	Asian girl	2
PN22	Asian girl	2
PN23	Asian girl	2
PN24	White girl	2
PN25	Asian girl	2
PN26	Asian girl	2
PN27	Asian girl	2
PN28	White girl	2
PN29	White girl	2

PN30	White girl	2
PN31	White boy	2
PN32	White boy	2
PN33	White boy	1
PN34	No recording	
PN35	White boy	2
PN36	Afro-Caribbean girl	2
PN37	White girl	1
PN38	White girl	1
PN39	Asian boy	2
PN40	Afro-Caribbean boy	2
PN41	Afro-Caribbean boy	2
PN42	Asian girl	2
PN43	Afro-Caribbean girl	1
PN44	No recording	
PN45	Afro-Caribbean boy	2
PN46	Afro-Caribbean boy	2
PN47	Afro-Caribbean boy	2
PN48	White boy	1
PN49	White girl	2
PN50	White girl	2
PN51	Afro-Caribbean boy	2
PN52	White girl	1
PN53	Afro-Caribbean boy	2
PN54	Afro-Caribbean boy	1
PN55	Asian boy	2
PN56	White boy	2
PN57	Afro-Caribbean girl	2
PN58	Afro-Caribbean girl	2
PN59	White boy	2
PN60	Asian boy	2
PN61	Asian boy	2
PN62	Asian boy	2
PN63	White boy	2
PN64	Afro-Caribbean boy	2
PN65	Afro-Caribbean boy	2
PN66	Afro-Caribbean girl	2
PN67	Afro-Caribbean boy	1
PN68	Afro-Caribbean girl	2
PN69	Afro-Caribbean girl	2

PN70	Afro-Caribbean girl	2
PN71	Afro-Caribbean girl	2
PN72	Afro-Caribbean boy	2
PN73	White boy	2
PN74	White boy	2
PN75	White girl	2
PN76	Afro-Caribbean girl	2

Appendix II

Continuation of interview of PN72 from chapter 6.

KKB: Do you think unemployment's got anything to do with it? With the riots?

PN72: No. No. Because if a lot of blacks was employed more the police would still push them about. A lot of it is police harassment I think.

KKB: Why do you think they're like that – why do you think they are like that?

PN72: I don't know – it's just the way they are. The superiors in the police might teach them to be like that. Because they know that some blacks are bad, that sort of gives all the blacks a bad name. Just like in the paper if someone gets mugged and a black guy did it they say 'black youth', but if a white guy does it they just say a youth – I don't agree with that either.

KKB: Do you watch the news? Do you read the papers?

PN72: Yeh. Every day.

KKB: What do you read? What do you watch?

PN72: I watch Granada Reports and if I'm in I watch the News at One. And I always read *The Sun* every day.

KKB: Why?

PN72: I don't know. 'Cause that is delivered every morning so Ernie's got it now and when he's finished with it I read it. I always read that Woodrow Wyatt on a Saturday I think it is 'cause he's always on about the riots – and that Professor Vincent. I don't like that Enoch Powell either – he's cheeky. He said that they should pay all the blacks so many thousand, tell them to go back, that's the only way you're going to stop riots. But if the police were more friendly... well no, I would like the police to be more friendly and then if they were more friendly it would mean that we'd get more friendly with them. I don't want to be friendly with them. It's like.. to me the police are like Hitlers sort of – don't like 'em. Like little dictators. Just don't like 'em.

KKB: What do you think about what's happening in South Africa?

PN72:   Apartheid and all that? Yeh, that's very wrong and they have got a real reason to riot. I don't think it's right 'cause it's their country in the first place ain't it? So they should have the freedom. But I think in time they will overcome the government there 'cause it's obvious now it's building up and up and up. And up. Did you watch that A Plus Four on Tuesday? With that Oliver Tambo?

KKB: No I didn't see it but I know who you mean.

PN72:   Well I was watching that and he was on about it – dead interesting. He was saying that he's in the MSC [ANC] or something and he's the leader and he's saying that the hassle that he's had is just unbelievable and he said that the only way to overcome it is to stop all this segregation and all that – that's the only way to overcome it. It was on for half an hour. I didn't mean to watch it but I just turned it over and I started watching it – dead interesting so...

KKB: Do you like that programme?

PN72:   I don't watch it every week. I read it in the paper.

Bibliography

All the references below are not necessarily cited in the text. However, they are being included as many of them influenced the development of the research.

Abercrombie, N., Hill, S. and Turner, R.S. (1983) 'Determinacy and indeterminacy in the theory of ideology'. *New Left Review* No. 142, Nov/Dec, pp. 55–67

Abrams, M. (1966) 'Social trends and electoral behaviour' in R. Rose (ed.) *Studies in British Politics*. London: Macmillan.

Aiken, M. and Ferman, L.A. (1966) 'The social and political reactions of older negroes to unemployment'. *Phylon* Vol. 57, pp. 333–46

Aries, P. (1973) *Centuries of Childhood*. Harmondsworth: Penguin Books

Ashton, D. and Maguire, M. (1983a) 'The vanishing youth labour market'. Occasional Paper No. 3 Youthaid

Ashton, D. and Maguire, M. (1983b) 'Competition between young people and adults: a research note on the structure of the youth labour markets'. *International Review of Applied Psychology*, Vol.32, pp. 263–9

Banks, M. (1984) 'The effects of unemployment on young people'. Paper delivered at ACPP meeting, London, 15 February

Banks, M. and Jackson, P.R. (1982) 'Unemployment and risk of minor psychiatric disorder in young people: cross sectional and longitudinal evidence'. *Psychological Medicine* Vol.12, pp. 789–98

Banks, M., Ullah, P. and Warr, P. (1984) 'Unemployment and less qualified urban young people'. *Employment Gazette,* pp. 343–6

Banks, M., and Ullah, P. (1987) 'Political attitudes and voting among unemployed and employed youth'. Draft paper

Bates, I., Clarke, J., Cohen, P., Finn, D., Moore, R. and Willis, P. (eds.) (1984) *Schooling for the Dole?: The New Vocationalism*. London: Macmillan

Beechey, V. (1984) 'Women's employment in contemporary Britain'. Paper presented to BSA Conference, Bradford, April

Bhavnani, K-K. (1985) 'Psychology, unemployment and young people: which is the problem?'. Paper presented to Day School organised by Regional Association of Child Psychology and Psychiatry. Norwich, January

Bhavnani, K-K. (1986) 'Power in the research process'. Paper presented at the Annual Conference, Social Section, British Psychological Society. Brighton, September

Bhavnani, K-K. (1987) 'Disaffection or disenfranchisement?'. Paper presented to Annual Conference, Social Section, British Psychological Society. Oxford, September

Bhavnani, K-K. (1988) 'Empowerment and social research: some comments'. *Text* Vol.8, No. 1, pp. 41–50

Bhavnani, K.K. (1990) 'What's power got to do with it?' in Parker and Shotter (1990)

Bhavnani, K-K. and Coulson, M. (1986) 'Transforming socialist feminism: the challenge of racism'. *Feminist Review* No. 23, pp. 81–92

Billig, M. (1978) *Fascists: a social psychological view of the National Front*. London: Harcourt Bruce Jovanovich

Billig, M. (1982) *Ideology and Social Psychology*. Oxford: Basil Blackwell

Billig, M. (1984a) 'Political ideology: social psychological aspects' in H. Tajfel (ed.) *The Social Dimension: European developments in social psychology*. Vol.2. Cambridge: Cambridge University Press, pp. 446–64

Billig, M. (1984b) 'Political ideology' in H. Belosso and J. Nicholson (eds.) *Psychology Survey No. 4*, pp. 245–63.

Billig, M. (1986a) 'Political psychology and social psychological theory' in M. Brouwer et al. (eds.) *Political Psychology in the Netherlands*. Antwerp: Mola Russa

Billig, M. (1986b) 'Very ordinary life and the Young Conservatives' in H. Beloff (ed.) *Getting Into Life*. London: Methuen, pp. 67–93

Billig, M. (1987) *Arguing and Thinking: a rhetorical approach to social psychology.* Cambridge: Cambridge University Press

Billig, M. (1989) 'The argumentative nature of holding strong views: a case study'. *European Journal of Social Psychology* Vol. 19(3), May–June, pp. 203–24

Billig, M. and Cochrane, R. (Dec 1982) 'Lost generation'. *New Socialist*, pp. 38–41

Blackburn, R.M. (1982) 'Review of Verba, S. and Schlozman, K.L. (1979)'. *British Journal of Economics* Vol. 33, No.1, pp. 135–56

Blackwell, T. and Seabrook, J. (1985) *A World Still to Win: the reconstruction of the post-war working class.* London: Faber and Faber

Blalock, H.M. (1975) (ed.) *Measurement in the Social Sciences: theories and strategies.* London: Macmillan

Bowlby, J. (1963) *Child Care and the Growth of Love.* Harmondsworth: Penguin

Bowler, M.K. (1981) 'Review of Verba, S. and Schlozman, K.L. (1979)'. *Political Science Quarterly* Vol.96, No.2, pp. 323–4

Brah, A.K. (1984) 'Unemployment and racism: Asian youth on the dole'. Paper delivered at BSA conference on Work, Employment and Unemployment, April

Brake, M. (1980) *The Sociology of Youth Culture and Youth Subcultures: sex and drugs and rock 'n' roll.* London: Routledge and Kegan Paul

Brake, M. (1985) *Comparative Youth Cultures The Sociology of youth culture and youth subcultures in America, Britain and Canada.* London: Routledge and Kegan Paul

Breakwell, G. (1982) 'The consequences of threats to identity in adolescence'. Paper given to B.P.S. Social Psychology Conference, September 1982, Edinburgh

Breakwell, G. (1986) 'Political and attributional responses of the young short term unemployed'. Unpublished manuscript

Brody, R.A. (1980) 'Review of Verba, S. and Schlozman, K.L. (1979)'. *American Political Science Review* Vol.74, No.3, pp. 832–3

Brody, R.A. and Sniderman, P.M. (1977) 'From life space to polling place: the relevance of personal concerns for voting behaviour'. *British Journal of Political Science* Vol.7, pp. 337–60

Brown, G.W. and Harris, T. (1978) *Social origins of depression; a study of psychiatric disorder in women.* London: Tavistock

Brown, P. (1986) 'It is a job being adult: the social and educational consequences of changing labour market conditions for school leavers'. Paper given at BSA Annual Conference. Loughborough, March

Bulmer, M. (ed.) (1977) *Sociological Research Methods: an introduction.* London: Macmillan

Bunker, N. and Dewberry, C. (1983) 'Unemployment behind closed doors'. Paper given to SSRC Workshop in 1983 in *The Journal of Community Education* Vol.2, No.4

Burgess, R.G. (1982a) *Field Research: a sourcebook and field manual.* London: Allen and Unwin

Burgess, R.G. (1982b) 'Elements of sampling in field research' in Burgess (1982a)

Burgess, R.G. (1984) *In the Field: an introduction to field research.* London: Allen and Unwin

Burstein, P. (1982) 'Review of Verba, S. and Schlozman, K.L.(1979)'. *Social Forces* Vol.60, No.3, pp. 924–5

Buss, T.R., Hofstetter, C.R. and Redburn, F.S. (1980) 'The form of mass unemployment: some political and social implications'. *Political Psychology* Fall/Winter, pp. 95–113

Butters, S. (1975) 'The logic of enquiry of participant observation' in Hall Jefferson (1975), pp. 253–73

Byrne, L., Burchell, B. and Morley, I. (1985) 'The social psychological effects of unemployment on YTS leavers'. Unpublished paper

Campbell, B. (1984) *Wigan Pier Revisited.* London: Virago

Carugati, F. (1986) 'Parental identity and social representations of intelligence and development'. Paper delivered at British Psychological Society (Developmental Section) Annual Conference, Exeter, England. September

Castles, S. and Wustenberg, W. (1979) *The Education of the Future: an introduction to the theory and practice of socialist education.* London: Pluto Press

Centre for Contemporary Cultural Studies (1982) *The Empire Strikes Back: race and racism in '70s Britain.* London: Hutchinson

Clarke, J., Hall, S., Jefferson, T. and Roberts, B. (1975) 'Subcultures, cultures and class' in Hall and Jefferson (1975), pp. 9–74

Clifford, J. and Marcus, G. (eds.) (1986) 'Writing culture. The poetics and politics of ethnography'. School of American Research Advanced Seminar. Berkeley: University of California Press

Coard, B. (1971) *How the English Educational System Makes the West Indian Child Educationally Subnormal.* London: New Beacon Press

Cochrane, R. and Billig, M. (1982a) 'Adolescent support for the National Front: a test of three models of political extremism'. *New Community* Vol.X, No.1, Summer

Cochrane, R. and Billig, M. (1982b) 'Extremism of the centre: the SDP's young followers'. *New Society* 20 May, pp. 291–2

Cochrane, R. and Billig, M. (1983) 'Youth and politics'. *Youth and Policy* Vol.2, No.1, pp. 31–4

Cochrane, R. and Billig, M. (1984) 'I'm not National Front myself, but...'. *New Society* 17 May, pp. 255–8

Cockburn, C. (1977) *The Local State. Management of Cities and People.* London: Pluto Press

Coffield, F. (1983) 'Learning to live with unemployment: what future for education in a world without jobs?' in F. Coffield and R. Goodings (eds.) (1983) *Sacred Cows in Education. Essays in Reassessment.* Edinburgh: Edinburgh University Press, pp. 191–207

Coffield, F., Borrill, C. and Marshall, S. (1983) 'How young people try to survive being unemployed.'. *New Society* 2 June, pp. 332–4

Coffield, F., Borrill, C. and Marshall, S. (1986) *Growing up at the Margins.* Milton Keynes: Open University Press

Cohen, P. (1983) 'Losing the generation game'. *New Socialist* No.14, Nov/Dec, pp. 28–36

Cohen, P. (1985) 'Towards Youthopia'. *Marxism Today*, October, pp. 33–7

Coleman, J. and Coleman, E.Z. (1984) 'Adolescent attitudes to authority'. *Journal of Adolescence* Vol. 7, pp. 131–41

Commission for Racial Equality (1980) 'Ethnic minority youth unemployment'. CRE London, July

Conger, J. (1973) *Adolescence and Youth. Psychological development in a changing world.* New York: Harper International Edition

Connell, R.W. (1983) *Which Way is Up: essays on sex, class and culture.* Sydney: George Allen and Unwin

Cooley, M. (1980) *Architect or Bee: The Human/Technology Relationship.* Slough: Hand and Brain Publications

Corrigan, P. (1979) *Schooling the Smash Street Kids.* London: Macmillan

Corrigan, P. and Frith, S. (1975) 'The politics of youth culture' in Hall and Jefferson (1975), pp. 231–9

Coulson, M. (1983) 'Women, social policy and the capitalist state'. Book outline

Coulson, M. and Bhavnani, K.K. (1989) 'Making a difference – questioning women's studies' in E. Burman (ed.) *Feminists and Psychological Practice.* London: Sage

Davidson, D. (1970) 'Mental events' in *Essays on Actions and Events.* Oxford: Clarendon Press, Ch. 10, pp. 207–27

Davis, A.Y. (1974) *Angela Davis: an autobiography.* New York: Random House

Davis, A.Y. (1981) *Women, Race and Class.* London: The Women's Press

Deacon, A. (1981) 'Unemployment and politics in Britain since 1945' in Showler and Sinfield (1981), pp. 59–87

Dean, D.G. (1961) 'Alienation: its meaning and measurement'. *American Sociological Review* Vol.26, pp. 753–8

Deaux, K. (1976) *The Behaviour of Women and Men.* California: Belmont

Declaration for International Youth Year. 1985

Demos, J. and Demos, V. (1969) 'Adolescence in historical perspective'. *Journal of Marriage and the Family.* November

de Muth, C. (1978) *'Sus': a report on section 4 of the Vagrancy Act 1824.* London: Runnymede Trust

Department of Employment (1977) *Economic Trends.* London: HMSO. October

Department of Employment (1985) *Department of Employment Gazette.* London: HMSO. October

Department of Employment (1986) *Department of Employment Gazette.* London: HMSO. August

Department of Employment (1987) *Department of Employment Gazette.* London: HMSO. September
Department of Employment (1987) *Department of Employment Gazette.* London: HMSO. October
Department of Employment (1987) *Economic Trends Annual Supplement.* London: HMSO
Deschamps, J.C. (1982) 'Social identity and relations of power between Groups' in H. Tajfel (ed.) *Social identity and intergroup relations.* Cambridge: Cambridge University Press, pp. 85–98
Deutscher, I. (1984) 'Foreword' in Farr and Moscovici (1984), pp. xiii–xviii
Dex, S. (1983) 'The second generation: West Indian female school leavers' in Phizacklea (1983)
Dickinson, J. (1986) 'Individual representations of social inequality'. EAESP Summer School. Bologna, Italy. August–September 1986
Di Giacomo, J-P. (1980) 'Intergroup alliances and rejections within a protest movement (analysis of social representations)'. *European Journal of Social Psychology* Vol. 10, pp. 329–44
Doise, W. (1978) *Groups and Individuals: explanations in social psychology.* Cambridge: Cambridge University Press
Doise, W. (1982 – English Translation 1986) *Levels of Explanation in Social Psychology.* Cambridge: Cambridge University Press
Doise, W. and Moscovici, S. (1983) (eds.) *Current Issues in European Social Psychology,* Vol. 1. Cambridge: Cambridge University Press
Doise, W. and Moscovici, S. (1987) (eds.) *Current Issues in European Social Psychology,* Vol. 2, Cambridge: Cambridge University Press
Donovan, A. and Oddy, M. (1982) 'Psychological aspects of unemployment: an investigation into the emotional and social adjustment of school leavers'. *Journal of Adolescence* Vol. 5, pp. 15–30
Dyhouse, C. (1981) *Girls Growing Up in Late Victorian England.* London: Routledge and Kegan Paul
Economic and Social Research Council (1987) *What Next? An Introduction to Research on Young People.* London: Economic and Social Research Council
The Economist (1982) 'Jobless too placid', p. 13 and pp. 23–4. 4 December
Elkin, F. and Westley, W.A. (1955) 'The myth of adolescent culture'. *American Sociological Review* Vol.55, No.6, December
Elshtain, J.B. (1981) *Public Man, Private Woman. Women in Social and Political Thought.* Oxford: Martin Robertson
Erikson, E.H. (1971) *Identity: youth and crisis.* London: Faber and Faber
Eysenck, H.J. (1954) *The Psychology of Politics.* London: Routledge and Kegan Paul
Fagin. L. (1978) 'The psychology of unemployment'. *Medicine in Society* Vol. 4., No.2, pp. 8–13
Fagin, L.H. (Winter 1979–1980) 'The experience of unemployment: the impact of unemployment'. *New Universities Quarterly*
Fairweather, H. (1976) 'Sex differences in cognition'. *Cognition* Vol. 4, p. 231–80
Farish, M. (1984) 'The Youth Training Scheme: a critical response'. Paper delivered at BSA Conference on Work, Employment and Unemployment Bradford, April
Farr, R.M. (1977) 'Heider, Harre and Herzlich on health and illness: some observations on the structure of "representations collectives"'. *European Journal of Social Psychology* Vol. 7, pp. 491–504
Farr, R. and Moscovici, S. (eds.) (1984) *Social Representations.* Cambridge: Cambridge University Press
Femia, J. (1975) 'Hegemony and consciousness in the thought of Antonio Gramsci'. *Political Studies* No.23, pp. 29–48
Fineman, S. (ed.) (1987) *Unemployment Personal and Social Consequences.* London: Tavistock
Finn, D. (1983) 'The Youth Training Scheme – a new deal?'. *Youth and Policy* Vol.1, No.4, Spring, pp. 16–24
Finn, D. (1984) 'Britain's misspent youth,'. *Marxism Today* February, pp. 20–4
Finn, D. (1986) 'The Manpower Services Commission and youth unemployment'. Seminar for Graduate Students, SPS Committee, May 1986
Flacks, R. (1983) 'Moral commitment, privatism and activism: notes on a research program' in N. Haan, R. Bellah, P. Rabinow, and W. Sullivan (eds.). New York:

Columbia University Press, pp. 343–59

Foucault, M. (1977) *Discipline and Punish*. London: Penguin

Foucault, M. (1980) *Michel Foucault: Power/Knowedge*, ed. C. Gordon. Sussex: Hassocks

Frankenberg, R. (1979) 'Methodology: social or individual'. Paper delivered to BSA/SSRC Methodology Conference, January 1979

Frankenberg, R. (1988) *White Women Race Matters*. Doctoral Dissertation, University of California, Santa Cruz. To be submitted in June

Fraser, C. (1980) 'The social psychology of unemployment: Marienthal, an extreme case?' in M. Jeeves (ed.) *Psychology Survey No.3*. London: George Allen and Unwin

Fraser, C. (1986) 'Social representations and social attitudes'. Paper delivered at 'Attitudes and attributions: a symposium in honour of Jas Jaspars'. BPS Annual Conference, Sheffield, April 1986

Fraser, C. and Marsh, C. (1983) *Cambridge Evening News*. Survey for General Election June 1983

Free, L.A. and Cantril, H. (1967) *The Political Beliefs of Americans*. New Brunswick: Rutgers University Press, cited in Mann (1982)

Frith, S. (1984) *The Sociology of Youth*. Ormskirk: Causeway Books

Fryer, D. (1985a) 'The positive functions of unemployment'. *Radical Community Medicine* Spring, pp. 3–9

Fryer, D. (1985b) 'Stages in the psychological response to unemployment: a (dis)integrative review article'. *Current Psychological Research and Reviews*

Fryer, D. (1986a) 'Employment deprivation and personal agency during unemployment: a critical discussion of Jahoda's explanation of the psychological effects of unemployment'. *Social Behaviour* Vol.1, pp. 3–23

Fryer, D. (1986b) 'On defending the unattacked: a comment upon Jahoda's defence'. *Social Behaviour* Vol.1, pp. 31–2

Furnham, A. (1985) 'Youth unemployment: a review of the literature'. *Journal of Adolescence* Vol.8, pp. 109–24

Gallagher, A. (1987) 'Who defines the group? Social identity and the conflict in the north of Ireland'. Paper presented to Annual Conference, Social Section, British Psychological Society. Oxford, September

Garratty, J.A. (1978) *Unemployment in history: economic thought and public policy*. New York: Harper and Row

Galtung, J. (1967) *Theory and Methods of Social Research*. London: George Allen and Unwin

Gershuny, J.I. and Pahl, R.E. (1979/1980) 'Work outside employment: some preliminary speculations'. *New University Quarterly*, Winter pp. 120–35

Giddens, A. (1979) *Central Problems in Social theory: Action Structure and Contradiction in Social Analysis*. London: Macmillan

Gillies, P., Elwood, J.M. and Hawtin, P. (1985) 'Anxieties in adolescents about unemployment and war'. *British Medical Journal* Vol. 291, pp. 383–4

Gilroy, P. (1984) 'The myth of black criminality' in R. Miliband and J. Savile (eds.) *Socialist Register, 1983*. London: Merlin Press, pp. 47–56

Gilroy, P. (1987) *There Ain't No Black in the Union Jack*. London: Hutchinson

Glaser, B.G. and Strauss, A.L. (1967) *The Discovery of Grounded Theory, Strategies for Qualitative Research*. Chicago: Aldine

Goot, H. and Reid, E. (1984) 'Women: if not apolitical, then conservative' in J. Siltanen and M. Stanworth (eds.) *Women and the Public Sphere: a critique of sociology and politics*. London: Hutchinson, pp. 122–39

Gorz, A. (1982) *Farewell to the Working Class: an essay on post-industrial socialism*. London: Pluto Press

Grewal, S., Landor, L., Lewis, G., Kay, J. and Parmar, P. (eds) (1988) *Charting the Journey: Writings by black and third world women*. London: Sheba

Griffin, C. (1981) Progress Report to ESRC for Project on Young Women and Work: with special reference to gender and the family

Griffin, C. (1985a) 'Qualitative methods and cultural analysis: young women and the transition from school to unemployment', in R. Burgess (ed.) *Field Methods in The Study of Education*, Brighton: Falmer Press

Griffin, C. (1985b) *Typical Girls: young women from school to the job market*. London: Routledge and Kegan Paul

Griffin, C. (1985c) Research proposal: 'Effects of youth unemployment on family life and leisure: with special reference to gender and class differences'. First draft

Griffin, C. (1986a) 'Broken transitions: from school to the scrap heap'. Paper presented to the BSA Conference, University of Loughborough, March 1986

Griffin, C. (1986b) 'Innovations in social psychology: a study of young women from school to the job market'. Draft paper

Griffin, C. (1986c) 'Qualitative methods and female experience: young women from school to the job market' in S. Wilkinson (ed.) *Feminist Social Psychology: developing theory and practice*. Milton Keynes: Open University Press

Griffiths, D. and Saraga, E. (1979) 'Sex differences and cognitive abilities: a sterile field of enquiry?' in O. Hartnett, G. Boden and M. Fuller (eds.) *Sex Role Stereotyping*. London: Tavistock, pp. 17–45

Grimshaw, R., Hobson, D. and Willis, P. (1980) 'Introduction to ethnography at the Centre' in S. Hall, D. Hobson, A. Lowe and P. Willis (eds.) *Culture, Media, Language*. London: Hutchinson

Gross, A.E., Collins, B.E. and Bryan, J.H. (1972) *An Introduction to Research in Social Psychology: exercises and examples*. New York: John Wiley and Sons

Gudgin, G. (1983) Seminar in SPS on Cambridge Economic Policy Group's view of 'What causes unemployment?'. October

Gurney, R.M. (1980a) 'The effects of unemployment on the psycho-social development of school leavers'. *Journal of Occupational Psychology* Vol. 53, pp. 205–13

Gurney, R.M. (1980b) 'Does unemployment affect the self esteem of school leavers?'. *Australian Journal of Psychology* Vol. 32, No.3, pp. 175–82

Gurney, R. and Taylor, K. (1981) 'Research on unemployment: defects neglect and prospects'. *Bulletin of the British Psychological Society* Vol.34, pp. 349–52

Hall, S. (1983) 'The battle for socialist ideas in the 1980s' in R. Miliband and J. Savile (eds.) *Socialist Register*, 1982. London: Merlin Press, pp. 1–19

Hall, S. (1984) 'The culture gap'. *Marxism Today* January, pp. 18–22

Hall, S. (1985) 'Authoritarian populism'. *New Left Review* No. 151, pp. 115–24

Hall, S. (1986) 'Thatcherism amongst the theorists'. Paper delivered at Social and Political Sciences Committee, University of Cambridge. 28 November

Hall, S., Critcher, C., Jefferson, T., Clarke, J. and Roberts, B. (1978) *Policing the Crisis. Mugging, the State and Law and Order*. London: Macmillan

Hall, S., Hobson, D., Lowe, A. and Willis, P. (eds.) (1980) *Culture, Media, Language: working papers in cultural studies, 1972–1979*. London: Hutchinson

Hall, S. and Jefferson T. (eds.) (1975) *Resistance Through Rituals: youth subcultures in post-war Britain*. London: Hutchinson

Harding, S. (1987) (ed.) *Feminism and Methodology*. Milton Keynes: Open University Press

Hartley, J. (1980) 'Psychological approaches to unemployment'. *Bulletin of the British Psychological Society* Vol.33, pp. 412–14

Hartsock, N. (1983) 'The feminist standpoint: developing the ground for a specifically feminist historical materialism' in S. Harding and Hintikka, N. (eds.) *Discovering Reality: Feminist Perspectives on Epistemology, Metaphysics, Methodology and Philosophy of Science*. Dordrecht: Reidel, pp. 283–310

Hawkins, K. (1984) *Unemployment*. Harmondsworth: Penguin

Hayes, J. and Nutman, P. (1981) *Understanding the Unemployed – the psychological effects of unemployment*. London: Tavistock

Heather, N. (1976) *Radical Perspectives in Psychology*. London: Methuen

Heffernan, W.J.Jr (n.d.) 'Political behaviour of the poor'. Discussion Paper for Institute for Research on Poverty, University of Wisconsin, Madison

Herzlich, C. (1973) *Health and Illness: A Social Psychological Analysis*. London: Academic Press

Hewstone, M. (1985) 'On common sense and social representations: a reply to Potter and Litton'. *British Journal of Social Psychology* Vol. 24, pp. 95–7

Hewstone, M., Jaspars, J. and Lalljee, M. (1982) 'Social representations, social attribution and social identity: the intergroup images of "public" and "comprehensive" schoolboys'. *European Journal of Social Psychology* Vol.12, pp. 241–71

Himmelweit, H.T., Humphreys, P., Jaeger, M. and Katz, M. (1981) *How Voters Decide: a longitudinal study of political attitudes and voting extending over fifteen years*. London: Academic Press

Hirsch, D. (1983) 'Youth unemployment: a background paper'. Youthaid

Hobson, D. (1978) 'Housewives: isolation as oppression' in Women's Studies Group, Centre for Contemporary Studies, (ed.) *Women Take Issue: aspects of women's subordination*. London: Hutchison

Hobson, D. (1980) 'Housewives and the mass media' in Hall (1980), pp. 105–14

Hoinville, G., Jowell, R. and Associates (1977) *Survey Research Practice*

Honigmann, J.J. (1982) 'Sampling in ethnographic fieldwork' in Burgess (1982)

hooks, b. (1989) *Talking Back: Thinking Feminist Thinking Black*. Boston: South End Press

Hudson, B. (1984) 'Femininity and adolescence' in A. McRobbie and M. Nava (eds.) *Gender and Generation*. London: Macmillan, pp. 31–53

Hughes, A. (1975) *Psychology and the Political Experience*. Cambridge: Cambridge University Press

Hull, G.T., Scott, P.B. and Smith, B. (eds.) (1982) *All the Women are White, All the Blacks are Men, But Some of Us are Brave*. Old Westbury, N.Y.: The Feminist Press

Humphries, S. (1981) *Hooligans or Rebels? An Oral History of Working Class Childhood and Youth 1889–1959*. Oxford: Basil Blackwell

Hyman, H. (1979) 'The effects of unemployment: a neglected problem in modern social research' in R.K. Merton, J.S. Coleman and H. Rossi (eds.) *Qualitative and Quantitative Social Research: papers in honour of Paul F. Lazarsfeld*. New York: The Free Press

Jack, I. and McCullin, D. (1981) 'Youth: scenes from the life of a beleaguered generation'. Photo Essay. *Sunday Times Magazine* November

Jackson, J.S. III (1973) 'Alienation and black participation'. *Journal of Politics* Vol. 35, pp. 849–85

Jackson, M. (1985) *Youth Unemployment*. Beckenham: Croom Helm

Jackson, P. (1986) 'Towards a social psychology of unemployment: a commentary on Fryer, Jahoda and Kelvin and Jarrett'. *Social Behaviour* Vol. 1, pp. 33–9

Jahoda, M. (1979) 'The impact of unemployment in the 1930s and the 1970s'. *Bulletin of the British Psychological Society* Vol. 32, pp. 309–14

Jahoda, M. (1982) *Employment, and Unemployment: a social-psychological analysis*. Cambridge: Cambridge University Press

Jahoda, M. (1986) 'In defence of a non-reductionist social psychology'. *Social Behaviour* Vol. 1, pp. 25–9

Jahoda, M. and Rush, H. (1980) 'Work, employment and unemployment', SPRU Occasional Paper Series No. 12

Jahoda, M., Lazarsfeld, P.F. and Zeisel, H. (1933) *Marienthal: The Sociography of an Unemployed Community* (English translation 1972). London: Tavistock

James, C.L.R. (1960) 'The Battle for Survival' in C.L.R. James (1984) *At the Rendezvous of Victory*. London: Allison and Busby, p. 131

James, H.E.O. and Moore, F.T. (1940) 'Adolescent leisure in a working class district'. *Occupational Psychology* Vol. 14, No. 3. pp. 132–45 and Part II

Jaspars, J. and Fraser, C. (1984) 'Attitudes and social representations' in Farr and Moscovici (1984), pp. 101–23

Jenkins, R. (1983a) *Lads, Citizens and Ordinary Kids: working class youth life-styles in Belfast*. London: Routledge and Kegan Paul

Jenkins, R. (1983b) 'Goals, constraints and occupational choice: the first 12 months in the Belfast labour market'. *British Journal of Guidance and Counselling* Vol. 11, No. 2, pp. 184–95

Jennings, M.K. and Niemi, R.G. (eds.) (1974) *The Political Character of Adolescence: the influence of families and schools*. Princeton: Princeton University Press

Jodelet, D. (1984) 'The representation of the body and its transformation' in Farr and Moscovici (1984)

Johnson, R. (1979) '3 problematics: element of a theory of working class culture' in J. Clarke (ed.) *Working Class Culture: studies in history and theory*. London: Hutchinson, in association with the Centre for Contemporary Cultural Studies, pp. 201–37

Jones, C. (1983) 'Thatcherism and the attack on expectations' *Bulletin on Social Policy* No. 14, pp. 1–11

Jordan, J. (1986) 'Problems of language in a democratic state (1982)' in J. Jordan (ed.) *On Call. Political Essays*. London: Pluto Press, p. 28

Kamin, L. (1976) *The Science and Politics of IQ.* Harmondsworth: Penguin

Keddie, N. (ed.) (1973) *Tinker, Tailor... the myth of cultural deprivation.* Harmondsworth: Penguin

Kellmer-Pringle, M. (1975) *The Needs of Children.* London: Hutchinson

Kelvin, P. and Jarrett, J. (1985) *Unemployment: its social psychological effects.* Cambridge: Cambridge University Press

Kettle, M. and Hodges, L. (1982) *Uprising!: the police, the people and the riots in Britain's cities.* London: Pan

Kidder, L. (1981) 'Qualitative research and quasi-experimental frameworks' in M. Brewer and B. Collins (eds.) *Knowing and Validating: A Tribute to Donald Campbell.* San Francisco: Josey Bass

Kirby, R. and Roberts, H. (1984) 'YB on YTS? Why Not?'. Paper delivered at BSA Conference on Work, Employment and Unemployment, April

Klandermans, B. (1980) 'Unemployment and the unemployed movement'. Unpublished manuscript, Free University (Amsterdam) – Department of Social Psychology

Kolakowski, L. (1978) *Main Currents of Marxism.* Oxford: Oxford University Press

Kollontai, A. (1926) 'The aims and worth of my life' reprinted in English in A. Kollontai (1972) *Autobiography of a Sexually Emancipated Woman,* London: Orbach and Chambers, p. 8

Kurtines, W.M. and Gewirtz, J.L. (eds.) (1984) *Morality, Moral Behavior and Moral Development.* New York: John Wiley and Sons

Labour Research, December 1982

Labovitz, S. and Hagedorn, R. (1976) *Introduction to Social Research.* New York: McGraw Hill

Lane, R.E. (1968) *Political Ideology: why the American common man believes what he does.* New York: The Free Press

Lawrence, E. (1982) 'Just plain common sense: the "roots" of racism' in *Centre for Contemporary Cultural Studies* (1982)

Leggett, J.C. (1964) 'Economic insecurity and working class consciousness'. *American Sociological Review* Vol. 29, pp. 226–34

Leggett, J.C. (1983) 'Uprootedness and working class consciousness'. *American Journal of Economics* Vol. 68, pp. 682–92

Leggett, J. (1981) 'Review of Schlozman and Verba's *Injury to Insult* (1979)'. *Contemporary Sociology* Vol. 10, part 5, pp. 636–40

Lowe, G.S. (1986) 'Young people's explanations of unemployment: some Canadian evidence'. Paper at Social Psychology Seminar, SPS Committee. February

Lowe, G., Krahn, H., Hartnagel, T. and Tanner, J. (1985) 'Blaming the victim: public explanations of unemployment in a Canadian city'. First Draft

McClosky, H. (1964) 'Consensus and ideology in American politics'. *American Political Science Review* Vol. 58, pp. 361–82, cited in Mann (1982)

McGuire, W.J. (1983) 'A contextualist theory of knowledge: its implications for innovation and reform in psychological research' in L. Berkowitz (ed.) *Advances in Experimental Social Psychology.* Vol. 16. New York: Academic Press

McGuire, W.J. (1986) 'The vicissitudes of attitudes and similar representational constructs in twentieth century psychology'. *European Journal of Social Psychology* Vol. 16, pp. 89–130

McKee, L. and Bell, C. (1983) 'Marital and family relations in times of male unemployment'. Paper at SSRC Workshop in Employment and Unemployment (Labour Markets Workshop). Manchester, December

McRobbie, A. (1978) 'Working class girls and the culture of femininity' in Women's Study Group, Centre for Contemporary Cultural Studies. *Women Take Issue.* London: Hutchinson

McRobbie, A. (1982) 'The politics of feminist research: between talk, text and action'. *Feminist Review* No. 12, pp. 46–62

Makeham, P. (1980) *Youth Unemployment.* Department of Employment. Research Paper No. 10. London: HMSO

Mani, L. (1990) 'Multiple mediations: feminist scholarship in the age of multi-national reception'. *Feminist Review* No. 35, July

Mann, M. (1970) 'The social cohesion of liberal democracy'. *American Sociological Review,* Vol. 35, pp. 423–39

Mann, M. (1982) 'The social cohesion of Liberal democracy' in A. Giddens and D. Held (eds.) *Classes, Power, and Conflict: classical and contemporary debates.* London: Macmillan

Manpower Services Commission (1987) *Labour Market Quarterly.* Sheffield, June

Marsh, C., Fraser, C. and Jobling, R. (1985) 'Political responses to unemployment' in B. Roberts, R. Finnegan and D. Gallie (eds.) *New Directions in Economic Life.* Manchester: Manchester University Press

Marsden, D. and Ryan, P. (1986) 'Where do young workers work? Youth employment by industry in various European economies'. *British Journal of Industrial Relations* Vol. 24, No. 1, March

Marsh, C. (1982) *The Survey Method: The Contribution of Surveys to Sociological Explanation.* London: Allen and Unwin

Marsh, C., Fraser, C. and Jobling, R. (1983) 'Political responses to unemployment'. Paper for SSRC Conference on Local Labour Markets, Manchester, December

Maxwell, S. (1981) 'The politics of unemployment in Scotland'. *Political Quarterly* Vol. 52, pp. 88–9

Meiksins Wood, E. (1981) 'The separation of the economic and the political in capitalism'. *New Left Review* No. 127, May/June, pp. 66–96

Miles, I. (1983) *Adaptation to Unemployment?* SPRU. University of Sussex, March

Miliband, R. (1977) *Marxism and Politics.* Oxford: Oxford University Press

Millham, S., Bullock, R. and Hosie, K. (1978) 'Juvenile unemployment: a concept due for recycling?' *Journal of Adolescence* Vol. 1, pp. 11–24

Mills, C. Wright (1959) *The Sociological Imagination.* New York: Oxford University Press

Minford, P. (1981) 'The problems of unemployment'. Selsdon Group Policy Series, No. 5. London

Mitchell, J. (1971) *Women's Estate.* Harmondsworth: Penguin

Moore, F.T. (1941) 'The Hulme youth problem'. *Social Welfare* Vol. 4, No. 7, January

Moraga, C. and Anzaldua, G. (eds.) (1981) *This Bridge Called My Back: Writings by Radical Women of Colour.* Watertown, Mass.: Persephone Press

Moscovici, S. (1976) *Social Influence and Social Change.* London: Academic Press

Moscovici, S. (1981) 'On social representations' in J. Forgas (ed.) *Social Cognition: perspectives on everyday understanding.* London: Academic Press, pp. 181–209

Moscovici, S. (1982) 'The coming era of representations' in J-P Codol and J-P Leyens (eds.) *Cognitive Analysis of Social Behaviour.* The Hague: Nijhoff

Moscovici, S. (1984) 'The phenomenon of social representations' in Farr and Moscovici (1984), p. 3–69

Moscovici, S. (1985) 'Comment on Potter and Litton'. *British Journal of Social Psychology* Vol. 24, pp. 91–2

Moscovici, S. and Hewstone, M. (1983) 'Social representations and social explanations: from the "naive" to the "amateur" scientist' in M. Hewstone (ed.) *Attribution Theory: Social and Functional Extensions.* Oxford: Basil Blackwell

Moser, C.A. and Kalton, G. (1971) *Survey Methods in Social Investigation.* London: Heinemann

Moss, P. (1986) 'Marital relations during the transition to parenthood'. Social Psychology Seminar. SPS Committee, January

Mugny, G. (1982) *The Power of Minorities.* London: Academic Press

Murdock, G. and McCron, R. (1975) 'Consciousness of class and consciousness of generation' in Hall and Jefferson (1975), pp. 192–207

Murray, N. (1986) 'Anti-racist and other demons: the press and ideology in Thatcher's Britain' *Race and Class*, Winter, Vol. 27, No. 3, pp. 1–19

Nachmias, D. and Nachmias, C. (1976) *Research Methods in the Social Sciences.* London: Edward Arnold

Namjoshi, S. (1988) 'Among Tigers' in S. Grewal, J., Kay, L. Landor, G. Lewis and P. Parmar (eds.) *Charting the Journey.* London: Sheba, p. 262

Nava, M. (1981) 'Girls aren't really a problem'. *Schooling and Culture* No. 9, Spring, pp. 5–11

Newby, H. and Vogler, C. (1983) 'From class structure to class action: a critique of recent theories'. Paper at SSRC Workshop on Labour Markets, University of Manchester, December

Niemi, R.G. and Sobieszek, B. (1977) 'Political socialisation'. *Annual Review of Sociology* Vol. 3, pp. 209–33

Oakley, A. (1981) 'Interviewing women: a contradiction in terms' in H. Roberts (ed.) *Doing Feminist Research.* London: Routledge and Kegan Paul, pp. 30–61

O'Brien, G.E. (1986) *Psychology of Work and Unemployment.* Chichester: John Wiley

Olsen, M.E. (1969) 'Two categories of political alienation'. *Social Forces* Vol. 47, pp. 288–99

Ortner, S. (1976) 'Is female to male as nature is to culture?' in M. Rosaldo and L. Lamphere (eds.) *Woman, Culture and Society.* Stanford: Stanford University Press, pp. 67–88

Orum, A.M. and Cohen, R.S. (1973) 'The development of political orientations among black and white children'. *American Sociological Review* Vol. 38 (Feb.), pp. 62–74

Osmond (1981) 'Wales: will unemployment create unrest or apathy?'. *Political Quarterly* Vol. 52, No. 1, pp. 127–34

Palmonari, A. and Zani, B. (1987) 'Social representations and cognitive social psychology'. Paper presented at the Annual Conference, Social Section, British Psychological Society. Oxford, September

Palmonari, A., Carugati, F., Riccibitti, P.E. and Sarchielli, G. (1984) 'Imperfect identities: a socio-psychological perspective for the study of problems of adolescence' in H. Tajfel (ed.) *The Social Dimension: European Developments in Social Psychology,* pp. 111–136. Vol. 1. Cambridge: Cambridge University Press

Parker, I. (1984) 'Representation, sociology and social psychology'. Paper delivered to BPS Social Psychology Conference, Oxford, September

Parker, I. (1989) *The Crisis in Modern Social Psychology – And How to End It.* London: Routledge

Parker, I. and Shotter, J. (1990) (eds.) *Deconstructing Social Psychology.* London: Routledge

Parmar, P. (1982) 'Gender, race and class'. *Centre for Contemporary Cultural Studies* (1982), pp. 213–78

Parry, G. and Warr, P. (1980) 'The measurement of mothers' work attitudes'. *Journal of Occupational Psychology* Vol. 53, pp. 245–52

Passerini, L. (1979) 'Work ideology and consensus under Italian Fascism'. *History Workshop* No. 8, Autumn, pp. 82–108

Passerini, L. (1987) *Fascism in Popular Memory: the cultural experience of the Turin working class.* Cambridge: Cambridge University Press

Pearson, G. (1983) *The British Hooligan.* London: Macmillan

Peck, J.A. (1984) 'A dynamic approach to the study of unemployment'. Paper presented at WHO Conference on Unemployment

Phizacklea, A. (1983) *One Way Ticket Migration and Female Labour.* London: Routledge and Kegan Paul

Phoenix, A. (1988) 'Narrow definitions of culture: the case study of early motherhood' in S. Westwood and P. Bhachu (eds.) *Enterprising Women: Home, work and culture among minorities in Britain.* London: Routledge and Kegan Paul

Piven, F.F. and Cloward, R.A. (1977) *Poor People's Movements: how they succeed, why they fail.* Oxford: Basil Blackwell.

Platt, J. (1986) 'What can case studies do?' Paper at ESRC Field Research Seminar, University of Warwick, 14 March

Platt, S. (1983) 'Unemployment and parasuicide in Edinburgh 1968–1982'. *Unemployment Unit Bulletin* No. 10, November, pp. 4–5

Pollock, L.A. (1983) *Forgotten children: parent-child relations from 1500 to 1900.* Cambridge: Cambridge University Press

Potter, J. and Litton, I. (1985a) 'Representing representations: a reply to Moscovici, Semin and Hewstone'. *British Journal of Social Psychology* Vol. 24, pp. 99–100

Potter, J. and Litton, I. (1985b) 'Some problems underlying the theory of social representations'. *British Journal of Social Psychology* Vol. 24, pp. 81–90

Potter, J. and Wetherell, M. (1987) *Discourse and Social Psychology: beyond attitudes and behaviour.* London: Sage

Prendergast, S. and Prout, A. (1980) 'What will I do? Teenage girls and the construction of motherhood'. *Sociologial Review* Vol. 28, No. 3, pp. 517–35

Pulzer, P.G.J. (1968) *Political Representations and Elections in Britain.* London: Allen and Unwin, p. 107

Raffe, D. (1984a) 'The transition from school to work and the recession: evidence from the Scottish School Leavers Survey 1977–1983.' *British Journal of Sociology of Education* Vol. 5, No. 3, pp. 247–65

Raffe, D. (1984b) 'Change and continuity in the youth labour market'. Paper given to BSA Conference, Bradford, April

Raphael, D.D. (1970) *Problems in Political Philosophy*. London: Pall Mall Press

Rees, R.L. and Atkinson, P.C. (1982) *Youth Unemployment and State Intervention*. London: Routledge and Kegan Paul

Reicher, S. (1988) 'It's not what you do, it's how you say it.' Paper presented at the Annual Conference of the British Psychological Society, April, Leeds, UK

Ricci-Bitti, P.E. (1983) 'Adolescent's motivation: the plans of self realisation ten years after'. Paper delivered to International Society for the Study of Behavioural Development. 7th Biennial Meeting. Munich, 31 July – 4 August

Richardson, K., Spears, D. and Richards, M. (1972) (eds.) *Race, Culture and Intelligence*. Harmondsworth: Penguin

Ridley, F. (1979/1980) 'View from a disaster area: unemployed youth in Merseyside'. *New Universities Quarterly* Winter

Riley, D. (1983) *War in the Nursery: theories of the child and mother*. London: Virago Press

Roach, J.K. and Roach, J.L. (1980) 'Turmoil in command of politics: organising the poor'. *Sociological Quarterly* Vol. 21, Spring, pp. 259–70

Roberts, B. (1975) 'Naturalistic research into subcultures and deviance' in Hall and Jefferson (1975), pp. 243–53

Robins, D. and Cohen, P. (1978) *Knuckle Sandwich: growing up in the working-class city*. Harmondsworth: Penguin

Rodman, M. (1963) 'The lower class value stretch'. *Social Forces*, December, pp. 208–15, cited in Femia (1975)

Roiser, M. (1987) 'Common sense, science and public opinion'. *Journal for the Theory of Social Behaviour*, in press

Rose, H. and Rose, S. (1979) 'The IQ myth' in D. Rubinstein (ed.) *Education and Equality*. Harmondsworth: Penguin, pp. 79–93

Rose, R. and McAllister, I. (1986) *Voters begin to choose: from closed-class to open elections in Britain*. London: Sage

Rosenstone, S.J. (1982) 'Economic adversity and voter turnout'. *American Journal of Political Science* Vol. 26, No. 1, Feb

Rosenthal, R. (1966) *Experimental Effects in Behavioural Research*. New York: Appleton

Ryan, P. (1983) 'Youth labour, trade unionism and state policy in contemporary Britain'. Paper presented to 5th Conference of the International Working Group on Labour Market Segmentation. Aix-en-Provence, July

Ryan, W. (1971) *Blaming the Victim*. London: Orbach and Chambers

Sandoval, C. (1982) *The Struggle Within: Women Respond to Racism*. Oakland, Ca.: Centre for Third World Organising

Scarborough, E. (1988) 'Attitudes, social representations and ideology'. Draft paper

Schlozman, K.L. and Verba, S. (1979) *Injury to Insult*. Cambridge, Mass. and London: Harvard University Press

Scott, S. (1984/5) 'The personable and the powerful: gender and status in sociological status' in C. Bell and H. Roberts (eds.) *Social Researching*. London: Routledge and Kegan Paul

Scott, S. and Porter, M. (1983) 'On the bottom rung: a discussion of women's work in Sociology'. *Women's Studies International Forum* Vol. 6, No. 2, pp. 211–21

Seabrook, J. (1982) *Unemployment*. London: Quartet Books

Seidel, G. (1985) 'Political discourse analysis' in T.A. van Dijk (ed.) *Handbook of Discourse Analysis* Vol. 4. London: Academic Press

Semin, G.R. (1985) 'The 'phenomenon of social representations': a comment on Potter and Litton'. *British Journal of Social Psychology*, Vol. 24, pp. 93–4

Shepherd, G. (1981) 'Psychological disorder and unemployment'. *Bulletin of the British Psychological Society* Vol. 34, pp. 345–8

Shils, E. (1968) 'The concept of consensus'. International Encyclopaedia of the Social Sciences. Quoted in Passerini (1979), p.5

Shotter, J. (1986) 'Warranting accounts: justifying privileged forms of speech'. Paper delivered at the British Psychological Society (Social Psychology Section) Annual

Conference. Brighton, September

Showler, B. and Sinfield, A. (eds.) (1981) *The Workless State: studies in unemployment.* Oxford: Martin Robertson

Siltanen, J. and Stanworth, M. (1984) 'The politics of private woman and public man' in Siltanen and Stanworth (1984), pp. 185–208

Simon, B. (1971) *Intelligence, Psychology and Education.* London: Lawrence and Wishart

Sivanandan, A. (1985) 'RAT and the degradation of black struggle'. *Race and Class* Vol. 26, Spring, No. 4, pp. 1–33

Smith, D. (1987) *Everyday World as Problematic.* Milton Keynes: Open University Press

Solomos, J. (1986) 'The social and political context of black youth unemployment: a decade of policy developments and the limits of reform' in S. Walker and L. Barton (eds.) *Youth, Unemployment and Schooling.* Milton Keynes: Open University Press

Spradley, J.P. (1979) *The Ethnographic Interview.* New York: Holt, Rhinehart and Winston

Squire, C. (1989) *Significant Differences – Feminism in Psychology.* London: Routledge

Stacey, B. (1978) *Political Socialisation in Western Society: An Analysis from a Life Span Perspective.* London: Edward Arnold

Stafford, E.M. and Jackson, P. (1983) 'Job choice or job allocation? work aspirations and job seeking in an area of high unemployment'. *International Review of Applied Psychology* Vol. 32, pp. 207–32

Stafford, E.M., Jackson, P. and Banks, M. (1980) 'Employment, work involvement and mental health in less qualified young people'. *Journal of Occupational Psychology* Vol. 53, pp. 291–304

Stokes, G. (1983) 'Out of school – out of work: the psychological impact'. *Youth and Policy* Vol. 2, No. 2, Autumn

Stone, K. (1983) 'Motherhood and waged work: West Indian, Asian and white mothers compared' in Phizacklea (1983), pp. 33–52

Stradling, R. (1970) 'The political awareness of the school leaver'. Hansard Society

Tajfel, H. and Fraser, C. (1978) (eds.) *Introducing Social Psychology.* Harmondsworth: Penguin

Tajfel, H., Jaspars, J. and Fraser, C. (1984) 'The social dimension in European social psychology' in H. Tajfel (ed.) *The Social Dimension.* Cambridge: Cambridge University Press, pp. 1–5

Tanner, J., Lowe, G.S. and Krahn, H. (1984) 'Youth unemployment and moral panics'. *Perception* Vol. 7, No. 5, pp. 27–9

Taylor, M. (1983) *Growing Up Without Work.* London and Paris: Community Projects Foundation

Thomas, W.I. and Znaniecki, F. (1918–1920) *The Polish Peasant in Europe and America.* Boston: Badger

Thompson, J. (1984) *Studies in the Theory of Ideology.* Oxford: Polity Press

Tremblay, M.A. (1982) 'The key informant technique – a non-ethnographic application' in Burgess (1982)

Ullah, P. (1984) 'A qualitative study of unemployed black youth in Sheffield. Report to the Dept. of Employment.' MRC/ESRC SAPU Memo, No. 654

Ullah, P. (1985) 'Disaffected black and white youth: The role of unemployment duration and perceived job discrimination'. *Ethnic and Racial Studies* Vol. 8

Ullah, P. (1987) 'Unemployed black youths in a Northern City' in D. Fryer and P. Ullah (eds.) *Unemployed People.* Milton Keynes: Open University Press

Ullah, P. and Banks, M. (1985) 'Youth unemployment and labour market withdrawal'. *Journal of Economic Psychology*

Ullah, P., Banks, M. and Warr, P. (1985) 'Social support, social pressures and psychological distress during unemployment'. *Psychological Medicine.* MRC/ESRC SAPU Memo 636

Unemployment Unit (1986) *Statistical Supplement* November

Wainwright, H., Segal, L. and Rowbotham, S. (1979) *Beyond the Fragments: Feminism and the making of socialism.* London: Merlin Press

Walker, A. (1981) 'South Yorkshire: the economic and social impact of unemployment'. *Political Quarterly* Vol. 52, No. 1, pp. 74–87

Wallace, C. (1986) 'From girls and boys to women and men: the social reproduction of gender roles in the transition from school to (un)employment' in S. Walker and L. Barton (eds.) *Youth, Unemployment and Schooling.* Milton Keynes: Open University

Press, pp. 92–117

Warr, P. (1982) Editorial: 'Psychological aspects of employment and unemployment'. *Psychological Medicine* Vol. 12, pp. 7–11

Warr, P. (1983a) 'Work, jobs and unemployment'. *Bulletin of the British Psychological Society* Vol. 36, pp. 305–11

Warr, P. (1983b) 'Job loss, unemployment and psychological wellbeing' in E. van de Viliert and V. Allen (eds.) *Role Transitions.* New York: Plenum Press

Warr, P. (1983c) 'Work and unemployment' in P.J.D. Drenth, H. Thierry, P.J. Willems and C.J. de Wolff (eds.) *Handbook of Work and Organisation Psychology.* London: Wiley

Warr, P. (1984) 'Economic recession and mental health: a review of research' to appear in *Tijdschrift voor Sociale Gezondheidszorg*

Warr, P., Banks, M. and Ullah, P. (1985) 'The experience of unemployment among black and white urban teenagers'. *British Journal of Psychology* Vol. 76, pp. 75–86

Warr, P. and Jackson, P. (1984) 'Men without jobs: some correlates of age and length of unemployment.' *Journal of Occupational Psychology* Vol. 57, pp. 77–85

Warr, P. Jackson, P. and Banks, M. (1982) 'Duration of unemployment and psychological wellbeing in young men and women'. *Current Psychological Research* Vol. 2, pp. 207–14

Warr, P. and Payne, G. (1983) 'Social class and reported changes in behaviour after job loss'. *Journal of Applied Social Psychology* Vol. 13, pp. 206–22

Watts, A. (1978) 'The implications of school leaver unemployment for careers education in schools'. *Journal of Curriculum Studies* Vol. 10, No. 3, pp. 233–50

Watkins, S.J. (1982) 'Recession and health: the policy implications'. Paper presented to WHO Workshop on Health Policy in Relation to Unemployment in the Community, Leeds

Weiner, G. (1985) (ed.) *Just a Bunch of Girls: feminist approaches to schooling.* Milton Keynes: Open University Press

Weinreich-Haste, H. (1982) 'Adolescence: an overview of psychological approaches'. Paper presented to Annual Conference, Developmental Section, British Psychological Society. Durham, September

Weinreich-Haste, H. (1984) 'Morality, social meaning and rhetoric: the social context of moral reasoning' in Kurtines and Gewirtz (1984), pp. 325–47

White, J. (1980) *Rothschild Buildings: Life in an East End Tenement Block 1887–1921.* London: Routledge and Kegan Paul

Willer, D. and Willer, J. (1973) *Systematic Empiricism: Critique of a Pseudoscience.* Prentice Hall

Williams, R. (1983) 'Problems of the coming period'. *New Left Review* No. 140, July/Aug, pp. 1–10

Willis, P. (1977) *Learning to Labour: how working class kids get working class jobs.* Westmead, Hampshire: Saxon House

Willis, P. (1980) 'Notes on method' in Hall (1980), pp. 88–95

Willis, P. (1984a) 'Youth unemployment: thinking the unthinkable'. *Youth and Policy* Vol. 2, No. 4, Spring, pp. 17–36

Willis, P. (1984b) 'Youth unemployment'. *New Society* Vol. 67, Series of articles Nos. 1114, 1115, 1116, on 29 March, 5 April and 12 April respectively

Wober, J. M. (1980) 'Televison and teenagers' political awareness'. IBA Audience Research Department. December

Wright, P.J. (1975) 'Political socialisation research: the primacy principle'. *Social Focus* Vol. 54, pp. 243–55

Zhang Jie (1987) *Leaden Wings.* London: Virago, p. vii

Index